P9-DTG-513

3 1404 00910 2861

The
Reference Shelf®

MAR 1 1 2013

WITHDRAWN

JUN 1 7 2024

DAVID O. McKAY LIBRARY
BYU-IDAHO

Reality Television

The Reference Shelf
Volume 85 • Number 1
H. W. Wilson
A Division of EBSCO Publishing, Inc.
Ipswich, Massachusetts
2013

The Reference Shelf

The books in this series contain reprints of articles, excerpts from books, addresses on current issues, and studies of social trends in the United States and other countries. There are six separately bound numbers in each volume, all of which are usually published in the same calendar year. Numbers one through five are each devoted to a single subject, providing background information and discussion from various points of view and concluding with an index and comprehensive bibliography that lists books, pamphlets, and articles on the subject. The final number of each volume is a collection of recent speeches. Books in the series may be purchased individually or on subscription.

Library of Congress Cataloging-in-Publication Data

Reality television.
    pages cm -- (The reference shelf ; v. 85, no. 1)
  Includes bibliographical references and index.
  ISBN 978-0-8242-1212-4 (issue 1, pbk.) -- ISBN 978-0-8242-1211-7 (volume 85)
1. Reality television programs--Social aspects. 2. Reality television programs--Psychological aspects. 3. Reality television programs--Political aspects.
  PN1992.8.R43R385 2013
  791.45'6--dc23
                        2012045303

Cover: Melissa Rycroft and Tony Dovolani were crowned champions of this all-star season, on the Season Finale of 'Dancing with the Stars: All-Stars,' November 27, 2012 on the ABC Television Network. (Adam Taylor/©ABC/Getty Images)

Copyright © 2013, by H. W. Wilson, A Division of EBSCO Publishing, Inc.
All rights reserved. No part of this work may be used or reproduced in any manner whatsoever or transmitted in any form or by any means, electronic or mechanical, including photocopy, recording, or any information storage and retrieval system, without written permission from the copyright owner. For permissions requests, contact proprietarypublishing@ebscohost.com.

Printed in the United States of America

Contents

3

Consuming Reality

4

The Play on Realism

5

Reality Identities

6

The Business of Reality Television

Preface

The Rise of the Docu-Drama

During the Olympic finals of the women's gymnastics competition in 2012, Rachel Syme noted in the *New Yorker* how the reality principle had influenced NBC's coverage of the American women vying for the gold ("Women's Gymnastics: The Olympics as Reality TV"). To marvel at the extraordinary acrobatics on display was no longer enough: Americans needed a storyline, one that might touch the collective gut of spectators and frame the deeper reality of the competition. The drama of the competition was not simply the battle for the gold medal, but a battle of character and mind as well. "What NBC is producing," Syme observes, "is a reality-television program, with high stakes and teen stars, a daredevil version of *Gossip Girl* (or less-fatal *Hunger Games*). The performance of Gabby Douglas, while remarkable on its own terms, is all the more remarkable after the devastating turn experienced by her teammate Jordyn Wieber who, in the early storyline, was heavily favored to win the all-around. Holding the team together, Douglas is suddenly cast as America's all-around sweetheart. "There are strong young women behind those stories," Syme continues, "and a lifetime of work. But that can be hard to remember when the circus is in town."

The circus moved into town, by all accounts, back in 1992. That year, MTV premiered the half-hour program *The Real World*, following the lives of a group of young adults collected to live in an apartment in New York. The show offered a hybrid of popular and documentary form in the youthful, irreverent energy familiar to MTV viewers, recorded in an unscripted, spontaneous fashion. We can trace a number of signature features in reality programming today to this groundbreaking show. *The Real World* adopts the model of an earlier reality program from 1973, *An American Family*, which documented the lives of Pat and Bill Loud and their five children in affluent Santa Barbara, California. PBS captured the family in a period of dramatic change over several months, with the coming out as gay of son Lance Loud and the disintegration of the parents' marriage, culminating in divorce. The producer of the program, Craig Gilbert, asserted that the documentary project was a sociological study of the changing family in 1970s America. The claim to documentary status aside, when the Louds invited Americans into their home, the line between private and public blurred in ways not previously seen on television. Twenty years later, *The Real World* captured the fly-on-the-wall, documentary quality of its antecedent, suggesting a life-as-lived verisimilitude—young adults dealing with real young adult issues. However, the documentary-like subtleties in *The Real World* end there.

From its inception, *The Real World* unhesitatingly toyed with the lines between authenticity and staging. Certainly, strangers placed in a well-appointed New York apartment will immediately suggest a concocted environment. Yet the important innovation of the program was in the careful selection of housemates designed to heighten the tension and drama of young people cohabitating, and the dramatis personae nailed their roles. Producers James Solomon and Alan Carter described their vision for the series in archetypal gestures, a feature that would shape reality TV a decade later: "We needed relatable kids from urban to suburban, financially challenged to wealthy white-yellow-black-brown and in-between, gas jockeys to disc jockeys" (*The Real World: The Ultimate Insider's Guide*). Consequently, the program would depart from earlier incarnations of reality programming by emphasizing a managed artifice: However spontaneous the actions, however dramatic the confrontations, and however revealing the outcomes, a sense of staginess crept into the unscripted program—and this was just fine with its teenage and college audience.

One may be hard pressed to find anyone betting nowadays on the side of "realism" with a capital R. Twenty years following the premier of *The Real World*, the evolution of reality programming has accompanied a cultural swing toward revelation and voyeuristic consumption that has complicated the divide between public and private experience. The development of social networking, for example, promotes a voyeuristic impulse to peek into the lives of others. Both reality programming and social networking promote readymade selves as the modus operandi of living a collected life. Whether on *The Real World* or Facebook, people are called upon to project a watchable self. It is no wonder, then, that the contemporary logic of reality TV would have at its base a free-for-all of self-revelation.

Reality programs based on the everyday lives of ordinary people should be distinguished from the competition shows on which contestants rely on some level of skill—the wildly successful shows *American Idol*, *Survivor*, and *The Amazing Race*, for example, which are based on various forms of elimination. The lines of descent from *The Real World* are programs that generate an appetite for "real life," from the mundane to the extraordinary, and in the process create a hyper-reality out of the quotidian minutia of life. Switching between channels on any given afternoon, viewers will encounter the hillbilly milieu of *Here Comes Honey Boo Boo* in McIntyre, Georgia, the unpleasantness of *True Grime: Crime Scene Clean Up*, and the posh settings of *The Real Housewives of Beverly Hills*. If *The Real World* led the way in concocting ready-made archetypes for a pseudo-experiment in human interaction, today's reality TV has streamlined the exploration into the human experience, generating a large cast of familiar characters eager for their time in the spotlight.

While the landscape for reality programming could be understood by its generic outlines, a few of the more successful subgenres are worth noting for their evolution of the public/private domains. *Deadliest Catch* premiered in 2005 on the Discovery Channel, and has been successful owing to its filming of an often hazardous job with a fishing fleet in the Bering Sea. The show's success initiated a turn to reality programming based on the idiosyncrasy of nonmainstream jobs, such as *Miami Ink* on TLC, *Ice Road Truckers* on History, and *True Grime: Crime Scene Clean Up* on Investigation Discovery. Given the extraordinary setting of weather, high seas, and a cast of characters as hard-bitten as any, *Deadliest Catch* was among the most "realistic" of reality programs, as each season viewers were taken for a tumultuous ride into the personal lives of men searching for that next big, lucrative haul of crab. For many, the success of the show occurred on the human level, represented most dramatically in 2011. Filmmakers followed closely the sudden death of Captain

Phil Harris, the gruff centerpiece to the series, and the reactions of his sons. Rather than a private moment, his death became a collective event shared with a mass television audience, and few faulted the producers for their decision (many wrote of the tactfulness of the show). While the jobs in these shows establish the occasion, audiences gravitate to the better of them because of the common human stories told in rather uncommon situations. The death of Captain Phil caught on film (he is shown briefly in the hospital in the throes of death) suggests the exploitative nature of reality TV, which may not be a revelation but is worth noting nonetheless. As the line between what is private and public blurs, reality programming's responsibility to its audience (if we are to account for one) becomes more complicated.

A case in point is the show that may well have struck the first blow against what is available for public consumption. The producers of *Cheaters*, premiering in 2000, clandestinely "investigated" the extramarital or extrarelational affairs of men and women. The format of the show worked in three parts: hidden camera investigation, revelation (the video "proof," the host would shake his head), and the confrontation by the now-overwrought wronged party. The program drew upon a multiethnic, generally lower-income cast of characters, features that meet the "type" for this variety of reality programming. The producers elevated the purpose of the show to "public-service broadcasting," which characterizes shows of this kind that deliver viewers into the seamier side of life; and, along the way, they present a debased variety of reality exploitation. *Intervention* constructs an elaborate ruse whereby the filmmakers follow the life of an addict on the pretext of filming a documentary on substance abuse; but in reality, the producers are working behind the scenes with loved ones to stage, with the help of an expert, an intervention and pressure the addict into rehab. *Hoarders* follows the same format, staging an intervention into the life of a clinically compulsive person suffering from a serious case of hoarding and in need of serious decluttering. The public service these shows deliver, presumably, is gaining insight into the addicts and hoarders in our own lives; or the power of recovery through love; or perhaps an education in virtue. Without question, these lives, left alone, leave a field of damage for their families and themselves. These shows, however, tap into an apparent fascination among viewers with the aberrant and abject in life. Viewers must enter a gray area, confronting what is appropriately exploitative and what prompts some to turn away.

Then we have the genre of reality TV that is a model of self-exploitation. *The Real Housewives of Orange County*, premiering in 2005, has generated a franchise for the Bravo Network with offshoots from New Jersey to Beverly Hills, shows that offered an inside look into the lives of the wealthy as they negotiate the rigors of boutique shopping, beauty salons, and plastic surgeons. The show may well have established a format for some of the most successful reality TV that followed: *Laguna Beach: The Real Orange County* on MTV, *The Girls Next Door*, and *Keeping Up with the Kardashians*, both on E! What these shows reveal is the power of voyeuristic entertainment, the desire to look into the ordinary, the quotidian, given a brightly lit sheen. To varying degrees, the shows represent the ascendency of the "celebutante," the young celebrity famous for money, looks, and, well, being a celeb.

The Kardashians serve as a case in point. In 2007, sisters Kim, Khloé, and Kourtney appeared seemingly out of nowhere fully formed as celebrities; their celebrity generates its own energy, cutting across multiple media platforms to such an extent that it is difficult to locate the origin of their notoriety. The drama on these shows occurs on the most mundane level (in the case of *Real Housewives*, it consists of lots of sniping), and they appear to generate interest as a form of benign social interaction, the kind of eye candy that can be quickly dismissed.

Today, a body of literature in the form of books and scholarship argue the case for a closer, more serious look to the social and cultural significance of reality programming. What is certain is that the dynamics of spectatorship and self-revelation have changed in ways unimagined just a decade ago. In 1993, David Foster Wallace observed that the medium of television catered to people who love to watch people but hate being watched. Television once worked in just this way, a form of sociality that preserved the private. Times have changed.

1

The Evolution of Reality TV

(Time & Life Pictures/Getty Images)

The Loud family (clockwise from top): Kevin, Lance, Michele, Pat, Delilah, Grant, and Bill, subjects of the 1973 PBS documentary *An American Family*, sitting in their living room.

Reality Television Then and Now

Reality television has changed the entertainment industry. Reality TV programming has influenced popular culture and the nature of celebrity, and its impact has led television audiences to expect a completely new viewing experience. Although the worldwide success of reality television occurred in the 2000s, the story of its evolution dates to the mid-1940s and the early decades of commercialized media.

The show most often cited as the first reality television show is *Candid Camera*, which debuted in 1948. Created by Allen Funt, the show depicted people reacting to various pranks and out-of-the-ordinary circumstances via footage shot with hidden cameras. Other examples of early reality TV shows include the *Miss America* pageant (1954) and *Confession* (1958), which featured interviews with real-life criminals. In 1964, the show *Seven Up!* debuted in the United Kingdom, featuring candid interviews with children. The work of artist Andy Warhol, who created various films featuring impromptu acting and unscripted dialogue, is also credited as an early example of the reality genre.

The 1960s saw the introduction of several game shows featuring everyday people as contestants, which are also considered forerunners of the genre. These included *The Dating Game* (1965) and *The Newlywed Game* (1966). In 1973, PBS aired the series *An American Family*, a twelve-part documentary about a real-life California family, the Louds, and their experience with divorce. Interest in the series inspired *The Family*, a BBC spin-off show that aired in 1974. *The Gong Show*, which featured a celebrity panel judging and conversing with amateur singers, comedians, and performers, debuted in 1976.

NBC debuted the series *Real People* in 1979. The show, which aired until 1984, featured vignettes about people throughout the United States with unique interests and occupations. *Cops*, one of the longest-running television programs in the United States, and an icon of the reality TV genre, debuted in 1989. The show features the work of law enforcement officials in major US cities, and has also filmed episodes in Europe. After debuting as a television special in 1989, *America's Funniest Home Videos* began airing as a weekly series in 1990. The show, which has aired for over twenty seasons, features footage of pranks and accidents, filmed and submitted by the public. The show's audience votes for the funniest video, and its producers are awarded a monetary prize. MTV's hugely popular reality television series *The Real World* first aired in 1992. Audiences became enthralled by the drama and raucous behavior of the "real-life," twenty-something roommates featured on the show, though producers were criticized for staging or arranging much of what occurred in front of the camera. *The Real World* helped to blur the distinction between scripted (or semi-scripted) scenarios and real-life behavior on television.

Reality television became a global phenomenon in the early 2000s, following the success of *Big Brother* and *Survivor*. *Big Brother* debuted in 1999. The show focuses on a group of people who elect to live in a house rigged with video recording equipment. Individuals are "evicted" from the house based on a periodic private vote, which is influenced by the relationships and cliques formed between houseguests. The American version of *Big Brother* spawned numerous incarnations in other countries, including Australia, Mexico, Bulgaria, Spain, Thailand, and Serbia. *Survivor*, which first aired in the United States in May 2000, features a group of competitors in a remote location, vying to provide themselves food, water, and shelter in the wild. In addition to testing their wilderness survival skills, contestants compete in an array of physical challenges and face meetings of the "tribal council," where group members are "voted off," or chosen by the others to leave the game. Like *Big Brother*, the last man or woman standing receives a monetary prize.

In March 2002, MTV aired the first episode of *The Osbournes*, which featured the day-to-day lives of rock star Ozzy Osbourne, his wife Sharon, and two of their three children, Kelly and Jack. In addition to merging everyday tasks like taking out the garbage with celebrity culture, the show depicted the family coping with Sharon's cancer diagnosis. It also gave audiences a firsthand look at how Osbourne and his wife counseled their children about drugs and sex. *The Osbournes* became a template for other family-oriented reality programming based around the families of celebrities. These include *Newlyweds: Nick and Jessica* (2003), featuring singers Nick Lachey and Jessica Simpson, and *Hogan Knows Best*, which featured the wrestler Hulk Hogan and his family. Other series such as *Jackass* (2000), *Fear Factor* (2001) and *Breaking Bonaduce* (2005) pushed the envelope of risky behavior and dangerous stunts on television, much to the delight of audiences.

The breadth of reality television content has spawned a new type of celebrity. Hotel heiress Paris Hilton attained worldwide fame for her role in the television series *The Simple Life* (2003). Hilton leveraged the success of the show in a variety of ways, becoming a fashion entrepreneur, author, musician, and a star of other reality television shows. Other examples of celebrities who got their start by appearing in reality television shows include Elisabeth Hasselbeck (a former *Survivor* contestant) and Michael "The Situation" Sorrentino (of MTV's *Jersey Shore*).

In addition to exploring and exploiting human relationships within families and between perfect strangers, reality television has exposed audiences to the inner workings of various jobs and industries that might have otherwise remained largely unknown. The Discovery Channel's *Dirty Jobs* (2003) featured host Mike Rowe trying his hand at a variety of stomach-turning professions. *Deadliest Catch* (2005), also on Discovery, showed the world the hard work and treachery involved in Alaska king crab fishing, and spawned spin-off shows such as *Ice-Road Truckers* (2007). The HGTV and Bravo networks have become full-time purveyors of programming that explores the business and practice of home improvement, real estate (*Million Dollar Listing*) the culinary arts (*Top Chef*), and marketing (*The Pitch*).

As some reality television franchises passed their ten-year anniversaries, some critics predicted that the reality genre may see its success begin to wane. However, it seems more likely that, far from fading away, the themes and concepts of reality programming have become so embedded in the television viewing experience and the larger popular culture that they will be an integral part of the media landscape for decades to come.

The Documentary Roots of *Survivor*

By Daniel Roberts
Berfrois.com, September 26, 2012

The competition show *Survivor* just began its 25th season in the United States, and while any stigma associated with watching the show has almost completely faded, it nonetheless still gets grouped into the wide expanse of "reality television." But that label, which tends to carry such negative associations, doesn't actually fit *Survivor*.

For those lucky enough not to be hooked on CBS's dump-'em-in-the-jungle battle of brains and brawn, or for those in the U.K. that missed the program's short run there, *Survivor* works like this: 18 people (originally it was 20) are brought to an island, where they will live together with no outside help for food and shelter, and they are all split into two tribes (this season there are three). The tribes compete against one other in daily physical challenges that come with rewards. At the end of each episode, the losing tribe heads to a council where the group votes out one of its own. That person leaves the island and is off the show (except for in seasons when they play with redemption). About halfway through, the tribes merge into one big group, and the challenges become an individual push, with only one person winning immunity from the council each episode, instead of a whole tribe.

From year to year that formula can change a bit, but only in the most superficial, gimmicky ways (this season there are two 'celebrity' contestants: a former child TV star from the sitcom *Facts of Life* and a recently-retired professional baseball player), but for the most part the show never alters much, and sticks with the same thing each time. After all, it works.

Survivor has distanced itself from other "reality" shows. *Keeping up with the Kardashians. Flavor of Love. The Real Housewives of Bumblefuck. Bethenny Ever After.* These are programs built around the appeal of voyeurism. *Survivor*, meanwhile, is more like a sports program. It depicts a supposed "reality," yes, showing you the castaways in their island shelters, letting you watch as they head into the woods for private chats to scheme against each other, but the core of the game is physical.

In a warped sense, *Survivor* has its roots in the PBS documentary series *An American Family*, much forgotten today, itself a "reality" show, the first ever, that followed around one family (the Louds of California), and not at all a competition program. The show gained some brief prominence a year ago when HBO put out *Cinema Verité*, a drama film about the making of *An American Family*. The movie was very good—James Gandolfini played the show's producer Craig Gilbert, and Diane Lane and Tim Robbins portrayed the miserable Mr. and Mrs. Loud—but it was more interested in the ethics of Gilbert's decisions, as well as his rumored affair

By Daniel Roberts. This piece originally appeared in Berfrois, online at berfrois.com, in September 2012.

with Pat Loud, than it was in the cultural significance of the show. To truly appreciate HBO's flick, you need to have seen *An American Family*. (But good luck with that: the show doesn't exist on DVD, which is puzzling, and there is a scarcity of YouTube clips; the only way to see the show is on dusty videotapes in a library basement; while in grad school, I did just that, watching all 12 hour-long episodes for a History of Journalism assignment.)

By all accounts, when *An American Family* first premiered in 1973, audiences were floored. A documentary about life as an American family; it sounds mundane now, but no one had done it then. People felt uncertain and uncomfortable about what they were seeing. (It helped that one of the sons, Lance, was fabulously, flamingly gay and rebellious, which nicely shook up scores of bigoted middle-class homes.) The events were straightforward, easy to decode, but no less upsetting (the parents' marriage eventually crumbles on-camera); seven members of a family went about their routine business. Jeffrey Ruoff wrote in *An American Family: A Televised Life* that the week-to-week size of the show's viewership "astonished" its creators.

An American Family thrived due to the simplicity of its concept. The show's fundamental ethos was to do very little: let the cameras roll, just record quotidian interactions. That simplicity was its most precious asset. Nothing was scripted, nothing planned out.

Now, you could certainly make the old argument that just by occurring in front of a camera, interactions cease to be natural. Maybe so. But unlike so many other reality shows that we have come to learn are at least lightly scripted, *An American Family* was not, and neither (previous contestants tell me) is *Survivor*. Shows like *The Real World*, in which horny people under 30 "stop being polite and start getting real," are also inspired by *An American Family* but are completely unlike it. Gilbert's documentary series has more in common with *Survivor* because the film crews do not give contestants any help finding food or making shelter. They're left alone, as was the Loud family. They don't stay in a fully furnished hotel suite or apartment with alcohol-stocked fridge, courtesy of MTV.

When Pat Loud visits her son Lance in New York (he stays at the Chelsea Hotel, which would soon become an unmistakable symbol of the counter-culture), Lance and his roommate (and lover?) Soren drag her along with them to go see a transvestite play. The cameras roll, and we see footage of Pat squirming in her seat. Though she is fully supportive of Lance's lifestyle, that doesn't mean she was quite ready, perhaps, for a tranny show, and her discomfort is clear. After the show, over dinner, Pat is quite happy to admit she didn't enjoy the performance. "Well," she asks the boys, "was there a message that I didn't get?"

Today, the more educated and accepting among us might find even her light discomfort to be distasteful. But when the show aired, in the 1970s, Pat represented the national mass audience, and in fact there were many viewers in that audience who were not accepting of Lance at all. We know this from newspaper articles of the time. Regardless, the moment of Pat's discomfort—not revulsion, by the way, not at all, but more like an uncertainty, a cautious willingness to watch and learn—is, like all moments in the show, completely natural, not manufactured by the cameras.

No one tells Pat what to say, just as no one instructed or expected her own son to respond to her question, in perfectly flamboyant fashion, "Oh, no, honey," as though she's a young child, not an adult who raised him and has more life experience.

Survivor makes similar choices, sometimes controversially, and often, surely, to the inevitable complaints that they choose inflammatory characters to amp up the drama. (They certainly do, but that's different from scripting it.) In the most recent season, *Survivor: One World*, a loudly gay young Southerner named Colton quickly became one of the rudest, most offensive people to ever appear on the show. He quickly developed, for no apparent reason (well, maybe one reason), a hatred for a fellow cast member, a black comedian named Bill. Colton called Bill "ghetto trash," told him to "get a real job," and repeatedly announced to Bill and others that

> *Now, you could certainly make the old argument that just by occurring in front of a camera, interactions cease to be natural. Maybe so. But unlike so many other reality shows that we have come to learn are at least lightly scripted,* An American Family *was not, and neither (previous contestants tell me) is* Survivor.

he did not like Bill. At a tribal council, Colton defends himself: "Yes, I did go to a private, like, all-white school, but I do have, like, African-American people in my life… my housekeeper." Yes, it was pretty bad. It didn't get much better when an old white man who went by the name Tarzan (and was one of the craziest contestants in the show's history) jumped in, afraid to badmouth Colton, who was running his alliance, and raged: "The whole thing about race irks me. I think it's time to quit talking about goddamn race… And I think this country is moving in that direction. We have a Black president!" Yikes.

In allowing these characters to reveal their true colors, appalling though those colors can be, the show hearkens back to the Craig Gilbert approach. Why feed people lines when the things they'll say spontaneously are fascinating enough? The "stranger than fiction" idiom comes to mind.

Survivor has competition and suspense; its players are rewarded based on actual merit, and often, they deserve to be sent home when they are, either because someone has outfoxed them socially or overcome them in athletic and mental races. Though *An American Family* had no game element, it required devotion, as does *Survivor*. It rewarded viewers who watched each episode, since they begin to feel emotionally attached to one character. Certainly one could argue that any reality show builds on an intimate connection with its characters, but shows like *The Real World* seem easier to "pick up and go" with; viewers often tune in having seen none of the current season's episodes and find themselves entertained nonetheless.

Of course, *An American Family* was more than just a predecessor of reality television. Lance Loud became a gay rights icon, and *Cinema Verité*, however briefly, reminded people of the show that rocked the nation in the late 70s. What remains of the show's legacy is the simplicity it lent to later shows, a heart that ticks purely from character appeal and a hands-off approach—the same mechanics that so many people, forty years later, identify in *Survivor*, whether they realize it or not.

Survivor is also reminiscent, just a bit, of the famous Richard Connell short story "The Most Dangerous Game," about a man who hunts people for sport. Connell's very wonderful story has influenced scores of TV and movies (you can skip *The Pest*, with John Leguizamo, even though I inexplicably found it hilarious in middle school and rented it again and again), and perhaps *Survivor* is one of its most successful influences. The contestants on the show are "surviving" not just the physical challenges but also the psychological and the catty elements of the island. They must weather the storms of petty, green-eyed pairings eager to lie and deceive. But they are also, in a sense, hunting each other, even as they must rely on their tribe (at least for the first half of the season, before the groups merge) to win challenges and thus rewards that can often sustain and reenergize people. *Survivor* may be the closest real-life approximation of the Connell story's plot.

Having had an impact on so much of today's television landscape, it's a travesty that *An American Family* isn't available on DVD. Get with the program, PBS.

Jeffrey Ruoff's *An American Family: A Televised Life* Reviewing the Roots of Reality Television

By Jason Landrum
Film and History, May 2002

"I feel very strongly that the television documentary, if it is to have any future it must go in this direction. It must be in a series form—repetition and involvement with characters is what holds viewers—and it must he concerned with the events in the daily lives of ordinary citizens."—Craig Gilbert "Reflections on An American Family*"*

The recent publication of film historian Jeffrey Ruoff's *An American Family: A Televised Life* (University of Minnesota Press) brings renewed and well-deserved attention to the groundbreaking, 1973 PBS documentary series produced by Craig Gilbert. Ruoff carefully examines the creation and production of this series, placing it within the documentary film tradition, while demonstrating its hybridity, and provides a detailed analysis of the critical response received by *An American Family*, positioning this series as a forerunner of television shows such as *Cops* (Fox, 1989-present) and *The Real World* (*MTV* 1992-present). As Richard B. Woodward notes in an April 2002 *New York Times* article, "Unavailable on video, *An American Family* has not received the attention it deserves from a younger generation."[1] Jeffery Ruoff's thoughtful work offers both a thorough study of *An American Family* and a bridge to ongoing discussions on reality television.

The origins and future of reality television as a media genre have become much-debated issues. As recently as the March 29, 2002, edition of *USA Today*, the death of the genre was pronounced in an article entitled "Reality TV cools its jets." The author, Gary Levin, explains that *Survivor* winner Richard Hatch has become a distant memory, and shows like *Making the Band, Chains of Love,* and *Boot Camp* have come and gone without even the faintest scratch on the television landscape. Within a two-year period, twenty-five shows dedicated to the lives of ordinary people vanished from the airwaves, leaving CBS's *Survivor* and MTV's *The Real World* as the only consistent ratings-draw. The tremendous glut and variety in the genre taught television networks some lessons about what types of reality television shows are most successful. According to Levin, two distinct styles of shows emerged from CBS, ABC, NBC, and Fox network productions: self-contained game shows that crown a winner in each edition, and serialized shows that aim for well-developed

From *Film and History* 32.1 (May 2002). Copyright © 2002 by *Film and History*. Reprinted with permission. All rights reserved.

real-life characters who can draw viewers in week after week (E2). The second format, the serialized shows, has a long history in American television, but Levin's article, and others that discuss the genre, fail to recognize this rich tradition and fascination with watching real people on television. Indeed, the lessons learned by television executives are not new, as Jeffrey Ruoff indicates in the historical over-view he provides in *An American Family: A Televised Life.*

To understand the vogue of reality television, one need not explore further than Gilbert's PBS series *An American Family* (1973). In 1971, Gilbert and his pro-duction team, led by Alan and Susan Raymond, descended upon Santa Barbara, California, to film the family of Bill and Patricia Loud. Drawing upon the tenets of *cinema verite,* Gilbert and the Raymonds recorded the everyday lives of an upper-middle-class family, hoping to develop a portrait of a family that captured "the breakdown of fixed distinctions between public and private, reality and spectacle, serial narrative and nonfiction, documentary and fiction, and film and television" (Ruoff xii). Moreover, the series demonstrated the uneasy meeting ground between the demands of *cinema verite* and television. Jeffrey Ruoff's insightful new study. *An American Family: A Televised Life,* charts the long process of making the series and contends that it "transformed the representation of family life on American TV" and "'is worth revisiting...because it opened doors to a variety of new nonfic-tion forms, not only reality programming but also confessional talk shows" (xii).

An American Family's influence as a forerunner to today's boom in reality pro-gramming is primarily due to the series' structure and form combined with its cul-tural values, and upon reflection and comparison with its subsequent inheritors, like *The Real World* and *Survivor,* a poetics of reality television emerges. Ruoff's foundational dissection *of An American Family* provides an architecture for not only Gilbert's 1973 series, but also of the genre as we know it today and, while he contends that *An American Family* should be remembered because of its influence upon documentary filmmaking, its formal and political influence upon its television offspring reveals the visual language by which Americans have come to understand a so-called "new" genre. Instead of remembering *An American Family* as a failure because of its transgressions against the codes and ethics of traditional documen-tary film, it might be more appropriate to appreciate the innovative series as the creator of a new genre—a new form that finds its ultimate expression in an age of cable television when factual and fictional modes have blurred and merged.

Controversial Cultural Content—A "Loud" Reassessment

Craig Gilbert, although aware of the work of film documentarians (Robert Drew, Richard Leacock, D. A. Pennebaker, and Frederick Wiseman), received his cin-ematic training solely in television production and direction. His credits, before *An American Family,* included Navy training films, *The March of Time, Victory at Sea, Lowell Thomas Remembers,* and documentary portraits of notables in the arts. His time at National Educational Television (NET) in New York City began with *Marga-ret Mead's New Guinea Journal* (1968) but his work offered no opportunities to ad-dress contemporary social or cultural issues. Although an Emmy-winner in 1970 for

The Triumph of Christy Brown, by 1971, Gilbert requested that he be laid off (Ruoff 6–12). Gilbert's supervisor. Curt Davis, hoping to keep his award winning producer:

> handed him a challenge he couldn't refuse: give me a plan for a show you always wanted to do but for whatever reason couldn't. Gilbert thought about it during the weekend in which he "drank a lot and wallowed in self pity" over his failed marriage. Somewhere, buried in the troubling question of why men and women have such a tough time maintaining relationships, was the germ of an idea for a show. He grabbed a pencil and began making notes. The result was the outline for *An American Family*. (Day 185)

Beyond his own experience with divorce. Gilbert understood that the social fabric of America was undergoing a radical change begun in the 1960s. Ruoff notes that Craig Gilbert was a devotee of Charles Reich's *The Greening of America,* a text that celebrated a cultural revolution in America—a revolution that involved a transformation of personal and social values(13). Gilbert's ambitious project proposed to document those changes, focusing on one American family, filmed over an extended period of time. James Day's approval of this proposal marked the first step toward the reality television of the 1990s and sought to add cinematic flesh to Charles Reich's manifesto for political, social, and corporate (including television production) change.

Gilbert, with the help of Susan Lester, his associate producer, prepared a twenty-one-page proposal describing the goals of his project. "Gilbert believed that the American family was disappearing, becoming 'obsolete.'" The experiences of the family he selected were to be set "in a historical context which would also tell the story of the social and cultural changes that... [had] taken place in the United States during the past fifty years" (Ruoff 13, 21). Craig Gilbert hoped to paint a portrait of America with a broader brush than even Charles Reich. While Reich freely addressed the issues of divorce, sexual permissiveness, gay and women's activism, the "Generation Gap," conspicuous consumption, drug use, environmental issues, and the War in Vietnam, not all of these issues received explicit attention in *An American Family.* With 300 hours of footage shot by Alan

> *Craig Gilbert hoped to paint a portrait of America with a broader brush than even Charles Reich. While Reich freely addressed the issues of divorce, sexual permissiveness, gay and women's activism, the "Generation Gap," conspicuous consumption, drug use, environmental issues, and the War in Vietnam, not all of these issues received explicit attention in An American Family.*

and Susan Raymond over eight months, editorial decisions (editing took more than one year) were made which focused on Bill and Pat Loud's divorce. This decision served a two-fold purpose: first, the divorce offered a narrative thread to tempt audiences of the first of the twelve episodes to tune in the following weeks to witness the dissolution of a marriage; more pragmatically, airing the final filming allowed

Gilbert to provide closure to the series no matter how many episodes would finally be produced. Gilbert originally hoped to complete fifteen episodes but changes in network management dictated the twelve that were broadcast in 1973 (Ruoff 40). Both the content of the series and the "politics" of production were unique. Gilbert submitted his plan for *An American Family* at a time when not only American culture at large was undergoing significant changes, but also at a period when public television was experiencing reorganization and political pressures. Indeed, the former president of NET, James Day, doubts that:

> an innovative series such as *An American Family* could have been made at any other time in the history of public TV, given the administrative structure of PBS and the turn to corporate underwriting for individual programs after President Richard Nixon vetoed the 1972 Corporation for Public Broadcasting budget. After 1973, staff producers at member stations were bound, through corporate ties, to conventional styles and non-controversial subject matter. (quoted in Ruoff 5)

Both network fears, under pressure from government and corporate sponsors, and the vociferous critical response to *An American Family* indicate a conservative broadcast tradition, an outgrowth of a shift from radio and print journalism to a visual medium, as well as the cultural blurring of public and private spheres, which reality television has capitalized on to expand Warhol's "fifteen minutes of fame" into a lengthy opportunity for public notoriety and possible financial gain through prize-money or future film contracts. At the time that Gilbert's series aired, media management and media critics defended standards unreflective of the changing attitudes of American television viewers.[2]

Although media management felt obligated to provide status quo programming and media critics felt the need to defend that status quo when writing about *An American Family,* the seventies audience recognized the issues being explored, both explicitly and implicitly. In Episode Nine, the debate over divorce comes to the forefront. The empathy built throughout the series for Mrs. Loud's marital dilemma, the choice between preserving a dysfunctional family or ending the charade of the typically 1950s style ideal family, casts her sister-in-law's assessment of women's roles in doubt, echoing the doubts and shifting values of the 1970s audience. Beneath the surface discussion of Pat's decision to divorce, additional questions of sexual morality and women's roles also come into play, explaining to her sister-in-law that she was too old for "women's lib," but too young to be ignored and marginalized by her husband. Throughout the series, the crackup of the Loud family, illustrated in the opening credits, carried the narrative with arguments over proper cheese storage (Episode Seven), bitter attacks and innuendos while dining out (Episodes Six and Seven), and daughter Delilah's admission of her embarrassment over the bickering between Pat and Bill (Episode Seven). Gilbert's sympathetic portrayal of Pat Loud shifted blame for the family problems away from this stay-at-home Mom, leaving one to consider cultural, social, and moral change as possible causes for the "generation gap" overtly presented in Episode Eight, as well as the visual but unarticulated issues of Lance's "gayness," the children's use of drugs and alcohol, and the material abundance of upper-middle-class consumerism. Reich's "Consciousness III" types would quickly identify the environmental issues raised by Bill Loud's delight in strip-mining.'³

According to Reich, Bill Loud would represent a "Consciousness II" type, the older generation, who "are inclined to think of work, injustice and war, and of the bitter frustrations of life, as the human condition" (220). The Loud children are representative of a younger Consciousness III generation. Gilbert's series champions individual liberation and challenges traditional values, and despite post-broadcast reservations, the William Loud family of 35 Wooddale Lane moved into the spotlight and "provided a framework for people to think about their lives" (Ruoff 105). *An American Family* also tempted viewers to ask themselves, "What would I have done?" Ultimately, this question forms the core of contemporary fascination with reality television, and *An American Family* proves that "[r]eality TV allows Americans to fantasize about gaining status through automatic fame. Ordinary people can watch shows, see people like themselves and imagine that they too could become celebrities by being on television" (Reiss and Wiltz 54). Indeed, Reich's notion of "Consciousness III" suggests that individual liberation is best enjoyed when noticed and shared by others, and reality television provides a mirror for which viewers can see a way to increase one's sense of importance, showing that "[w]e think we are important if others pay attention and unimportant if ignored" (Reiss and Wiltz 54). Consequently, the shifting cultural values reflected by *An American Family* translate to America's fascination with celebrity, diversity, and individual liberation—elements that form the spine of reality television shows in the 1990s such as *The Real World* and *Survivor*.

The Hybrid Form of Reality Television

The financial and ratings success of television shows like *The Real World* and *Survivor* depends upon the premise of gathering strangers into a new and foreign place, pointing the cameras at them, and watching them struggle to adapt to their new surroundings. Sometimes they ease into the new environment, making new friends and connecting successfully with their landscape, and other times, friction arises within the constructed televisual space. The camera patiently waits for the "considerable drama in the daily lives of ordinary citizens'" to erupt, and the show organizes its storytelling strategy around these dramatic situations (Gilbert 301). As Ruoff contends, *"An American Family* is not entirely unified or consistent... [it is] a distinctly hybrid work, the documentary represents, in the words of Yale drama professor Richard Gilman, a 'bastard union of several forms'" (xxiii). The hybrid form of storytelling in *An American Family* is a blend of observational cinema, multi-narrative focus, serial structure, and multiple characters. The blend leads to a television show that mimics the goals of daytime soap operas, following the lives of the many characters, building viewership through serial viewings, and hoping to dramatize the lives of the ordinary people on the screen. Indeed, the hybrid formal style of *An American Family* provides the model for subsequent reality based television shows.

Episode Eight of *An American Family* serves as a good model for the others in the twelve part series, not only because it covers Pat's plans to divorce Bill, but because it dramatizes the conflict through the use of editing, captures the reactions of their children, and leaves the audience suspended at the end of the episode. Episode eight effectively demonstrates Ruoff's contention that the series "represents a compromise among these different tendencies, bridging the stylistic conventions of independent documentary film and broadcast TV. Gilbert adapted the innovations of American *cinema verite* to the traditions of television" (57).

While Gilbert's cameras follow the Loud children—Lance in New York, Kevin going on his trip to Asia, Grant and his rock band, Delilah and her dance recital, and Michelle in her room—the series focuses intensely on Bill and Pat Loud's failing marriage. The multiple characters of the Loud family each receive attention, but the structure of the show relies upon Mom and Dad. Episode One establishes that Bill and Pat have separated, and each subsequent episode builds toward the climax of Pat's asking Bill for a divorce. In Episode Eight, Bill travels across the country to help his stalling business, and Pat plans for divorce by visiting her attorney and confessing her decision to her brother and sister-in-law. Like the previous episodes, the focus is shifted between the children, Pat, and Bill. However, Pat's confession to her brother runs for thirty minutes of this particular episode, privileging her point of view. The show begins with Bill on the road, attempting to secure new customers and to "schmooze'" with old ones. Echoing themes of prior portrayals of Bill, he complains about his kids, referring to Lance as a con artist and Grant as lazy, and subsequently repeating his desire to have his children out of his house. Bill is linked visually with the strip-mining parts that he sells (the "teeth" of the machines), and the editing through these sequences continually associates him with the exploitation of the environment—a definite sin of a "Consciousness II" person. Back in California, Pat is portrayed in much more sympathetic terms. She talks openly about herself, her lack of identity, and her fears of an "empty nest." While her brother and sister-in-law listen to and empathize with her confession, Pat is reduced to a lonely, isolated figure who Bill has ignored.[4]

The pattern of portraying Pat and Bill in this manner holds throughout the series; whether these are accurate depictions of either person is debatable, but what is important is that the filmmakers have chosen to dramatize Pat essentially as the good wife, worthy of the viewer's sympathy, and Bill as the bad husband, engendering the disdain of the many who watched the series. Moreover, the personalities and traits of Bill and Pat do not simply unfold before the camera, as the tenets of direct cinema would ask the viewer to believe. Instead, the filmmakers, in order to deliver a story—a story with a particular point-of-view—carefully construct their "characters" through deliberate editing choices. The episode ends with dramatic irony as Grant goes to pick up Bill at the airport, and the filmmakers have carefully crafted a highly suspenseful conclusion to this episode. In effect, Gilbert and company have employed Alfred Hitchcock's famous "bomb under the table" by which the audience knows that there is bomb about to explode underneath a table where two unsuspecting characters idly chat. Pat, the children, and the audience are all fully aware of what Bill is about to walk into, and the episode lingers, waiting for the bomb to explode, dramatizing the moment. However, like a soap opera, which asks the viewer to "tune-in tomorrow." Episode Eight ends on this note of suspense, which forms the beginning of Episode Nine—the famous divorce episode and series climax foreshadowed in the opening of the series.

Although most critics who disliked *An American Family* in 1973 referred to it as a soap opera, the series' adaptation of this dramatic narrative technique differentiates it from the goals of documentary and suggests that it forms a closer bond with the medium of television and storytelling codes. *An American Family* shares the following characteristics of a soap opera: consistent viewer involvement (twelve episodes), multiple characters (the Loud family—parents and five children), multiple and indefinite plotlines (Lance in New York, Pat in Taos, Bill in Hawaii, etc.), and intimate connections with the daily lives of characters (countless revealing phone conversations), and, ultimately, the value of character over story in soap operas, which Gilbert stresses above all in the series (Ruoff 58). This combination of melodramatic soap opera narrative techniques with "fly on the wall" filmmaking serves as the core of the subsequent explosion of reality television in the 1990s. Citing her fascination with the PBS series in an interview, *The Real World* creator, Mary-Ellis Bunim explains that her "background was soap operas. Jon [Murray—her co-creator] came out of news and documentaries. We were both intrigued by *An American Family* the old PBS series. I was consultant to MTV on a scripted soap opera, which is an expensive format. We pitched *The Real World* as a means to give them their own soap opera" (Roth 38). Each creator of the successful series—moving into its eleventh year—provides the necessary ingredients to fulfill the promise established by Gilbert's 1973 experiment, suggesting that the primary influence of *An American Family* is its combustible mixture of the narrative technique of television with observational style of direct cinema.

Who's to Blame?

In a recent article in *Fortune* magazine, Daniel Roth asks "who's to blame for all this reality TV?" (38). He goes on to explain that the real culprit for the glut of reality based television shows in the late 1990s is Mary-Ellis Bunim and Jon Munay of MTV's *The Real World*. This observation is myopic because it ignores the overriding influence of *An American Family*. By overlooking the foundational aspects of the groundbreaking series, Roth ignores the fact that nothing in the shows of the 1990s—aside from casting the "players" and adding game show incentives—was not already worked out in 1973. For example, *The Real World* casts seven strangers of diverse gender, race, and sexual orientation and puts them in a gorgeous house/sound stage in a large American city. The hope is that this diversity within the group of house members will lead to dramatic moments that will translate into storylines to be followed throughout the season. The show values marginalized voices outside those traditionally seen and heard on network television and promotes the notion "that anyone's inner life can be interesting" (Marsh 72). *The Real World* provides the same mirror that *An American Family* did in 1973, showing its audience that life is better when others pay attention, and compares favorably with ideas expressed in Reich's *The Greening of America*.

Structurally, the shows resemble each other in that they favor character over narrative, are arranged in an episodic fashion, have multiple character focus, and follow multiple narrative lines. Like the soap opera, which Bunim admits to mimicking. *The Real World* demands consistent viewer involvement, going so far as to hold all-day marathons on weekends to help casual viewers catch up with recent shows. To dismiss the Bunim-Murray influence, which has been extremely important to the current explosion of reality television, would be a gross misevaluation. However, to diminish the foundational aspects of Gilbert's experiments with nonfiction story-telling reduces the impact of *An American Family* on today's counterparts. While Gilbert may have broken certain rules cherished by the direct cinema tradition, his series opened doors for the future success of television shows like *The Real World*.[5] As Ruoff observes, *"An American Family* represents a new stage in the filming of everyday lives of ordinary individuals, a landmark in the history of nonfiction film" (137). By combining the demands of two different visual mediums, Gilbert, the Louds, and *An American Family,* established the poetics by which future reality television shows would organize themselves. With his thorough discussion of *An American Family: A Televised Life,* Jeffrey Ruoff's work not only offers commentary on an historical television documentary event, but also provides the springboard for an examination of current programming on network and cable television.

Works Cited

Cunin, Michael. *Packaging Reality: The Influence of Fictional Forms on the Early Development of Television Documentary.* Ed. James W. Tankard, Jr. Journalism Monographs 137. Columbia SC: Association for Education in Journalism and Mass Communications (AEJMC), 1993.

Day, James. *The Vanishing Vision: The Inside Story of Public Television.* Berkeley: U of California P, 1995.

Dovey, Jon. *Freakshow: First Person Media and Factual Television.* London: Pluto Press, 2000.

Gilbert, Craig. *"Reflections on* An American Family.*" New Challenges for Documentary.* Ed. Alan Rosenthal. Berkeley and Los Angeles: U of California P, 1988, 288, 307.

Levin, Gary. "Reality TV cools its jets." *USA Today* 29 Mar. 2002: E1+.

Marsh, Katherine. "What is Real?" *Rolling Stone* 22 June 2000: 71-79, 141.

Reich. Charles A. *The Greening of America.* New York: Random House, 1970.

Reiss, Steven, and James Wiltz. "Why America loves reality TV." *Psychology Today* Sep.-Oct. 2001: 52-4.

Roth, Daniel. *"Real World* Creator: Some Reality Biles." *Fortune* 14 Aug. 2000: 38.

Roth, Jeffrey. *An American Family*: A Televised Life. Minneapolis: U of Minnesota P. 2002.

Woodward, Richard B. "Tied to Television to the Very Last" *The New York Times on the Web* 14 April 2002. www.nytimes.com/2002/04/I4/ arts/television/14 WOOD

Notes

1. After Lance, the eldest Loud son, died in December 2001, many news accounts brought *An American Family* into American cultural awareness or recollection. Woodward, as have others, reports that, with death approaching, Lance Loud contacted filmmakers Alan and Susan Raymond to record his final days, thirty years after their first collaboration.

2. Michael Curtin, in *Packaging Reality,* provides explanations for the changing forms of documentary television as news staff shifted from the domination of radio celebrities and visual technicians. Jon Dovey, in *Freakshow,* describes the slippage between public and private spheres of personal experience emphasizing the "truth" of personal experience and the importance of "trauma" television.

3. Charles Reich celebrated the youthful "Consciousness III" generation's transformation of the rigid standards and lifestyles of postwar, middle class America (Consciousness II). Reich's wide-ranging discussion included capitalism, popular music, the drug culture, and blue jeans.

4. This episode also provides a brief portrayal of the typical television marriage as Pat's sister-in-law describes how to make a husband feel important as both head-of-the household and master-of-the-bedroom.

5. Although defining *cinema verite,* direct cinema, or observational film remains problematic in documentary film studies, Gilbert included techniques outside the usual understanding of these terms. *An American Family* includes the producer's opening monologue: voiceovers by Lance, Pat, and Bill Loud recorded after filming; and a parodie transvestite stage production filmed at a later time and at a new venue.

Obsessive Repulsive

By Will Self
New Statesman, May 14, 2012

Compulsive hoarding is pretty out there, no? I mean what kind of a weirdo saves all that cardboard and bubble wrap, ties it up with string and wedges it in on top of crappy old wing chairs and fake-veneer TV cabinets stacked high with bundles of old newspapers and books, then tops the whole teetering pile off with 30-or-so cat litter trays (full), leaving the felines themselves—perhaps 40 of them—to smarm along the alleys carved through this dreck (for this is but one room of an entire semi so engorged), shitting and pissing wherever?

A complete weirdo—that's who. And these people, together with their odd pathology, are of increasing interest to the general population, as is evidenced by the arrival on these shores of the British version of *Hoarders*, a US documentary series about compulsive hoarders that has already been running over there for four seasons and is currently embarking on its fifth. Not that this is Brit TV's first foray under the sinks of the seriously possessive—there was a standalone docco, *Obsessive Compulsive Hoarder* on Channel 4 back in 2011—and it may be because I'm taken by the phenomenon (a hoarder of programmes about compulsive hoarders) that it seems to me that I've snapped on the set on a number of other occasions only to find the camera's lens nosing along a skirting board behind which are stuffed sheaths of old discount coupons.

Marching Hoarders

Wherefrom comes this urge to expose such traumatic interiors? After all, hoarding can be nothing new—it's easy to imagine a Cyclops's cavern stuffed to the roof with sheep bones, cheese rinds and the remains of hapless Argonauts. The splurge of reality obesity shows the explanation is simple: schadenfreude. We look upon those poor wobblers being shaken to their core by life coaches and think to ourselves, I may be a little on the tubby side but—Jesus!—I'm not that bad. Actually, my suspicion is that the compulsive hoarder craziness is an even more craven attempt to affect such a catharsis. As the crack team of cleaners goes into the bungalow, black bags and bug spray at the ready, we sit on the sofa watching and, for a few dreamy minutes, can forget all about the landfill-in-waiting that surrounds us.

Every morning of my serene existence I open the door to my writing room and think, I can't stand this! It's an avalanche crushing me! The box files full of papers, the shelves piled with books (the floor piled with books), the desk stacked with

From *New Statesman* 141.5105 (14 May 2012): 51. Copyright © 2012 by *New Statesman* Ltd. Reprinted with permission. All rights reserved.

unanswered correspondence, the desk lamps corralled by tchotchkes—old toys, plastic figurines, broken watches, stones I've picked up as mementoes of the places I've been and yet forgotten, foreign coins, pine cones—the space below the desk humped with boxes full of camping gear all coiled in dust-furred computer cabling … Aaaargh! I want to scream, because there's no point in turning away from it, for there are scores of books not simply unread but which I will never read. Just as in the pantry there are bay leaves I will never put in a casserole, and in the shed there are trowels that neither I—nor anyone else—will ever delve with.

The splurge of reality obesity shows the explanation is simple: schadenfreude. We look upon those poor wobblers being shaken to their core by life coaches and think to ourselves, I may be a little on the tubby side but—Jesus!— I'm not that bad.

Sticky Moments

Yes, I know there are those who exhibit a different pathology: their homes are pristine, their socks are colour-coded, the second they acquire something superfluous they organise a tabletop sale. But the rest of us are charged with some sort of unearthly static electricity that makes paper clips, hairpins, half-used Sellotape rolls (especially the ones where you cannot detach the tape even after hours of flicking at it under operating-theatre-strength lighting), local newspapers, tins of baked beans missing their labels, jump leads, hair rollers, half-used tubes of athlete's foot cream, half-popped packs of headache pills, broken folding chairs, Jiffy bags, VHS tapes, etcetera, etcetera, et-bloody-cetera cling to us with terrifying inertia.

If you stand on the banks of the Thames east of Gravesend, roughly where Pip met Magwitch and Boris wants to build an airport, you can watch as giant container ships loaded with discarded electrical goods set out on the ebb tide for China, where all these washing machines, computers and consoles will be recycled into useful appliances for their upwardly mobile rural poor. Some might take heart at this—not I. I see the earth as a compulsive hoarder, spinning through the endless night of space, snaffling up meteorites as she goes.

What's Right with Reality TV

By James Poniewozik
Time, February 22, 2010

Ten years since the premiere of Survivor, *the genre has gone from guilty pleasure to quintessentially American entertainment*

The first thing you notice on MTV's *Jersey Shore* is the nicknames. Well, that and the hair, and the thongs, and the leathery tans, and the tattoos, and the hair gel, and the hot-tub sex, and the bar brawls, and the lustily embraced Italian-American stereotypes. But then: those nicknames. There's Nicole (Snooki) Polizzi. Mike (The Situation) Sorrentino. And most spectacularly, Jenni (Jwoww) Farley. For future copy editors of academic histories of mass media, that's two syllables, hyphen optional, and three w's, not in a row.

Like the tetragrammatic name of God, the moniker Jwoww has encoded in it everything you need to understand the world we live in today. The idea that an unknown 23-year-old from Long Island would come equipped with a tabloid-ready exclamatory nickname, like J. Lo or P. Diddy, might, in a more self-effacing era, have seemed presumptuous. Now it's just commonsense branding. If you might be on a reality show, you may as well have a name that pops and precedes you like a well-positioned set of silicone implants. (Oh, also: you should get the implants too.)

For the cast of *Jersey Shore*—gearing up to shoot Season 2 in the next few months—camera-readiness is second nature. These are the children of reality TV. In February 1992—literally a generation ago—*The Real World* introduced MTV's viewers to living in public. Ten years ago, *Survivor*—now in its 20th season—mainstreamed the idea for older viewers. *The Jersey Shore*-ites have never known a world in which hooking up drunk in a house paid for by a Viacom network was not an option. This year in the coveted post–Super Bowl time slot, CBS showcased not a new drama or sitcom but its reality series *Undercover Boss*. (The premiere attracted 38.6 million viewers, the most for a post–Super Bowl show since *Survivor: The Australian Outback* in 2001.) In March, Jerry Seinfeld returns to NBC—as producer of the reality show *The Marriage Ref*.

Reality is more than a TV genre now. It's the burgeoning career field that led Richard Heene to perpetrate the Balloon Boy hoax, and Tareq and Michaele Salahi to crash a White House dinner, Bravo TV cameras in tow. It's the content mill for the cable-tabloid-blog machine, employing human punch lines like Rod Blagojevich, the disgraced governor turned contestant on *Celebrity Apprentice*. It's everywhere.

From *Time* 175.7 (22 Feb. 2010): 92–97. Copyright © 2010 Time Inc. Reprinted with permission. All rights reserved.

When Scott Brown won an upset Senate victory in Massachusetts, he was joined onstage by his daughter Ayla, an *American Idol* semifinalist from Season 5.

In 1992, reality TV was a novelty. In 2000, it was a fad. In 2010, it's a way of life.

The Evolution of a Genre

The summer of the first *Survivor* season, I wrote a cover story about it for this magazine [Time]. The concerns that the show's popularity raised seem so quaint now: a professor worried its success would lead to "Let's try a public execution. Let's try a snuff film." We're still waiting for those. But *Survivor* is still on—considered, together with the likes of *Idol* and *The Amazing Race*, to be relatively tame, even family-oriented entertainment.

At the time, there were a handful of reality shows on TV. Since then, we've seen 20 *Survivors*, 16 *Amazing Races* and 14 *The Bachelors*. We've seen *Chains of Love, Rock of Love, Flavor of Love* and *Conveyor Belt of Love*. *American Candidate, American Gladiators* and *American Inventor*. *Anna Nicole, Kathy Griffin* and *Britney & Kevin*. *Design Star, Rock Star, Nashville Star* and *Dancing with the Stars*. *Joe Millionaire, Average Joe* and *The Joe Schmo Show*. *Shark Tank* and *Whale Wars, The Mole* and *The Swan*. *Fear Factor, The It Factor* and *The Benefactor*. (Coming in 2011: Simon Cowell's *The X Factor*!)

You can break down reality TV roughly into two major subgenres. The first—the big competition-event show—descends from *Survivor* and includes most of reality's big hits: *Idol, The Bachelor, The Amazing Race, The Biggest Loser, Project Runway*. These shows mainstreamed reality TV for bigger, broader (and older) audiences by applying it to familiar genres: game shows, singing competitions, cook-offs, dating shows.

The other type of reality show descends from *The Real World*'s naked voyeurism. Some of these shows are about celebrities, former celebrities or pseudo celebrities. Some are about therapy, about work or about parenting. And many are just about life. Bravo's *Real Housewives* series is still spreading across the country like *Cheesecake Factory* franchises. (The Salahis snuggled up to the President as candidates for *The Real Housewives of D.C.*) When Jon and Kate Gosselin drew 10 million viewers to watch their marriage end on TLC, reality TV proved it wasn't going into middle age quietly.

From Personality to Persona

Big as reality TV is, it's also just a facet of a larger shift in popular culture: changing attitudes toward privacy and self-expression. If you grew up with reality TV and the Internet, your default setting is publicity, not privacy. Mark Zuckerberg, the founder of Facebook, recently argued that sharing has become the "social norm."

Zuckerberg was defending a controversial change in Facebook's privacy settings to make the company's trove of user information more valuable. Still, he has hundreds of millions of users and their college beer-bong photos proving his point every day. Facebook's competitor Twitter is a worldwide agora of valuable information and TMI. You can make your tweets private if you want, but why would you?

Thus comes what you might call the realitization of reality: the evolution of once private, or at least obscure, acts into performance. The diary becomes the blog. The home-movie collection becomes the YouTube channel. The résumé becomes the public search-result page.

And the personality becomes the persona. Every time you sign up for a new social-networking service, you make decisions about, literally, who you want to be. You package yourself—choose an avatar, pick a name, state your status—not unlike a storyteller creating a character or a publicist positioning a client. You can be professional on LinkedIn, flippant on Facebook and epigrammatic on Twitter. What's more, each of these representations can be very different and yet entirely authentic. Like a reality producer in a video bay, you edit yourself to fit the context.

In the workplace, for more than a decade, job-insecure Americans have been told to cultivate "the brand called you." Decide what your strengths are. Focus on your core competencies. Be aware of the bullet points of your identity. The message of both business and leisure today is, Distinguish between the actual and the for-public-consumption self.

Put all these factors together, and reality TV's endless stream of candidates seems inevitable. Every winter, *American Idol*'s audition rounds attract a deluge of self-created characters, who have the formula for getting on national TV down to a science. "I'm the crazy accordion lady/ This is my song," yowls a blue-haired young woman cradling a squeeze-box. The advanced descendants of the costumed screwballs who tried to get Monty Hall's attention on *Let's Make a Deal*, today's reality performance artists put on virtual costumes—the Bitch, the Horndog, the Drama Queen—to get noticed. In reality TV, privacy and even likability are commodities that can be traded for something more valuable.

Which is? Reality TV is now a valid career choice. The *New York Times* estimated that at any given time, there are 1,000 people on air as reality TV stars. (That may not seem like a huge number, but compared with, let's say, full-time TV critics, it's quite a healthy field.) For a few talented individuals—say, *Idol*'s Kelly Clarkson or the cooks of *Top Chef*—this has made possible actual real-life opportunity. Jennifer Hudson lost on *Idol* but won an Oscar as an actress. Elisabeth Hasselbeck went from eating bugs on *Survivor* to chewing out Joy Behar on *The View*.

And for others, it has enabled a life of lucrative famousness for famousness. Members of the cast of *The Hills*, for instance, reportedly earn up to $90,000 an episode; the *Real Housewives*, about $30,000. *Hills* star Heidi Montag has released an album, launched a clothing line, even, God help us, co-written a book. Co-star Audrina Patridge at one point received $10,000 to party at a nightclub for two hours. Reality star Kim Kardashian reportedly nets $10,000 for each product she endorses on Twitter. How much money did you make in the last 30 seconds?

Will Offend for Fame

Of course, you don't reach that level of success without working for it. Kardashian, for instance, didn't get her show until a sex tape of her and an R&B singer became public. Which is another lesson of reality TV: outrageousness pays.

And the more reality TV there is, the more outrageous you have to be to break out. Nadya Suleman, or Octomom, parlayed a horrifyingly dangerous multiple birth into a reality special, ending up—like her apparent model, Angelina Jolie—on the cover of *Star* magazine, showing off "My New Bikini Body! How I Did It!" Richard Heene convinced the world that his 6-year-old son was hurtling toward his death in a balloon. But as the veteran of ABC's *Wife Swap* knew, the show he was pitching—eccentric storm-chasing scientist and his wacky family—wouldn't even raise an eyebrow on a cable schedule.

> *But what message is it all sending? The viralization of people like* American Idol's *General Larry (Pants on the Ground) Platt and William Hung before him has led to the charge that reality TV invites us to laugh at little people for sport. The fame of* Jersey Shore's *tanning-bed casualties and others brings the critique that reality TV celebrates violence, sluttiness (male and female) and other bad behavior.*

But what message is it all sending? The viralization of people like *American Idol*'s General Larry (Pants on the Ground) Platt and William Hung before him has led to the charge that reality TV invites us to laugh at little people for sport. The fame of *Jersey Shore*'s tanning-bed casualties and others brings the critique that reality TV celebrates violence, sluttiness (male and female) and other bad behavior.

These charges are so contradictory as to cancel each other out. How, exactly, can reality TV mock its participants and celebrate them at the same time? In fact, the audience's relation to reality shows is more complicated. People don't watch *Jersey Shore* because they consider the Situation a role model. It's entertaining because the show is basically satire, a pumped-up spoof of bigger-is-better American culture. (Quoth Jwoww: "I see a bunch of, like, gorilla juice heads, tall, completely jacked, steroid, like multiple growth hormone—that's, like, the type I'm attracted to.")

One of the biggest proponents of the idea that reality TV appeals to the worst in us is ... reality TV. Case in point, Susan Boyle. When she showed up, unpolished and dowdy, and blew the doors off *Britain's Got Talent* in her singing audition, it was hailed as a sign that we were finally getting sick of the ugly, snarky culture of reality TV. Did you see her wipe the smirk off Simon Cowell's face? The judges were ready to laugh at her, but she showed them that looks aren't everything! Well, yes, except that Boyle's entire "subversion" of reality TV was set up, framed and milked by a reality show.

Reality shows showcase plenty of bad behavior, but they also presume a heavy moralism on the part of the audience. *Survivor* is known for its self-rationalizing, situational ethics. Anything you do to win can be justified as playing the game. But part of the reason fans become involved in the show is that they get invested in the good guys and bad guys.

Look at the title of *Survivor*'s 10th-anniversary season, starting this month: "Heroes vs. Villains"—that is, those who played decently vs. those who "just played the game." Plenty of fans were entertained by Richard Hatch, who lied his way to the first-season title (often while buck naked). But a million dollars and one tax-evasion conviction later, do they admire him?

The main dangers of reality TV aren't to the viewers but to the participants and those around them. The Heenes were lucky the Balloon Boy hoax was just embarrassing and not deadly. But the sleaziest, and saddest, aspect of their whole story was the implication that their kids were being raised to think it was all a normal thing that people do to help the family business. As Falcon Heene blurted to his dad on *Larry King Live*, "You guys said that we did this for the show."

DJ Adam Goldstein, a.k.a. DJ AM, died last year of an overdose resulting from a drug relapse—while making a reality show about drug abuse for MTV that brought him close to his old temptations. NBC's *The Biggest Loser* casts ever heftier contestants and subjects them to ever-more-stressful challenges, to the point where it seems a competitive-eating reality show would be healthier. Sometimes it's the producers, not the viewers, who could use the reminder that it's not O.K. to do whatever it takes to win the (ratings) game.

Why Reality TV Is Us

But there's more to reality TV than fame-crazy lunatics, 'roid-raging meatheads and silicone drama queens wearing little more than craftily deployed censors' pixelation. A decade after *Survivor*, reality TV has become too vast and diverse a genre to be defined by any one set of especially lousy shows. And for all of everyone's worries 10 years ago, reality TV hasn't crowded "quality shows" off the air. The past 10 years of scripted shows—*The Wire*, *Battlestar Galactica*, *The Office*, *Mad Men*—are the strongest TV has ever had. (One genre that reality may be crowding out is soap operas. *As the World Turns* is ending, as did *Guiding Light*, their appeal supplanted by the immersive serial dramas of *Jon & Kate*, among others.)

In the best cases, reality and scripted television have reached a kind of symbiosis. It's not just that reality shows have learned to structure themselves like sitcoms and dramas. Many of the best TV shows of the '00s lift heavily from reality TV or would have been impossible without it.

Lost, for instance, began as an attempt to create a drama version of *Survivor*. Several of TV's best comedies—the American and British versions of *The Office*, *Parks and Recreation*, *Arrested Development* and *Modern Family*—have borrowed directly from reality TV's format of vérité filmmaking and "confessional" interviews with the characters.

Maybe the best example yet of the reality-fiction alliance is Fox's high school choir spoof *Glee*, which, in essence, is *American Idol* in teen-dramedy form. It is a literal re-creation of the pop appeal of *Idol* (just like *Idol*'s, *Glee*'s songs fly to the top of iTunes on a weekly basis). And it's also a critique of the *American Idol* culture that made it possible. In the words of Rachel (Lea Michele), "Nowadays, being anonymous is worse than being poor."

The best reality shows can be much more engrossing, complex and diverse than your average TV cop show. Last year *The Amazing Race* included the team of bisexual screenwriter Mike White and his gay minister father Mel White, giving a more nuanced, less stereotypical portrayal of both sexual orientation and faith than most big-network dramas would.

The past decade has seen experiments like documentary maker Morgan Spurlock's *30 Days* for FX, a brilliant trading-places switcheroo. (For instance, an anti-immigration militant spent a month living the life of an illegal alien.) *Wife Swap* is an intriguing show about American subcultures (homeschoolers, political activists, etc.) and the natural tendency of parents to secretly judge one another. TLC's *19 Kids and Counting*, about the fecund Duggars, may be an extreme-parenting freak show, but it's also a series about the life of a deeply religious family, a rare subject for TV dramas today.

Even MTV, home of *Jersey Shore*, has the high-minded *16 and Pregnant* (which often features working-class families, who scarcely exist in network drama nowadays); *The Buried Life*, about four friends who travel the world helping people accomplish things they want to do before they die; and *My Life as Liz*, a sort of reality *My So-Called Life* about a high school outcast in small-town Texas.

Are any of these MTV shows as big or as widely hyped as *Jersey Shore* (which got nearly 5 million viewers for its season finale)? No. But that is on you and me, not on reality TV. And even in the cheesiest reality shows, there is an aspirational quality, a democratic quality, a quality that's—yeah, I'll say it—American. "American" in the sense that what is true of countries is true of TV genres: their worst traits are inseparable from their best ones.

In the basic criticism of reality TV—that it makes people famous for nothing rather than rewarding hard work—is a Puritan streak that is as old as Plymouth Rock: Seek thou not the Folly of Celebrity, but apply thyself with Humility to thy Industry! Well, that's one strain of American values. But there are other American ideas that reality TV taps into: That everybody should have a shot. That sometimes being real is better than being polite. That no matter where you started out, you can hit it big, get lucky and reinvent yourself. In her own way, Jwoww is as American a character as the nobody Jay Gatsby heading east and changing his name.

And most important, that you can find something interesting in the lives of people other than celebrities, lawyers and doctors. In CBS's new *Undercover Boss*, executives go incognito to work in entry-level jobs in their companies. In the premiere, Larry O'Donnell, president and COO of Waste Management, picks up litter and cleans toilets. He learns that a woman driving a garbage route has to pee in a coffee can to keep on schedule; trash sorters are docked two minutes' pay for every minute they're late from their half-hour lunch. He's horrified; he's humbled; he vows to help his workers out.

There's plenty to criticize in *Undercover Boss*. The show is moving but it's also manipulative and infuriating. Yes, O'Donnell hands out raises and rewards to the nice people we've met. It makes him (and us) feel good. But company-wide—economy-wide—there's no reason to believe things will get better for the overstressed workers who didn't get on TV.

But here's the thing: you, watching the show, have the tools to come to that conclusion. You've held a job. You know how companies work. And one thing reality TV has trained people to do is to be savvy about its editing. That's how people watch reality TV: you can doubt it, interrogate it, talk back to it, believe it, or not.

And either way, what you're left with is a prime-time TV show about topical concerns, at a time when people would like to see some humility in our CEOs; a show, like Discovery's *Dirty Jobs*, about toilet cleaners and garbage pickers and other people that "quality TV" rarely takes notice of; a show, at heart, about how absolutely crazy-hard ordinary people work.

You also—in the worn-out but cheerful employees—see a testimony to the incredible camera-readiness of the American public. How did O'Donnell manage to work unsuspected among his employees? He told them he was "Randy," a host making a reality show, natch, about entry-level jobs.

And what could be more natural than that? What could be more normal, in an age of ubiquitous media, than to take a stranger for a ride on your garbage truck and complain about your supervisors to the cameras? TV calls, and you must answer. It is as if, as a society, we had been singing in front of a mirror for generations, only to discover that now the mirror can actually see us. And if we are really lucky, it might just offer us a show.

2
15 Minutes:
Celebrity Culture and Reality Stars

(Getty Images)

Susan Boyle attends an album signing at HMV on November 20, 2012, in Glasgow. Fans stood in line to get signed copies of her new album titled *Standing Ovation*.

Reality Television

Fifteen Minutes and Beyond

In 1968 American artist Andy Warhol famously observed that "in the future, everyone will be world-famous for fifteen minutes." His comment, made decades before the advent of reality television, would prove eerily prescient as notions of celebrity shifted at the turn of the century. Warhol's "fifteen minutes of fame"—as the idea is commonly known—took on new meaning with the rise in popularity of candid and competitive reality television and the attendant popularity of its stars. Reality television put a new category of individuals in the spotlight: ordinary people. Whether or not they are seeking the spotlight, and whether or not they have talent worthy of attention, these people have been placed in the public eye and have changed contemporary concepts of celebrity and success.

The traditional American narrative of success in show business was different before reality television became popular. In the traditional narrative, ordinary but talented people achieve fame through hard work and persistence, often waiting to be "discovered" or get their "big break." Reality television stars often become famous without following this traditional trajectory, achieving celebrity status seemingly overnight. Those who gain fame through appearing on a reality television show do so in a number of ways. For some—notably those who appear on talent competitions—reality television is a means to jumpstart a career, often in addition to years of performing and auditioning. Other types of reality stars are ordinary people put on television, people who are famous for being famous, and former stars looking to restart their careers.

The first and best-established way to become famous on reality television is through exhibiting talent. Competitive programs such as *American Idol*, *The X Factor*, or *Britain's Got Talent* present previously undiscovered performers looking for the limelight. *American Idol* alumni include Carrie Underwood, Kelly Clarkson, and Chris Daughtry (of the band Daughtry), all of whom have sold millions of records and have garnered multiple Grammy awards and nominations. Former contestants Katharine McPhee and Jennifer Hudson have become popular actresses, with Hudson winning an Academy Award for best supporting actress in 2007. It should be noted that, in the cases of Daughtry, McPhee, and Hudson, ultimately losing the competition was not an obstacle to later success. *Britain's Got Talent* boasts perhaps the quickest rise to fame in singer Susan Boyle, a middle-aged Scottish woman. Boyle's 2009 audition for the show astonished viewers and the media, as her plain appearance gave no hint of the beauty and power of her voice; the YouTube video of her performance was viewed millions of times in a matter of days and ultimately led to four albums and several tours. Boyle went on to be nominated for multiple Grammy awards as well.

Other shows, like *Project Runway*, *Top Chef*, and *So You Think You Can Dance*, showcase people active in their respective fields—be they fashion design, cooking, or dance—and offer prizes and opportunities for them to get ahead. Competitors on these shows most often become famous by appealing to the audience while also excelling at their craft. For these people, their fifteen minutes in the reality spotlight can often become long-term careers. *So You Think You Can Dance*, for example, features experienced dancers who must undergo a rigorous audition process to be a contestant on the show. Dancers from the show use the competition as a respectable means to further their careers in dance—appearing in commercials, television programs, music videos, and Broadway musicals. Former contestant Travis Wall is a successful, Emmy-nominated choreographer; Chelsie Hightower, Lacey Schwimmer, and Dmitry Chaplin have worked as professional dance partners on *Dancing with the Stars*; Kathryn McCormick starred in the film *Step Up Revolution*, joining many other *So You Think You Can Dance* alumni who appeared in the *Step Up* franchise. For people like these, reality television provided an opportunity to reach a wide audience.

In contrast to reality stars who become famous based on skill are those who become celebrities despite their unremarkable backgrounds. These ordinary people often find themselves thrown into a spotlight that they were not necessarily seeking. This can be seen in the MTV documentary-style program *16 and Pregnant*, a show designed to shed light on teen pregnancy, and its spinoff series *Teen Mom* and *Teen Mom 2*. The subjects of these shows have become television stars, with many, including Maci Bookout, Farrah Abraham, Amber Portwood, and Jenelle Evans, appearing in magazines and tabloid websites that chronicle their relationships and, in some cases, their arrests. Another MTV series, *Jersey Shore*, followed eight Italian American housemates over the course of a summer and became the network's most popular show. The housemates' wild personalities and behavior catapulted them to fame and notoriety, most notably in the cases of Nicole "Snooki" Polizzi and Michael "The Situation" Sorrentino. This state of fame can also be found in former dating show contestants and stars. Ali Fedotowsky and Emily Maynard each appeared as contestants on the dating show *The Bachelor* (seasons 14 and 15, respectively), and went on to star in *The Bachelorette* in seasons 6 and 8.

It should be noted that these ordinary-people-turned-celebrities tend to struggle the most under public scrutiny. Pressure and attention from fans and the media often have adverse effects on people trying to lead a normal life. In the cases of Fedotowsky and Maynard, both women have had high-profile breakups after being unable to sustain a relationship under a microscope. This can similarly be seen in the case of Jon and Kate Gosselin. The Gosselins were featured on several television specials—including *Surviving Sextuplets and Twins* and *Sextuplets and Twins: One Year Later*—about the multiple births in their family. These specials led to the reality television series *Jon & Kate Plus 8* (later *Kate Plus 8*), which ran from 2007 to 2011. The show and its publicity caused trouble in the Gosselins' marriage and documented their increasingly strained relationship and eventual divorce. Even Susan

Boyle, who sought a singing career, was admitted to a psychiatric clinic after losing the title on *Britain's Got Talent*. For reality stars like these, fifteen minutes of fame can be too long when coupled with near-constant media speculation, paparazzi harassment, public backlash and criticism, and the lack of privacy that often go hand in hand with being a celebrity.

Another group of people who reach a heightened state of celebrity through reality television are those who, in popular terminology, are famous for being famous. These individuals achieve celebrity status often without merit, with their notoriety itself often becoming enough for them to continue garnering attention. Among the first of these reality stars were socialites Paris Hilton and Nicole Richie, who appeared on the 2003 reality series *The Simple Life*. Hilton in particular became notorious for her on-screen persona and frequent presence in tabloids; despite being generally regarded as overexposed and overrated, she continued to appear in the media. Hilton and Ritchie—often pejoratively called "celebutantes"—played up their images as being both vapid and spoiled, using the attention to create brands for themselves and make lucrative forays into fashion, singing, and acting.

A prominent example of reality television stars who achieve fame simply through being famous is the program *Keeping up with the Kardashians*. The show, which premiered in 2007, stars socialite sisters Kim, Kourtney, and Khloé Kardashian, along with their mother, Kris Jenner, and their stepfather, former Olympian Bruce Jenner; various stepsiblings, half siblings, and significant others are also fixtures on the show. The Kardashian sisters have appeared on seven seasons of *Keeping up with the Kardashians* and spawned three spinoff series as of 2012: *Kourtney and Kim Take New York*, *Khloé & Lamar*, and *Kourtney and Kim Take Miami*. The shows have resulted in both high ratings and high earnings, especially for Kim Kardashian, the most famous of the sisters. The Kardashian sisters have extended their fifteen minutes of fame through fashion and cosmetics lines, television appearances, and high-profile relationships and marriages as they continue to capitalize on their fame. A study by the Ipsos marketing company indicated that Hilton and Kim Kardashian were among the least popular celebrity personalities, and in 2012 *Forbes* listed Hilton and all three Kardashian sisters among the "most overexposed celebrities." Despite negative attitudes toward these reality stars, audiences continue to tune in to watch their lives unfold on camera, raising questions about voyeurism and the persistence of interest in such figures.

An additional group of reality television celebrities are former stars who appear on shows to reenter the public eye. There are entire series that feature familiar personalities instead of unknowns, including *Celebrity Apprentice*, *The Surreal Life*, *Dancing with the Stars*, and *I'm a Celebrity. . .Get Me Out of Here!* All of these programs cast minor celebrities, often termed "has-beens" or "D-listers," including singer La Toya Jackson, actor Gary Busey, musician Bret Michaels, and host Melissa Rivers—all of whom have appeared on multiple reality shows. Appearing on these shows is an opportunity for these celebrities to restart their careers and become popular with a new audience. This kind of revival in the media is also an opportunity for rebranding and a chance for celebrities to promote themselves, alter their public image, and extend their fifteen minutes. Indeed, the exposure itself is ultimately more rewarding than the meager monetary payout from these shows. Reality contestants whose time on these shows brought significant career boosts include actor Mario Lopez, talk show host Ricki Lake, and singer and fashion designer Kelly Osbourne.

It is noteworthy that most of these celebrities have appeared on multiple shows, each time attempting to capitalize on more fame. Bret Michaels, for example, not only competed on *Celebrity Apprentice* in 2010, but between 2007 and 2009 was the star of his own VH1 dating show, *Rock of Love with Bret Michaels*, as well as its follow-up, *Bret Michaels: Life As I Know It*. These shows often begat other, similar shows; reality programs are inexpensive to produce and generally quick to film, so they are profitable for networks and for stars seeking to increase their time on the small screen. In the example of *Rock of Love with Bret Michaels*, season 2 runner-up Daisy de la Hoya was given her own dating series *Daisy of Love*, thus keeping herself visible. VH1 is especially guilty of populating its competitive reality shows with castoffs from earlier series and seasons, creating complicated interrelationships. For example, some contestants on the VH1 program *I Love Money* originally appeared on the dating show *Real Chance of Love*, which was itself a spinoff of the show *I Love New York*; *I Love New York* starred Tiffany Pollard, who was the runner-up on the dating show *Flavor of Love*, which starred rapper Flavor Flav—who was seeking a career revival in appearing on the show in the first place. Similar reappearances of reality stars occur on other networks as well, with people willing to reprise their on-screen personas in such programs as MTV's *The Challenge* (which features former stars of *The Real World* and *Road Rules*) and all-star seasons of shows including *Project Runway*, *America's Next Top Model*, *Survivor*, and *Big Brother*.

Despite participants' various reasons for entering—and in many cases remaining in—the public eye, an important and pervasive element of reality television is branding. The fifteen minutes of fame sought by reality stars is often the product of carefully crafted personas and closely managed packaging. In talent competitions like *American Idol*, contestants are given makeovers and are coached and costumed according to "type"; the singers often take on roles and even personalities based on their genre, be it rock, country, or pop. Often touted by judges, producers, and the media as "the next" version of a popular performer, reality contestants must appeal to audiences in the same way that brands are marketed. Likewise, candid reality stars often brand themselves by exaggerating personality traits in order to fill a niche (the typical roles of villain, backstabber, or "bad boy" on dating or competition shows, for example) and get more time on camera to fulfill their narrative role.

The concept of branding is an important and almost ubiquitous aspect of reality television in which stars construct their on-screen stints in order to secure further appearances and opportunities. For many, this is how they measure their success. Individuals like Nicole Polizzi and Kim Kardashian are self-created and self-perpetuating celebrities, whose television personas are crafted for entertainment and exposure. Polizzi in particular illustrates that, in the twenty-first century, celebrity is not necessarily equated with talent or merit. Instead, it can be as scripted, edited, and produced as a television show.

Dreaming a Dream:
Susan Boyle and Celebrity Culture

By Su Homes
The Velvet Light Trap, Spring 2012

Susan Boyle's audition of "I Dreamed a Dream" (*Les Misérables*) on the popular reality format *Britain's Got Talent* (2007-2009) rapidly became a phenomenal YouTube hit, catapulting her into media visibility on a global scale. Indeed, viewings of her audition performance leapt from 1.5 million to 5 million in under twenty-four hours (Hollywood). But after being variously hailed as an exceptional talent or a "hairy angel" (Smith), the speculation surrounding the forty-eight-year-old Scottish church volunteer took on a different tone as media coverage speculated whether she would "triumph or crack" (Brook and Carrell) as the eve of the final loomed.

Debates about the value, "state," and future of modern fame have become increasingly pervasive in academic and popular media contexts, and "ordinary" people have emerged as a fertile site for the circulation of such discourses. Whether seen as emblematic of the "cultural decline" thesis (in which we have witnessed a "regrettable" depreciation in the currency of fame) or as attesting to the emergence of a "populist democracy" (in which fame has become a social process that pivots on an egalitarian rhetoric of "leveling down") (Evans), "ordinary" people have been foregrounded as emblematic of "change" in celebrity culture.

Yet despite this emphasis on the "new" it is important to recognize continuity—especially with regard to the mythic or ideological functions of fame. For example, the mediation of the "ordinary" person-turned-star has historically dramatized the possibilities of the success myth (Dyer), in which "lucky breaks," hard work, "talent," and "ordinariness" are the central hallmarks of stardom. This is especially true of the reality talent shows such as *Pop Idol, X Factor,* and *Britain's Got Talent,* which (unlike *Big Brother,* for example) continue to peddle more traditional myths of fame. Indeed figures such as Boyle are invoked as culturally reassuring evidence of the fact that "talent"—in itself an ideological construct that is never clearly defined—still exists (and is waiting to be "discovered") in a context in which "merit" appears to be an absent discourse where celebrity is concerned.

Yet such programs undoubtedly work through more traditional myths of fame within a more self-consciously commercialized modern celebrity culture. In this regard they are often paradigmatic of a competing war between more traditional myths of fame (in which fame is explained by the existence of an "innate" attribute or

Originally published as the article "Dreaming a Dream: Susan Boyle and Celebrity Culture", by Su Holmes, in *The Velvet Light Trap*, Volume 65, pp. 74–76. Copyright © 2010 by the University of Texas Press. All rights reserved.

talent) and the increasing prevalence—since the postwar period—of manufacture as an explanation for fame (with an emphasis on image construction, packaging, "hype") (see Gamson). Given that the prevalence of manufacture and commerciality offers a potential challenge to more elite (and thus less egalitarian) explanations of fame, particular representational tropes have emerged to paper over the apparent disjuncture here. As Joshua Gamson has explained, one such trope is the increased emphasis on audience agency ("*you* choose"), which appears to insist, "If you don't like me, *you* can throw the spotlight onto someone more 'worthy'" (271, emphasis in original).

But in relation to reality TV, the question of audience agency is also invoked with regard to the relationship between "ordinary" people and the ethics of fame. In contrast to the emphasis on a "democratizing" impulse, reality TV has often been yoked to the worst "excesses" of a deeply commercialized celebrity culture in which ordinary people are exploited and used up before being "spat out" by the media machine. Indeed, when it was announced that Boyle was admitted to the Priory clinic after losing to dance troupe Diversity in the final of the show, it was not simply the producers of the program who were invoked as dangerously exposing the singer (who had reportedly also suffered from a mental defect since birth) to the pressures of fame: the viewing public was also seen as colluding in this "irresponsible" act. (After all. hadn't "we" ultimately failed to judge her as the winner?) Either way, the trajectory of Boyle's experience with notoriety reignited debates about the ethics of care provided by reality shows.

> *Indeed, when it was announced that Boyle was admitted to the Priory clinic after losing to dance troupe Diversity in the final of the show, it was not simply the producers of the program who were invoked as dangerously exposing the singer (who had reportedly also suffered from a mental defect since birth) to the pressures of fame: the viewing public was also seen as colluding in this "irresponsible" act.*

This framework is particularly resonant with regard to the audition clip that catapulted Boyle into media visibility. As Boyle appears on the audition stage, the choreography of the sequence immediately invites the question, What sort of pleasures will this performance provide? She explains that she is unemployed and single, has "never been kissed," and lives with her cat, Pebbles; she then elaborates on her dream to become a successful singer in the mold of Elaine Page. We then shift between a series of reaction shots in which the panel of judges as well as members of the audience express a combination of disbelief and scorn at what is seen as the apparent disjuncture between Boyle's physical appearance, social status, and professed aspirations. In this regard the sequence offers a somewhat predetermined subject position in which a superior, judging gaze is directed at a seemingly "deluded" subject, her middle-aged status and physical appearance apparently making her desires even more unacceptable than those of the typically young, fame-seeking "wannabe."

In this respect it is clear that the cultural construction of Boyle intersects with wider gender ideologies that presently structure the meanings of celebrity culture. Both academic and popular attention is now being given to the *highly gendered* imbalance that differentiates the coverage of male and female celebrities, given that current codes for celebrity representation tend to synthesize sexist and ageist logics (Negra and Holmes). Although this is a wider topic that cannot be considered in detail here, it is clear that current celebrity representation is "punishing of young and midlife women in related, but distinctly different, ways" (Negra and Holmes). Indeed, it is worth noting that the apparent "disjuncture" between perceived appearance and perceived talent was not cued as so pronounced when Paul Potts, the overweight opera singer who won the first series of *Britain's Got Talent,* auditioned in 2007: judge Simon Cowell noted, "I wasn't expecting that," while fellow panelist Piers Morgan agreed, "You have an incredible voice." Yet the fact that Boyle's performance was seen as so utterly incongruous with her physical appearance was not completely overlooked by journalists writing in the "quality" press. As Tanya Gold observed in the *Guardian,* "Why are we so shocked when 'ugly' women can do things, rather than sitting at home weeping and wishing they were somebody else? Men are allowed to be ugly and talented. Alan Sugar looks like a burst bag of flour. Gordon Ramsay has a dried up riverbed for a face." Yet, the initial reaction of the crowd at Boyle's audition suggested that she might "be hanged for her presumption" that she might be worthy of the media spotlight (Gold). Furthermore, when Boyle wiggled her hips and explained that her "ordinary" life was "only one side of [her]," judge Piers Morgan winced while the audience tittered with embarrassment, and as Gold later noted:"Didn't Susan know that she wasn't supposed to be sexual?" In observing how Boyle subsequently had her appearance "picked over" in many media forums, it was later observed that "fairy stories are full of woodcutter's daughters who get transformed into princesses, but what's happened to poor Susan Boyle has much more in common with a freakshow" (Smith).

The promise and expectation of physical transformation referenced in this quote may also elucidate the fervor with which Boyle attracted attention in America (especially when reality TV stars are conventionally national, rather than international, in appeal). Indeed, the expectation that Boyle might dramatize the possibilities of the reflexive self (Giddens) so central to the transformative, consumerist, and individualist ethos of makeover culture appeared to be especially pronounced in her US circulation and reception. To be sure, the fact that constructions of fame are gendered is hardly a startling revelation, but the circulation of Boyle (and the intensity of her media visibility and rapid temporal rise to fame) appears to articulate these in a condensed and thus microcosmic form. Furthermore, while Boyle might initially be invoked as reassuring evidence of the fact that real "talent" still exists (and that it can be discovered by reality shows), she has simultaneously been constructed as the "freakish exception that proves the rule" (Gold). In this regard, her construction and reception shore up conceptions of acceptable/"unacceptable" norms of femininity (especially as endorsed by celebrity culture), while she is simultaneously hailed as evidence of a democratized fame culture—even though by "raising Susan up, we will forgive ourselves for grinding every other Susan into the dust" (Gold). As Turner reminds us, fame is a very curious culture site in which to look for evidence of "democratization," given that, no matter how much it appears to expand, celebrity will always be a "hierarchical and exclusive phenomenon, no matter how much it appears to proliferate" (78).

Works Cited

Brook, Stephen, and Severin Carrell. "Susan Boyle Dreamed a Dream, Now TV Show Stress Has Become a Nightmare." *Guardian* 29 May 2009. Web. guardian. co.uk.

Dyer, Richard. *Stars,* 2nd ed. London: Routledge. 1998.

Evans, Jessica. "Celebrity, Media. History." *Understanding Media: Inside Celebrity.* Ed. J. Evans and David Hesmondhalgh. Buckinghamshire: Open UP, 2Ü05. 7-32.

Gamson, J. *Claims to Fame: Celebrity in Contemporary America.* Berkeley: U of California P, 1994.

Giddens, Anthony. *Modernity and Self-Identity: Self and Society in the Late Modern Age.* Cambridge: Policy, 1991.

Gold, Tanya. "It Wasn't Singer Susan Boyle Who Was Ugly on *Britain's Got Talent* So Much As Our Reaction to Her." *Guardian* 16 June 2009. Web. guardian.co.uk.

Holmwood, L. "Susan Boyle's *Britain's Got Talent* Performance a Hit for ITV Website." *Guardian* 16 Apr. 2009. Web. guardian, co.uk.

Negra, D., and S. Holmes. "Introduction: Going Cheap? Female Celebrity in the Tabloid. Reality and Scandal Genres." *Genders* 48 (Fall 2008). Web. http://www. genders.org/g48/g48 _negraholmes.html.

Smith, J. "The Susan Boyle Freakshow." *Guardian* 1 June 2009.

Baby Mamas

By Feifei Sun
Time, July 18, 2011

"This is the happiest day of my life!" So says Maci Bookout, according to a recent cover of *OK!* magazine, where the 19-year-old *Teen Mom* star and rumored bride-to-be flashes a beauty-queen smile. Sharing cover space with Bookout—and sporting a bikini, plus a **baby** on each hip—is Leah Messer, 19, whose dream wedding was featured in last spring's season finale of *Teen Mom 2*. (One month later, she filed for divorce.) Elsewhere in the celebrity mediasphere, one might find *Teen Mom*'s Farrah Abraham, 20, staging a photo op for paparazzi on a Florida beach, or Abraham's castmate Amber Portwood, 21, posing for photographers outside her latest court hearing; she was recently sentenced to probation after pleading guilty to felony domestic battery against the father of her child.

A spin-off of MTV's popular reality series *16 and Pregnant*, *Teen Mom* recently entered its third season. With more than 3 million viewers each week, it's the network's top-rated show after *Jersey Shore*, and its subjects provide endless fodder for the tabloids. But MTV's teen-pregnancy franchise is a more discomfiting venture than most artifacts of the reality-TV age. Not quite famous for being famous, as the denizens of *The Hills* and *Jersey Shore* are, these young mothers became famous for making unplanned detours into parenthood—and inviting cameras along for the ride. Though MTV recruited them to be the subjects of cautionary tales, the network has turned them into success stories: television stars and cover girls, gainfully employed just for being themselves. (Last December, Portwood disclosed that she earned $140,000 from a six-month contract with MTV.) The contradictions of *Teen Mom*–brand fame might be encapsulated in a 2010 cover of *Us Weekly*: Bookout and Abraham stand back to back, cradling their adorable toddlers and grinning sunnily above the somber headline INSIDE THEIR STRUGGLE.

It's an uneasy mix of messages from programs intended to document and deter teen pregnancy, not exalt it. Lauren Dolgen, senior vice president of series development at MTV and the creator of *16 and Pregnant* and *Teen Mom*, got the idea for the shows after reading that each year, 750,000 15-to-19-year-olds become pregnant in the U.S. "This is an epidemic that is happening to our audience, and it's a preventable epidemic," Dolgen says. "We thought it was so important to shed light on this issue and to show girls how hard teen parenting is."

Each episode of *16 and Pregnant* tracks one teen from the latter stages of pregnancy to the first months of her child's life. The series does not sugarcoat the challenges its subjects face: the slights and scorn of peers, friction with disappointed

From *Time* 178.3 (18 Jul. 2011): 58–60. Copyright © 2011 by *Time* Inc. All rights reserved. Reprinted with permission.

(grand)parents, colic, drudgery, arguments, sleep deprivation and—with dismayingly few exceptions—the burden of a feckless, absent or outright abusive boyfriend. Both *16 and Pregnant* and *Teen Mom* (which features alums of *16 and Pregnant* such as Bookout, Abraham and Portwood) beckon viewers to the website ItsYourSexLife.com, which offers sex-ed resources and promotes dialogue between teens and their parents about sex.

The approach works. An October 2010 focus-group study commissioned by the National Campaign to Prevent Teen and Unplanned Pregnancy found that 4 in 10 teenagers who watch an episode of *16 and Pregnant* talk about the show with a parent afterward and that more than 90% of them think teen pregnancy is harder than they imagined before watching the series. "Any show that provides an opportunity to get more direction from a responsible adult, whether it's a parent or an educator—that's a terrific opportunity," says Leslie Kantor, national director of education initiatives for Planned Parenthood Federation of America.

But Kantor adds that despite their quest for gritty realism, the shows may create a distorted view of teen sexual activity. "Showing the consequences of risky behavior can be helpful to some young people," she says. "What you don't want is to send the message that everybody is having unprotected sex. These shows create a perception that tremendous numbers of teens are becoming pregnant or becoming parents."

> *The series does not sugarcoat the challenges its subjects face: the slights and scorn of peers, friction with disappointed (grand)parents, colic, drudgery, arguments, sleep deprivation and—with dismayingly few exceptions—the burden of a feckless, absent or outright abusive boyfriend.*

And actually, they're not. The teen pregnancy rate in the U.S. has consistently declined over the past 20 years, except for a small spike from 2005 to 2007. Approximately 7% of girls 15 to 19 years old became pregnant in 2006—a significant number but perhaps not an epidemic. Nor does the casting of the shows reflect the actual racial breakdown of teen pregnancy. While *Teen Mom* focuses heavily on white girls, unplanned pregnancies affect African-American and Hispanic teens at nearly three times the rate of whites.

Liz Gateley, a former executive producer of *16 and Pregnant* and *Teen Mom* who is no longer with MTV, says the network specifically targeted middle-class girls through church groups and parenting organizations. "If we did inner-city people who really had difficulty with their upbringing," she says, "we thought the public will discount this as, 'Oh, that doesn't apply to me.'" According to Gateley, the model for the series was *Juno*, the Oscar-winning 2007 film about a white, middle-class teenage girl who gets pregnant—right down to the animated-sketchbook style of the movie's credits. (Dolgen would not directly contradict Gateley's account, but she maintains that the show casts a wide net in recruiting subjects.)

Bookout, subject of the premiere episode on June 11, 2009, was cast after her mother happened upon a Craigslist ad for the program while searching online for maternity-modeling jobs for her daughter. "When I first watched [the premiere], I had no idea it was going to be as big of a deal as it is now—such a controversial phenomenon," Bookout says.

But she has no regrets. During her two years in the limelight, she has left the father of her now 2-year-old son Bentley and fallen in love with a new man (though she says she has no wedding plans). She's appeared on dozens of magazine covers, spoken alongside Bristol Palin to groups about teen-pregnancy prevention and enrolled at Chattanooga State Community College, where she's studying English literature and creative writing. "I don't necessarily think I would change anything," Bookout says of her stint as a reality star. "I'm very proud of what my life has become and what the show has done."

Her castmate Catelynn Lowell, 19, is proud too. "I've changed girls' lives since the show started," she says. "I go to schools and talk about adoption, preaching contraceptives and abstinence." In many ways, Lowell is the outlier of the group. Unlike Bookout and the other *Teen Mom* parents, Lowell arranged an open adoption for her 2-year-old daughter Carly, and her relationship with her child's father remains intact; they plan to marry after graduating from college. The tabloids, for the most part, leave them alone. "I don't know why that is," Lowell says. "Probably because we don't get into trouble."

Other cast members can't say the same. Portwood is a fixture on TMZ.com and other tabloid sites; primary custody of her daughter Leah currently rests with the girl's father, and in June, Portwood was hospitalized after a reported suicide attempt. In March, *Teen Mom 2* star Jenelle Evans, 19, was arrested for assault, and in February 2010, Abraham's mother Debra Danielson struck a plea deal after she allegedly choked and hit her daughter.

These skirmishes may not come as a complete surprise to regular viewers of the shows. Tension, despair and sometimes explosive conflict are among the ingredients that make the series such addictive, even shocking television. That's why Bookout, the most glamorous star in the *Teen Mom* firmament, is also the last person to suggest that the shows glamorize their subjects.

"In every episode, someone is trying to figure out if they can pay their rent or go to school or find a job or when they're going to be able to take their next nap, because they haven't slept in 24 hours," Bookout says. "In every episode, someone has their heart broken."

Reality Shows Pay with Resuscitated Careers

By Andrew Gumbel
The WRAP TV, March 17, 2009

Not so long ago, reality TV was the last place any self-respecting celebrity would wish to end up.

"Hollywood Squares" was another term for Hollywood Hell. "Celebrity Boxing"—remember that little delight from 2002?—was a garbage collection point for tabloid cast-offs: Paula Jones, Joey Buttafuoco, Tonya Harding and the hapless Darva Conger, the former California nurse best known for thinking, wrongly, that she wanted to marry a multi-millionaire on live TV.

Now, though, the famous—and almost-famous—are lining round the block to get on the most popular shows, like "Dancing With the Stars" or "Celebrity Apprentice," sniffing out any opportunity to put themselves on the map or—in the case of fading mid-career entertainers—sell themselves in a different guise to a whole new generation of fans.

There seems to be no limit to the possibilities. Legendary funk master George Clinton angling for … a *Nashville* recording session on "Gone Country." Apple Computers co-founder Steve Wozniak on "Dancing With the Stars." (Yes, it's as bad as you'd think.) Andy Dick letting his addictions hang out and regularly breaking into tears on "Sober House"—along with the likes of Rodney King, and even an "American Idol" reject from last season. Joan Rivers shaking it up in the boardroom with Donald Trump.

One thing's for sure: It isn't for the money.

Every reality show is different. A celebrity with a show built around his or her life is likely to get producer credit and maybe something on the back end. Participants on an existing show generally get a flat fee without residuals.

In a show with a knock-out element like "Dancing With the Stars," the fee usually goes up the longer the participant survives. Someone who makes it to the finals on "DWTS" is looking at a fee in the $250,000-$300,000 range. Naturally, the fee is far lower, for example, on the VH-1, Bravo and E! shows than on a prime-time network.

And compare that to nonreality TV. Stars on a multi-character scripted drama can make upwards of $50,000 an episode—sometimes *way* upward.

"Between scripted shows and reality shows," said a leading TV agent, "in the success scenario there's just no comparison—and that's the way it should be. On scripted shows, they have to have talent."

The real money, though, often lies in what comes after. "It's all about the endorsements and other appearances. There's a lot of heat coming off that show," one TV agent said.

From *The WRAP TV* (17 March 2009). Copyright © 2009 by *The WRAP TV*. Reprinted with Permission. All Rights Reserved.

The real money, though, often lies in what comes after. "It's all about the endorsements and other appearances. There's a lot of heat coming off that show," one TV agent said.

Lauren Conrad has gone from nobody to television mega-celebrity by committing her young adult life to video on the MTV series "Laguna Beach" and its follow-up "The Hills." No longer simply an aspiring fashion designer, she has launched her own clothing line on the back of her cable network visibility.

Her fellow cast members Heidi Montag, Audrina Patridge and Whitney Port have similarly diversified into music, film acting, fashion design, earning themselves millions of dollars in the process.

Jerry Springer used "Dancing With the Stars" to help him escape the pigeonhole of his notorious daytime circus and turned it into a hosting slot on "America's Got Talent." It also put him in a position to be fielding, for the first time in his career, movie offers. Joey Fatone used the show as a springboard to become the host of "The Singing Bee."

And the list goes on: "DWTS'" Julianne Hough got a boost to her fledgling country music career; Mario Lopez was tabbed to host "Extra."

The thing that has changed from the "Battle of the Network Stars" days is, in a word, volume. "There's more of it out there," said one television agent who has set up reality shows for his clients. "With more out there come more opportunities for people who wouldn't otherwise have had an in on television. Now they are given their shot, their 15 minutes. And some people are parlaying those 15 minutes into 30 minutes or hours or full careers."

Though, for some, like Gary Busey, the options for reinvention seem limited to a stint on "Celebrity Rehab with Dr. Drew"—a hit show that is unlikely to do very much for its participants other than reinforce stereotypical views.

The television agent said he will spend several hours in development meetings trying to identify career goals and branding options for his clients before coming up with a reality show pitch. His greatest successes have come when he has been able to resuscitate a career—he did not want to name names, but he has done so several times by now.

"Some shows have been proven to be safe and have developed reputations as career rejuvenators," a television insider said. "'Dancing With the Stars' is a show people can do. 'Celebrity Apprentice' is safe to do. Of course, it's up to you to conduct yourself in a way consistent with your celebrity brand."

Indeed, there's no question a cleverly crafted reality show stint can do wonders—especially if the celeb is willing to open up the idiosyncrasies of his or her personal or professional lives to public scrutiny.

"At a time when the business is contracting and opportunities for a lot of celebrities are disappearing," the insider said, "there is greater pressure to take advantage of those kinds of shows."

"This Was My Worst Nightmare":
The Bachelor's Emily

By Monica Rizzo
People, July 11, 2011

It wasn't supposed to be like this. The last time Emily Maynard was in sunny Southern California, she was a contestant on the ABC reality dating show *The Bachelor*. That's where the Charlotte, N.C., single mom began a whirlwind TV romance with an eager-to-wed Brad Womack—a love affair that culminated in the Austin, Texas, bar owner popping the question on the show's season finale. It may have been an on-air love affair, but Maynard makes it clear she thought she had found The One. Instead, her return to the lavish mansion where the show is filmed—captured in an emotional one-on-one interview with host Chris Harrison that will air during the July 11 episode of *The Bachelorette*—reveals no such happy ending. Sobbing and shaking as cameras rolled, Maynard opens up about the rumors that have dogged the couple for weeks: that she and Womack had broken up. "We're no longer engaged," she tells PEOPLE, tearing up after her talk with Harrison. "The last time I got out of a car here was to meet Brad for the first time," she says. "I thought the next time [I came here] we would be planning a wedding, getting married. This was my worst nightmare. I thought there was no way Brad and I wouldn't work out."

For his part, Womack, 38, is also reeling from the breakup. "The demise of our relationship was completely my fault," says the former *Bachelor*, who declined to attend the ABC taping with Maynard, 25. "I gave Em every reason under the sun to get out much sooner than she did. She hung in there with me much, much longer than she should have."

Both say they tried hard to make their relationship work but that it had begun to unravel not long after their *Bachelor* season began airing last January. While viewers watched Womack romance her onscreen, Maynard—who had to remain apart from her fiance to keep the show's ending a secret—was devastated by scenes of him in intimate situations with other contestants. "Going through it, everything was very real for me," Maynard told PEOPLE in March. "Even when there were 30 girls, he still made me feel special. But then, watching it back, he had a tendency to say the same thing to a couple of girls. So I felt less and less special." Unable to comfort Maynard in person, Womack sent lavish gifts and flowers from Texas in an attempt to reassure her. "It was torturous," he says. "Not being able to be there physically to reassure Emily was the biggest test I've ever been through."

From *People* 77.1 (11 Jul. 2011): 50–54. Copyright © 2011 by Time Inc. Reprinted with permission. All rights reserved.

After watching the finale and reliving the moment when Womack got down on one knee and popped the question with a $50,000 Neil Lane diamond engagement ring, Maynard thought she was finally ready to put the past behind them. "I felt this is a whole new relationship—like I fell in love with him all over again," she says. "I never brought up the show again. I just wanted to fade into normal life."

Unfortunately, her idea of a normal life had ceased to exist. Photographers and camera crews followed Womack around in Austin and Maynard and her 6-year-old daughter Ricki in Charlotte. "I had photographers outside of my house waiting for me to go somewhere," says Maynard, who felt deeply conflicted about uprooting her daughter and relocating to Texas. "I thought, 'Oh, it will die down.' But it didn't."

> *The paparazzi "became a huge game-changer," says Womack, who experienced similar scrutiny during his first go-round as the* **Bachelor** *in 2007, when he famously didn't choose either of his final two potential suitors. "I failed [Emily] in the respect that I should have protected her." Angered by the tabloids, he sometimes directed his frustration at Maynard . . . .*

The paparazzi "became a huge game-changer," says Womack, who experienced similar scrutiny during his first go-round as the *Bachelor* in 2007, when he famously didn't choose either of his final two potential suitors. "I failed [Emily] in the respect that I should have protected her." Angered by the tabloids, he sometimes directed his frustration at Maynard . . . .

Meanwhile, the couple were coping with other major stumbling blocks, including Womack's inability to fully embrace the concept of being a 24-7 parent to Ricki. "He didn't understand why I couldn't go on a random vacation the next day," says Maynard. "It's hard for me to say, 'I am so tired, I want to go to bed at 8,' and for him to understand."

That stress was compounded by their long-distance relationship. Maynard had initially planned to move to Austin in the summer but ultimately decided it wasn't in her or Ricki's best interest because of the couple's on-off status. "I need stability," she says. "I can't just say I'll figure it out when I get there. I didn't feel it would be a good move to take my daughter away from her life for a guy if I don't know if it's going to work out a month down the road."

As the months wore on, both began to feel that their differences were too great to overcome. "There's nothing worse than fighting with someone you love so much. When we were together, we were really happy," says Maynard. "But the second we were apart, it got hard." Agrees Womack: "It drove me crazy. It was a sense of detachment I didn't like at all."

While some tabloid reports indicated that Maynard was always eager to break things off, Womack says she tried as hard as he did to keep their romance alive. "There were numerous moments that I threw my hands up and declared a breakup, but she stuck by my side," he says. After several months of trying to reconcile, however, Womack says he again suggested they part ways, and "she didn't disagree the last time." The split finally happened "not too long ago," Maynard says. "We didn't want to announce anything until we knew for sure. I was okay with it, but I think it was hard on him," she says, adding that they tried to make it work until the end. "We both went down swinging—that's for sure."

Maynard takes equal responsibility for the relationship's demise. "It wasn't him hurting me or me hurting him," she says about the decision to end the engagement (she has given the engagement ring back to *Bachelor* producers). "There was no huge blow-up fight. It was two adults having the maturity to step away and realize that just because we love each other doesn't mean we're right for each other."

She's quick to shoot down the idea that Womack is a commitment-phobe. "He's smart enough to know when it's right and when it's not," she says. "The first time he was on *The Bachelor*, it wasn't right. We both thought it was right this time. He's been such a gentleman. I feel confident had we lived in the same city and met at church, we could have made it."

Their breakup has added a sadness for Maynard, who lost her fiance, NASCAR driver Ricky Hendrick, in a 2004 plane crash, only to find out five days later that she was pregnant with their child. She remains close to Hendrick's parents, who "have seen me at the bottom and know how badly I want to fall in love again and get married," she says. "They know how much I want more children. They want it as much as I do for me."

For now, though, Maynard is trying to stay focused on enjoying the summer with her daughter, who "has been a huge help for me," she says. "I have more fun with her than I do with anyone else." The duo's plans include borrowing a pickup truck, putting a mattress in the back and taking Ricki and several of her pals to a local drive-in for her birthday. Maynard has also added a pet to the family, a kitten named Safari.

One thing she won't be doing, however, is signing on to be the next *Bachelorette*. "Right now my main focus is being a mom," she says of the gossip that she'll star in the series. "I'm just like any girl dealing with a heartbreak. The last thing on my mind is to do this all over again."

And while she and Womack have called it quits, Maynard plans to keep in touch with her ex-fiance. The two are still texting and calling each other. Could they ever reconcile? "I don't know," she says. "Right now I need a break from everything. I don't know what's going to happen in the future. I know that I love him, and more than anything he's been a friend to me."

She quietly starts crying as she recalls calling Womack her "angel" during the show. "He's taught me that I have it in me to love someone again," she says. "Just opening up my heart and not be scared of getting hurt. I think he's always going to be a part of my life." The feeling is mutual. "She was the one," says Womack. "She's the only woman I ever wanted to marry. I will always be in love with Em."

No matter what her future holds, Maynard is trying to stay positive. "It's okay," she says. "It's not the first relationship in the world that hasn't worked. People get through it. I know I will too, and he will." But that doesn't make the end of a fairy tale any less painful. "I'm sad," Maynard says quietly, "that we don't have a happy ending."

Why I Walked Away

By Charlotte Triggs, Monica Rizzo, and Gabrielle Olya
Time, December 12, 2011

After she got engaged to Roberto Martinez while filming *The Bachelorette* last May, a giddy Ali Fedotowsky couldn't stop talking about wedding plans. "Now that I've found the one for me, I can't wait!" Ali told *People* three months later. "I feel like, 'I gotta lock that down.'" But as time went on, the path to the altar stretched longer and longer. First the couple slowed down plans for a spring 2011 wedding. Then this past July, Ali needed knee surgery, forcing them to postpone their nuptials yet again. Finally plans for a holiday 2011 wedding, which would have been filmed for ABC, fell through over concerns about timing and the logistics of flying her Massachusetts-based clan and his relatives in Puerto Rico abroad for a destination affair. "It's just so frustrating," Ali confessed to *People* in September. "I'm not a planner. I just [want] to be there and marry the man of my dreams."

Now the dream is done. On Nov. 21, after being engaged for 18 months, Ali and Roberto announced they were breaking up. "I wouldn't be being truthful if I said this came out of nowhere," Ali told *People* through (many) tears in her first interview since the split, just days after moving out of their San Diego apartment. "We definitely had been having problems. But I had always believed that we could work it out." For his part, Roberto, 28, "kept believing and hoping that they'd find a way," says a source. "He's still in shock that it's really over."

To fans of the show, the bubbly, athletic blonde and her tall, dark and handsome beau seemed poised to beat the odds that stand in the way of reality-TV romance. (For the record: Two of seven *Bachelorette* couples are still together, and exactly zero of 15 original *Bachelor* pairs.) Ali and Roberto thought they would prevail too—until reality sank in. Off-camera the duo got off to a rocky start, with Ali admitting she wasn't thrilled with their tight quarters in an "industrial" area of San Diego, their chosen new hometown. Roberto, who had relocated from Charleston, S.C., worked to set up a new State Farm insurance office, while Ali, 27, who left her job at Facebook to take part in *The Bachelorette*, struggled to define her career path, working as a local news correspondent and signing a deal for a Style Network hosting gig that eventually fell through. "We were trying to establish ourselves individually," Ali concedes, "but a relationship should be solid regardless of circumstances."

When it came to day-to-day issues, their different interests started driving them apart. "A lot of times what I wanted to do and what he wanted to do didn't match up," she says plainly. "One of us was always compromising with the other, or we both ended up not doing what we wanted and staying home." When she injured her

---

From *Time* 76.24 (12 Dec. 2011): 88–94. Copyright © 2011 by Time Inc. All rights reserved. Reprinted with permission.

femur kickboxing and had to undergo surgery in July, "it really affected us," she says. "I couldn't really be active like I wanted to be. I hit a low." Before long, minor differences gave way to more challenging personality clashes. When it came to their free time, "he would rather be alone on weekends," says Ali. "He's more introverted. I love being around people and sharing stories and going out to dinner."

But a source close to Ali says one of their biggest issues was Roberto's temper—which was often triggered by arguments over his traditional, conservative values. "Roberto seemed bothered that Ali was career-minded and had a social life. He is very old-fashioned when it comes to a woman's place," says the source. Ali concedes that she often tried to play the part of dutiful helper: "I helped him build his business, and I'd bring him lunch all the time," she says. "I was so supportive of him." Even so, their fights had intensified lately. "In the past six months he kind of lost it," says the source. "He'd be really good and sweet in public, but their fights could be explosive."

When it came to day-to-day issues, their different interests started driving them apart. "A lot of times what I wanted to do and what he wanted to do didn't match up," she says plainly. "One of us was always compromising with the other, or we both ended up not doing what we wanted and staying home."

As their relationship began to disintegrate, the pair still held out hope of pulling together a TV wedding "to share with our fans," Ali told *People* in September. But when the plans began to unravel yet again, the once gleeful bride-to-be, who had already picked out shoes (sparkly Converses!) and a dress (Monique Lhuillier), instead declared the wedding was indefinitely on hold. "Something inside both of us said we still had more figuring out to do," Ali says. "We take marriage very seriously. It's not something we were going to do and just hope it works out."

All the while, Ali defended their relationship as rumors of strife hit the Internet. "It doesn't matter if you are the Bachelorette or a normal girl," she says. "When people criticize your relationship, even if it isn't in the best place, you want to believe that it is." She moved in with friends for a weeklong trial separation in November—then gave her relationship one more shot. "I went back to our apartment, and I cooked this Spanish dish that his mom makes to do something special for him, so we could have a dinner and talk," she recalls, breaking down in sobs. Instead the tension-filled meal only served as confirmation that they were over. "At the end of the day we both realized we were unhappy more than we were happy," Ali says. "And we both deserved more. I just knew that we needed to go separate ways." When she was moving out her belongings a few days later, Roberto stopped by. "We hugged each other. And he broke down, and I broke down. It was a very emotional experience." (Ali, for now at least, is hanging on to her $50,000 Neil Lane engagement ring and what it once represented: "It's a symbol of our love, and that's something that I still have.")

Now Ali, who is staying with friends in San Jose, Calif., will have many more decisions to make. "All of my things are going to be in storage until I figure out what to do," she says. "I literally don't even know where I want to live, never mind what I want to do." The first step, though, is healing. Ali and Roberto "still talk every day. I found real, true love, and I'm grateful that I had that experience," she says, adding emphatically, "There's no hate. I still love him, and I always will. But what matters is how we feel, and we both knew it wasn't right."

5 Worst Things about Reality Television

By Jessica Harpe and Brenna Rushing
Dallas Morning News, October 4, 2012

Has reality TV run its course? A Pegasus News writer lists her five worst things about music-related reality television shows like The Voice, American Idol, The X Factor, *and* America's Got Talent.

Just for fun, a writer who loves reality TV countered those arguments. It can't be all bad, can it?

No. 1: Winners of Reality Shows Get Famous and Quickly Lose Their Allure

Out of hundreds of contestants on *American Idol*, how many people can you name who have competed? Did you buy any of their music? Probably not.

Remember season two winner Ruben Studdard? I don't either. Since he won *American Idol* back in 2003, he has been signed to four different labels and released five albums. The only record to garner any serious attention was his debut album after he won. The others went unnoticed.

Know Lee DeWyze? Apparently he was the season nine winner. He has four albums, two of which were released post-Idol, though his last one didn't even manage to chart. Ouch.

America, you either stink at picking superstars or are terrible at supporting the people you voted for after they win.

On the Flip Side

According to the *Billboard* charts, many *American Idol* winners and/or runners up have record sales in the millions (including Studdard). Through July of 2012, Carrie Underwood has sold nearly 12.5 million records and Kelly Clarkson has sold more than 11 million. Studdard fell behind with 2.5 million records to date but has still reached multi-platinum status. Thirteen of the "Top 24 American Idols of All-Time" (according to Billboard.com) sold over a million records. I'd say that's success, especially for those singers that came from nothing. Oh, and how could we forget the Oscar that Jennifer Hudson took home in 2007 for her supportive acting and singing roles in *Dreamgirls*? She probably would not have had a chance at that audition without *American Idol*.

We can't leave out the *X Factor*'s British pop sensation, One Direction. Their debut album has sold 1.1 million copies this year, according to the *Billboard* charts,

From *Dallas Morning News* (4 October 2012).). Copyright © 2012 by *Dallas Morning News*. Reprinted with permission. All rights reserved.

which is currently 2012's second-biggest selling album in the US. One more example for good measure: Susan Boyle's debut album sold 701,000 copies in its first week according to Nielsen SoundScan. In 2009, it was the largest-ever sales debut for a female artist.

No. 2: Judges Don't Add Value

When Randy Jackson, Paula Abdul, and Simon Cowell judged *American Idol*, it was a good thing. Fine. You had a record producer/manager, a veteran choreographer/singer, and a music executive/manager helping America decide who was worthy of a record contract. Each judge had incredible insight to a fickle industry that could love you one day and leave you high and dry the next. However, when the trio called it quits and other reality singing competitions came into the picture, that's when judges were picked on ratings instead of the value they added to the show.

There are a few truly talented judges out there—CeeLo Green on *The Voice* is a good example—but who are the others? Sharon Osbourne, for instance, while fun to watch, isn't a musician. And though Christina Aguilera on *The Voice* is in fact talented, seeing her boobs all over TV is enough to turn us off to that show. Any advice Jennifer Lopez shells out can be easily ignored. She hasn't had a No. 1 hit in years.

On the Flip Side

We'll start with Lopez: She has kept her career while giving birth to twins in 2008, filing for divorce in April, and launching a world tour in June. She also released the single "On the Floor" featuring Pitbull in 2011. It was No. 3 on the *Billboard* Hot 100, which was her highest peaking song in eight years. She kicked off a headlining tour in June and is currently co-headlining a tour with Enrique Iglesias. We said this about their August 26 show in Dallas: "Lopez ran a tightly produced concert. A veteran performer who recently made headlines for leaving her judge's seat on *American Idol*, Lopez gave a polished performance appropriate for her superstar status."

Don't forget Cowell is now running the show on X Factor. His biting remarks and critical ear are still adding controversy to the primetime world, giving audience members even more reasons to hate him.

No. 3: Contestants Who Do Not Win Have Talent

The day *American Idol* made its debut was the day the music died. It became all about becoming a pop star as opposed to doing it for the music. Gone are the days of bands who work their way to the top; instead, they just get their lead singer to try out for a reality music competition. Musicians like Led Zeppelin, The Beatles, Pink Floyd, and Rolling Stones didn't need America to vote for them, they did it the old-fashioned way by writing their own songs and constantly touring. They didn't sell out to the masses, they sold out of records, and it took years to achieve the greatness that they reached.

Those musicians have longevity that no reality singing competition contestant will ever have.

On the Flip Side

Sure, the hard work of past rock 'n' rollers can't be compared to that of reality television stars, but it doesn't mean they don't have talent. *The Huffington Post* says AI's 2012 winner Phillip Phillips plays his own instrument and writes his own music. Clarkson has always been hands-on with her material—the *Washington Post* made note of her headline-grabbing veer from the typical mainstream hit-making processes by adding her darker, edgier words on a majority of tracks on her 2007 album *My December*.

> *The main offenders of making the show more about themselves than the contestants has got to be The Voice. Instead of just letting the contestants perform on their own, judges occasionally perform with them. It's got to be difficult to stand out while sharing the stage with a vocal powerhouse (and attention grabber) like Aguilera.*

AI's 2006 runner-up Katherine McPhee knows a thing or two about working her way up. With only 465,000 records sold to date, it seems she has been patiently waiting for that breakout performance to come her way, and last season's series premiere of NBC's *Smash* was just that. The Broadway-themed TV show gives McPhee all the time in the world to showcase her robust chords, as well as her surprisingly good acting skills.

No. 4: Judges Make the Show More About Themselves Than the Contestants

Since Cowell and Abdul left *American Idol*, the show can't find the right combination that has the staying power that the first eight seasons of AI had. The lineup now includes Nicki Minaj, Keith Urban, Randy Jackson, and Mariah Carey. Do we really care about Carey?

The main offenders of making the show more about themselves than the contestants has got to be *The Voice*. Instead of just letting the contestants perform on their own, judges occasionally perform with them. It's got to be difficult to stand out while sharing the stage with a vocal powerhouse (and attention grabber) like Aguilera.

As for *X Factor*, the show should really be called "Things Britney Does Now That She's Not Crazy Anymore."

On the Flip Side

Some judges really do seem to care about their protégés. Blake Shelton from *The Voice* brought Dia Frampton, his top contestant from season one of *The Voice*, along as his opening act on his nationwide tour. The winner of season one, Javier Colon, released his debut single with Adam Levine titled "Raise Your Hand." He also toured with Maroon 5 in August 2012.

America's Got Talent could easily boast of having the least amount of drama for a room full of star judges; the outspoken, yet oddly caring Osbourne, TV veteran Howie Mandel, and crass radio personality Howard Stern have had no drama to date (unless you count when Mandel reportedly got his feelings hurt or became jealous when Stern was picked up to replace Piers Morgan).

Unfortunately, the *American Idol* judges sit high above the rest in the diva category: Every day, we see new headlines about who is being added to the show or who is leaving and why. It doesn't seem to be getting any better, either. What drama will Minaj and Carey stir up by sitting at the same table for weeks on end?

No. 5: The Allure of Reality Television in General Is Over

Let's face it: we are done with reality television like Katie Holmes is done with Tom Cruise. It is tired, it is played out, and the talent pool that America has to offer is getting smaller and smaller. Pretty soon, *Honey Boo Boo* is going to make an appearance on *X Factor* and the world will realize just how unnecessary reality singing competitions really are. Sure it's entertainment, but it's cheap and getting worse as each season goes by.

On the Flip Side

The Nielsen TV ratings show that *American Idol* was the No. 2 highest watched primetime TV show (including non-reality shows) with 19.8 million viewers. It was only behind the almighty Sunday Night Football timeslot, so let's go ahead and consider them No. 1. The Voice came in at No. 9, *X Factor* was No. 19, and *America's Got Talent* trailed with the No. 40 spot. If this doesn't show that reality TV isn't dying, what does?

3

Consuming Reality

(Washington Post/Getty Images)

D.C. area residents react in different ways to the cast of *The Real World*, the flagship MTV reality series that's filming in and around Dupont Circle for four months. *Real World* castmates known as Mike (at left) and Ashley (at right) chat with local law enforcement officials at National Night Out in Dupont Circle on August 4, 2009.

Reality™

Since its introduction, television has been America's cultural barometer, reflecting attitudes and mores as they change over time. In the 1950s and '60s it was all Cleaver family dinners and rolling green acres. The next thirty years saw the rise of genre programming and edgy sitcoms that broke social taboos. Then, in the early 1990s, among more of the same drama and comedy programming, a new format emerged. The premier of MTV's *The Real World* in 1992 marked the beginning of a sea-change in television programming. In the decade that followed, reality television rose to an astounding level of prominence and popularity. By 2011, networks like TLC and Bravo were broadcasting almost exclusively reality content. Discussions over the meaning and social impact of the format abounded in academic circles as countless blogs followed every step of America's favorite reality darlings. Critics worried that reality shows glorified reckless excess and impulsive behavior, while proponents and producers saw an inexpensive way to make compelling television. But what does the format—with all its bawdy excess and celebrated drama—say about us? And is this garish version of reality safe for public consumption?

Early in season 16 (2012) of ABC's *The Bachelor*, eligible winemaker Ben Flajnik takes one of the twenty-five women competing for his affection on a walk around his adopted hometown of Sonoma, California. They're on their first date, and they've invited an entire production crew with them. And while the extra company may be offputting for most people, Flajnik knows what he's doing; this isn't his first time around the reality dating-show block. As the runner-up on season 7 (2011) of *The Bachelorette*—the requisite spinoff of *The Bachelor*—Flajnik suffered rejection at the hands of brunette bombshell Ashley Herbert, and now he's hoping for another shot at finding "The One"—the one in twenty-five, that is.

In its 2002 premier season, *The Bachelor* featured contestants fighting for the affections of gainfully employed dreamboat Alex Michel. By the end of the show's inaugural run, Michel had narrowed down his pool of potential spouses to one Amanda Marsh. The show is an elimination-style competition in which the eligible bachelor takes potential true loves on a series of group and individual dates. At the end of each episode, the bachelor hands out roses to the contestants he wants to remain on the show, sending one or more women home with each round of eliminations. The idea is that among this group of eager, carefully casted candidates, the bachelor just might find the person he wants to spend the rest of his life with. It's love with production value.

While Michel didn't propose to Marsh on the season 1 finale, and the two never wed, the couple did date for several months before calling it a wrap in early 2003. As of the end of season 16, not one of the bachelors has married the "winner" of the program. Season 13's bachelor eventually married the runner-up, but as of now, *The*

Bachelor's seasons-to-nuptials ratio is dismally imbalanced. But on television as in life, not every tale gets a storybook ending. Or at least not anymore.

Since its roots in the groundbreaking 1970s docudrama *An American Family*, reality programming has fundamentally changed the way we consume television—and life. As a documentary/scripted-action hybrid, reality television turns a funhouse mirror on experiential fact. It reflects, but stretches, the truth. Drama is amplified to the point of caricature, and real, living, human beings of depth and complexity are repackaged as immediately digestible vessels of infotainment.

The shift from fully scripted programming to shows that feature real people in at least temporally real situations might say something about our desire for self-examination. Genre shows and sitcoms are formulaic—there's the monster-of-the-week, the running plotlines, the cliffhanger. It operates within an established structure and frankly has become rather predictable. People, however, are more difficult to pin down. There's no way of knowing how any one reality cast member will react when presented with a certain set of circumstances. Reality television provides a sort of fishbowl voyeurism that allows audiences to observe other human beings acting in human ways—albeit in less than organic situations.

But if viewers want authenticity, then why does it seem that the majority of reality shows have been stripped of the entropic uncertainty of real life? In actual reality, there are no second takes, and no one is asked to reenact a previous encounter for the cameras. The effect that the mere presence of a camera crew has on the subject's behavior might even be reason enough to consider reality television anything but genuine.

If audiences are out for gritty realism, there's always the news. One could also go outside. Maybe go on a date and skip that episode of *The Bachelorette*, or sing some karaoke instead of watching *American Idol*. What the reality television boom seems to say is that it's not gritty realism that viewers want—it's branded realism.

In the world of reality television, people are walking statements. Participants come equipped with nicknames, catchphrases, and gimmicks. Michael Sorrentino is "The Situation" and Nicole Polizzi is "Snooki." Was Mr. Sorrentino "The Situation" before he made his *Jersey Shore* debut? Maybe. But he didn't have his own title card.

In the world of reality television, experience is compartmentalized. The dating scene is boiled down to cutthroat competition. Docusoaps like *The Hills* and the *Real Housewives* glam up the drama of daily living, making public breakdowns narratively convenient. MTV's *Jersey Shore* is the Saturday night to *The Apprentice*'s daily grind, and *Survivor* is humanity's most basic struggle in visually compelling, weekly installments. It's life with a shooting schedule.

Perhaps it's a byproduct of digital living. In an age of social media and user-produced content, average people have a global platform upon which to present the desired version of themselves. Our Facebook profiles are a multimedia chronicle of our lives, and individual identity is defined on Twitter by 140-character bursts of considered personality.

Like someone writing an online dating profile, reality television producers paint inevitably limited portraits of their subjects. They use the tools afforded by the medium—editing, music cues, and a dash of directorial oversight—to put cast members in established social roles. Almost every reality show has its ditz and its geek; its nice guy and its jerk. Viewers can tune in at any time and be presented with immediately recognizable archetypes acting in familiar yet ultimately unpredictable ways.

But if reality television is understood to be at least partially farce by the majority of its audience, then self-examination can't be the primary reason for viewing. In a 2008 study published in *Communication Quarterly,* researchers Lisa K. Lundy, Amanda M. Ruth, and Travis D. Park found that the majority of subjects in their sample of college students watched reality television for its escapist value.

While scripted television provides escape to any number of fanciful worlds, reality television keeps viewers in the real world—it just shows them a different, slightly filtered part of it. There is something to be said for the sheer scope of human diversity showcased on reality television. There appears to be a show about every type of job, hobby, lifestyle, disease, and social situation imaginable. Deep South pageant families. Uncommonly large families. Polygamist families. Little people families. Junk hoarders and junk hunters. Toilet paper eaters and Long Island mind readers—they're all accounted for and given their own time slot. If reality television is of any value, it is for the insight it provides into pockets of the population with which most viewers will never come into contact.

In their research, Lundy et al. found that many subjects in their focus group felt they could relate to reality "characters" on a deeper level, allowing them to live vicariously through the shows. Even if reality television requires a slight suspension of disbelief, viewers still know that the person eating live cockroaches on the other side of that screen is a human being with a history and a life, not a scripted fabrication.

Where traditional programming presents audiences with a version of the world culled from ideals, reality television retains most of life's imperfections. As evidenced by *The Bachelor*'s marriage record, reality shows don't always reach their intended conclusion. Throughout a season, any number of unforeseen events can entirely redirect the course of the series. When *Real Housewives of Beverly Hills'* Taylor Armstrong lost her husband to suicide just weeks before the show's season 2 premier, a prelude to the first episode was filmed so the other housewives could discuss Russell Armstrong's death. Early episodes from season 2 that focused on the Armstrongs' unraveling marriage were recut, even as the suicide story splashed across tabloid headlines.

In reality television, on-screen events have real-world implications. Following Russell Armstrong's suicide, it was revealed that the extravagant lifestyle demanded by his wife's participation in the show had left him over $1.5 million in debt. When a character on a fictional prime-time drama is killed off, the fallout is, at worst, a disappointed fan base. But on reality television, stakes are much higher. These stars aren't relieved of their existential burdens after the closing credits roll.

Therein lies another point of cultural significance in the reality format. Programming that features real people who do real things outside the confines of their respective shows allows audiences to interact with popular culture on an unprecedented level. Not only are talent-search shows like *American Idol* and *Dancing With the Stars* predicated on viewer involvement—both shows allow the public to vote for their favorite performers—but most reality programs garner an unusual amount of off-screen attention.

Since the reality renaissance of the mid 2000s, reality stars have rivaled tabloid favorites like Tom Cruise and Jennifer Aniston for front-page coverage. The young mothers featured on MTV's *Teen Mom* frequently grace the covers of *OK, InTouch*, and *People. Teen Mom* Amber Portwood's legal troubles stemming from charges that she physically abused the father of her child were the focus of intense media attention. A segment on *The Today Show* and countless magazine profiles preceded Portwood's eventual sentencing to five years in prison on unrelated drug charges, all independent of broadcasted content. In reality television, the show is never really over. Stars welcome viewers into their life for twenty-odd episodes a season, but that isn't enough. They've got a life beyond the cameras, and the public wants in.

Such is life for the cultural anomaly that is Kim Kardashian. Her entire career—launched by a sex tape and subsequent lawsuit—is built on the public's fascination with the intimate details of her personal life. Her every movement is documented by a multiplicity of blogs, news outlets, and gossip rags. When Kim's hip-hop superstar boyfriend Kanye West helps clean out her wardrobe, the world knows.

And while famous-for-being-famous types like Paris Hilton and the Kardashians are far from "ordinary people," they do exist in our world, not in an imagined prime-time universe. One couldn't bump into *Seinfeld*'s George Costanza on the streets of New York, but a chance brush with one of the many Kardashians is a very real possibility. Tila Tequila, the star of MTV's *A Shot at Love with Tila Tequila* wouldn't have been given a television show dedicated to her every romantic whim were it not for the notoriety she built on the social networking site MySpace. That's the allure of reality stars: They're out there—and they have Twitters. Just like us.

Reality programming has flattened the fourth wall—it's built a bridge between the televised and the tangible. Since humanity first turned a camera on itself, documentary media has shown the world as it is. But reality television doesn't have to show an authentic version of the world—just an entertaining one. The format unabashedly markets our selves to each other. It's reality: branded and packaged for consumption.

Factual Entertainment and Reality TV

By Daniel Beck, Lea C. Hellmueller, and Nina Aeschbacher
Communication Research Trends, June 2012

Introduction

In 2008, the *Popular Mechanics* magazine named *The Truman Show* as one of the 10 "most prophetic science-fiction movies ever" (*Popular Mechanics*, 2008, March 28). Peter Weir's movie starring Jim Carrey as an average guy, who has been bought by a company as an infant, is unknowingly filmed 24 hours per day for a popular TV show, and realizes at the age of 30 that his whole life has been a televised lie, was released in 1998. Soon afterwards, the world saw the breakthrough of a new kind of factual entertainment show that also pretended to depict real people in real situations and captured their intimate moments with the camera: *Big Brother*, *Survivor* and others were an instant success and became the prototypes of the reality TV genre already parodied in *The Truman Show*.

The new formats introduced around the year 2000 had several predecessors already featuring some of their characteristics. For example, the makers of *The Truman Show* must have been familiar with the MTV series *The Real World*, which documented the everyday life of ordinary people since the early 1990s; hence, they didn't need much imagination to create a fictional over-the-top version of a reality TV show. But they *were* prophetic with their assumption that reality TV was not a short-lived boom, and they anticipated the discussions about authenticity and ethical problems of the genre that were initiated by the popular shows of the early 21st century. Even the storyline of *The Truman Show* later appeared in an actual format: In 2003, Spike TV aired *The Joe Schmo Show* featuring a regular guy tricked into participating in a fake reality show.

Almost 15 years after *The Truman Show* and more than a decade after the beginning of the reality TV boom, the genre still flourishes. As of May 2012, 13 seasons of *Big Brother* and 24 seasons of *Survivor* have aired in the U.S., and CBS is preparing the next seasons of both shows (CBS, 2012). These pioneer formats still attract millions of viewers, although their audience ratings have dropped off over the years. They now have to compete with a huge number of new reality-based entertainment formats introduced during the past decade. To name a few, casting shows such as the *Idol*, *Top Model*, and *Got Talent* series have revived and modernized the genre of the televised talent contest by giving a deeper insight into the candidates' lives; dating game shows such as *The Bachelor* allow the viewers to share romantic moments with the participants; makeover and coaching programs provide advice for a

From *Communication Research Trends* 31.2 (June 2012): 4–27. Copyright © 2012 by Center for the Study of Communication & Culture. Reprinted with permission. All rights reserved.

better life in an entertaining way. New variations of the classical reality show depicting ordinary people's everyday life are also popular. Since 2009, millions of Americans have followed the adventures of "Snooki," "JWoww," "The Situation," and their friends in the MTV show *Jersey Shore*, and even President Obama publicly joked about the frequent solarium visits of the *Jersey Shore* cast in a speech at the White House Correspondents' Dinner (Djang, 2010). *Jersey Shore* also demonstrates that people may gain celebrity status by participating in a reality TV show; to name only a few examples more, one could mention successful casting show contestants such as pop singers Kelly Clarkson (*American Idol*, 2002) and Leona Lewis (*The X-Factor*, U.K., 2006), former British *Big Brother* candidate Jade Goody, whose death from cancer at age 27 was extensively covered by the media in early 2009 (Walter, 2010), or Kim Kardashian, whose TV show brought her enough fame to get her own wax figure at Madame Tussauds in New York (Vena, 2010).

But the success of reality TV is not limited to particular countries—it has become a global phenomenon. Local versions of the *Big Brother* format, which was originally developed in the Netherlands, of the British *Idol,* and of the American *Top Model* series, as well as of many other factual entertainment programs, have successfully aired on all continents. Factual entertainment is thus very attractive for viewers and has gained importance since the end of the last century—the audience is obviously interested in watching "real" events and "real" persons in television entertainment. The fact that some of these programs are controversially discussed due to concerns over their effects on society or criticized for voyeurism, contrived settings, or commercialism, may even have increased this interest. Both success and controversy of the new factual entertainment programs have also made them an important research topic for social scientists. The goal of this essay is to provide an overview of the most important findings in studies about factual entertainment and reality TV published in the past decade.

The research and literature review is divided in three parts. The first part, dealing with the concept of reality TV, starts with a discussion about definitions of reality TV in contrast to other forms of entertainment and documentaries, then traces the history of factual entertainment in the 20th century and makes an attempt to map the current reality TV landscape by presenting the various subgenres and their development. The second part deals with reality TV as a global phenomenon and discusses why non-fictional entertaining television formats could become successful all over the world and which strategies are applied to adapt them to local markets with different viewer habits and preferences. The third part finally gives an overview of studies about the audience of reality TV programs: Why do these programs attract such a wide range of audiences? Which gratifications are sought and obtained when people watch particular formats? What do viewers think about the authenticity of reality TV shows? The role of reality TV programs in promoting neoliberal values and imparting them to their audience will also be discussed in this part.

The Concept of Reality TV

Big Brother, American Idol, and *Jersey Shore*—the reality TV genre is waxing locally and globally. Reality TV as a contemporary media phenomenon is the focus of this part. Particularly, the following section examines components of reality TV, the development of the genre, and its definitional framework; finally, it provides a discussion of current manifestations of reality TV. Major subgenres in the current reality TV landscape and their development in the past decade are further presented. In fact, since the end of the 1990s, reality TV has undergone an enormous diversification, with dozens of new formats introduced every year. Hence, this essay provides an overview of a complex and dynamic research field.

General Characteristics of the Genre

While there is more or less consensus which programs can be categorized as reality TV, it seems difficult to find a common definition for such programs like *Rescue 911, The Real World, Big Brother, Survivor, Top Model, The Bachelor, Wife Swap, Judge Judy, The Osbournes,* or *1900 House*. Reality TV can in fact be seen as a metagenre including various subgenres. While early reality TV formats such as *The Real World* focused on "real life" and the portrayal of "ordinary," non-prominent people, these characteristics are no longer typical for the genre. Instead of an "attempt to 'capture' 'a life lived,'" recent formats of the genre can rather be seen as "televisual arenas of formatted environments in which the more traditional observational rhetoric of documentary jostles for space with the discourses of display and performance" (Holmes & Jermyn, 2004, p. 5).

In essence, reality TV is known for ordinary people being engaged in unscripted action and interaction (Nabi, 2007, p. 373), but some shows focusing on celebrities are also considered to be part of the genre. In any case, participants of reality TV shows may gain celebrity status due to television exposure, forming a new stratum of "ordinary" or "temporary" celebrity (Grindstaff, 2011; Riley, 2010; Hellmueller & Aeschbacher, 2010, pp. 12-16; Holmes, 2004). Nabi and colleagues provide a very general definition of the genre and describe it as "programs that film real people as they live out events in their lives, contrived or otherwise, as they occur" (2003, p. 304). Several key elements characterize such programs: (a) people portraying themselves, (b) filmed at least in part in their living or working environment rather than on a set, (c) without a script (or at least pretending to be without a script), (d) with events placed in a narrative context, (e) for the primary purpose of entertainment (Nabi, 2007, pp. 372-373).

The genre transcends the boundaries of classical television genres by means of documentary elements, merging information with entertainment, and reality with fiction (Krüger, 2010, p. 158). Reality shows differ from classical documentaries in regard to their main intention: Instead of stressing journalistic inquiry or intending to stimulate political debates, they are primarily made for entertainment and diversion (Corner, 2009, pp. 48-50). This intention leads to the use of more or less staged or artificial environments (pp. 45-46). The event covered by the broadcast is initiated by the medium itself, which is not the case in conventional documentaries (Krüger, 2010, p. 159).

On the other hand, the primary distinction of reality TV from fictional entertainment is the fixation on "authentic" personalities, situations, problems, and narratives.

But while program makers promise to depict reality, the plots of reality-based formats are influenced by the participants' awareness of being filmed and by the necessity for the producers to cut down the filmed footage to the length of a TV broadcast. Ganz-Blättler (2005, p. 27) argues that little is left to chance in reality TV formats: Like in fictional entertainment, location and cast are carefully selected before the shooting. But there are two main differences to fictional formats. The actors are non-professional and thus cheaper for the producers (but less controllable), and in most cases they act without a script. Still, a common characteristic of reality TV programs remains their claim to provide viewers an "unmediated, voyeuristic, and yet often playful look into what might be called the 'entertaining real'" (Murray & Ouellette, 2009, p. 5).

The claimed "authenticity" may also be seen as a primary selling point of the genre. In order to gain public attention for their reality TV shows, TV channels often present them as extraordinary media events, stressing their importance and uniqueness. Possible means for this "eventization" (Holmes & Jermyn, 2004, p. 3) are the extensive use of program trailers; features about the show in news broadcasts; talk show appearances of hosts, makers, or participants; and in some cases even spin-off magazines providing a deeper insight into the participants' lives. Other media, especially the tabloid press, regularly cover developments in reality TV shows. The shows are particularly newsworthy if they provide dramatic contents and moral controversies. The producers intend such controversies because they raise public interest and awareness. Along with dramatization, stereotyping, focus on emotions, and intimate details, calculated breaking of taboos has thus become one of the typical strategies of reality TV producers (Klaus & Lücke, 2003, p. 208). As a consequence, a "perfume of scandal" can be observed around many shows of the genre (Biltereyst, 2004, p. 7). However, in most cases the public discussion on controversial reality TV formats calms down after the initial phase of a broadcast. In essence, if a show is successful enough to be aired over several seasons, it is no longer disputed.

> *On the other hand, the primary distinction of reality TV from fictional entertainment is the fixation on "authentic" personalities, situations, problems, and narratives. But while program makers promise to depict reality, the plots of reality-based formats are influenced by the participants' awareness of being filmed and by the necessity for the producers to cut down the filmed footage to the length of a TV broadcast.*

Public interest is also given by the interactivity of some shows, allowing the viewers to feel that they can take part and influence the content of the show. This is especially the case in gamedocs such as *Big Brother* or in casting shows using televoting to evict candidates and to select the winner (e.g., Holmes, 2004). But there are also many popular reality TV formats without the possibility of televoting, e.g., programs without competition among the participants or contests in which the winner is elected solely by a jury. However, many reality-based formats involve their audience by discussing developments and candidates in online forums or, more recently, on social media pages, and providing other interactive features on the Internet, thus serving also as a testing ground for media convergence (Murray & Ouellette 2009, p. 2; Andrejevic, 2008; Tincknell & Raghuram, 2002, pp. 262-265; Foster, 2004). Although the possibilities to involve viewers actively have become much more sophisticated over the years, Griffen-Foley (2004, p. 544) refers to a long tradition of interactive media: As early as the late 19th century, print media invited their audience to participate in discussions and send in their own contributions, in order to foster a sense of audience engagement and to create a loyal community among viewers.

The Origins of Reality TV—A History of Factual Entertainment on Television

TV formats portraying ordinary people in unscripted situations are almost as old as TV itself. Allen Funt's *Candid Camera* about people confronted with funny, unusual situations and filmed with a hidden camera, first aired in 1948, is often seen as a prototype of reality TV programming (Clissold, 2004; McCarthy, 2009). In the beginning, some critics condemned his show as an invasion of privacy, but with the same recording technologies as used for espionage and surveillance, and playing with topics such as unquestioned authorities or uncontrollable machines, the show obviously fitted the zeitgeist of the Cold War era and became a long lasting success. The appeal of the program could also be explained—similarly to later reality TV shows—with the voyeuristic focus on unguarded, unscripted, and "intimate" experiences of other people, presented from unseen, unacknowledged vantage points.

Elements of modern reality TV can be discovered in both non-fictional entertainment shows (broadcast contests, quiz and game shows, talk shows) and documentaries about ordinary people. Thus, a history of reality TV would not be complete without a brief insight in the development of these genres with their long tradition. Like *Candid Camera*, the first talent contests in US television date back to the late 1940s. Notable beauty and musical contests have been televised since the 1950s: The *Miss America* pageant was first broadcast in 1954 (Riverol, 1992, p. 49), and the annual *Eurovision Song Contest*, with an estimated average of 125 million viewers in recent years one of the world's most popular nonsports events on television (EBU, 2012), started in 1956. While in the early years, the winners of such contests were mostly elected by a jury, the first forms of voting by the viewers appeared in the 1970s, and the widespread use of this interactive element, which has become so important in many modern reality TV shows, started in the 1990s, after the capacity of telephone networks had been remarkably improved. At *Eurovision Song Contest*, an international telephonic and SMS voting all over Europe was introduced in 1997 (EBU, 2012).

Quiz and game shows, giving ordinary people the possibility to present their knowledge and skills to a wide audience, were also very popular in the early years of television. In the U.S. they almost disappeared from prime time after many of the higher stake shows had been discovered to be rigged in the late 1950s, but shows with lower winning prizes soon made a comeback on daytime TV. In many other countries these shows had a much more permanent presence on both public service and private channels (Bourdon, 2004, pp. 287-289). But it was not before the 1990s when a worldwide renaissance of high stake prime time quiz shows was initiated by *Who Wants to Be A Millionaire?*, a British format created in 1998 and subsequently licensed or optioned in more than 100 countries (Cooper-Chen, 2005, pp. 237-238; Boddy, 2001, p. 81).

Besides classical trivia-based formats, some game shows included stunts and wacky games; others concentrated on general knowledge or even culture, vocabulary, and mathematics (Boddy, 2001, p. 80; Bourdon, 2004, p. 288). Shows such as *Queen for a Day* (NBC/ABC, 1956-1964) or *Strike It Rich* (CBS, 1951-1958), where the candidates had to describe an object or service they desperately needed and were awarded with personalized prizes, already anticipated elements of confessional talk shows and make-over programs (Watts 2009, p. 303). Dating shows such as *The Dating Game* (first on ABC, 1965) were another subgenre in which the candidates had to sacrifice some of their privacy (Gray, 2009, p. 261; James, 2003). With the game element omitted, it was a short step from such shows to the confessional talk show genre, focusing on ordinary people instead of the celebrity guests that appeared in the classical talk show formats. This subgenre, presenting intimate stories and often touching taboos, was mainly introduced by *The Phil Donahue Show* in 1967. The concept was popularized by *The Oprah Winfrey Show* (1986-2011) and became very successful in American and European daytime programs in the 1990s, after the focus of many shows had shifted from personal issues connected with social injustice to interpersonal conflicts, but declined in popularity afterwards (Shattuc, 2001). While confessional talk shows are not always seen as a subgenre of reality TV, they feature typical elements of the genre like helping ordinary people to screen presence and establishing problems of everyday life as communication topics (Grimm, 2010, p. 219).

Besides non-fictional entertainment shows, another important ancestry line in the genealogy of reality TV refers to documentaries. McCarthy (2009, p. 35) argues that in *Candid Camera* and other projects, Allen Funt wanted to document the behavior of "the average man in a crisis." His work attracted the attention of social scientists that started using hidden cameras for their research, including Stanley Milgram who became famous for his controversial experiments on obedience to authorities held at Yale University in the early 1960s. The scientific background of the wish to depict "real" life and "real" actions of ordinary people may be an explanation why some public service channels, with their mission of popular education (Bourdon, 2004, p. 285), were among the pioneers in the field of documentaries seen as precursors of modern reality TV formats. This stands in contrast to the present-day perception that reality TV formats as cheap, commercialized and sometimes ethically controversial programs are mainly broadcast by private TV stations.

An American Family, broadcast on PBS from 1971 to 1973, is often discussed as one of the first reality TV programs (Murray, 2009, p. 66). Originally intended to be a chronicle of the daily life of a typical American family, the 12-part series documented the separation of the parents Bill and Pat Loud, as well as the coming-out of their homosexual son Lance. The program stood in the tradition of observational ("fly-on-the-wall") documentaries introduced in the 1960s (Bruzzi, 2001b), but also borrowed structural elements of drama and soap opera with the intention to question the conventional depictions of family life in fictional entertainment (Kompare, 2009, p. 107). The series was very popular, but also provoked scandalized reactions: The Louds were criticized as either symbols of the cultural fallout of the 1960s or as victims of a manipulative sociological experiment conducted by unscrupulous producers (p. 102). Three decades later, a similar format demonstrated the fluid boundaries between documentary and reality TV: *American High*, a series about the lives of 14 high school students, was sold as a reality program since its first appearance on Fox in August 2000. In the following year, PBS picked up the program and marketed it as a documentary series (Murray, 2009, p. 70). From the present-day perspective, *An American Family* and later formats depicting people in their usual, more or less extraordinary living or professional environment may be categorized as *docusoaps*. Docusoaps differ from conventional documentaries as they prioritize entertainment over social commentary and take advantage of structural and dramaturgical elements known from soap operas such as the focus on character personality, short narrative sequences, intercuts of multiple plot lines, mini cliff-hangers and the use of a musical soundtrack (Bruzzi, 2001a, p. 132; Bruzzi, 2000, p. 89; Kilborn, 2003, p. 89-121).

Crime appeal programs were another early form of reality TV. A pioneer in this field was the German show *Aktenzeichen XY…Ungelöst,* which started on the public-service channel ZDF in 1967. The program consisted of film clips reconstructing serious unsolved crimes, interviews with police officers and victims' families, images of suspects, and appeals to the viewers to phone in and to volunteer information. The format was later sold to other countries, including the United Kingdom (*Crimewatch*, BBC, since 1984) and the U.S.A. (*America's Most Wanted*, Fox, since 1988). These programs were often criticized as cheap and voyeuristic—similar to the discussion about later controversial reality TV programs (Jermyn, 2004, p. 71; Bourdon, 2004, p. 298). Nevertheless, they remained on air for decades and paved the way for other formats showing police and other emergency forces at work, such as *Cops* (Fox, since 1989), *Rescue 911* (CBS, 1989-1996) and international adaptations such as the British *999* (BBC, 1992-2003) and the German *Notruf* (RTL, 1992-2006). These magazine-style programs combining camcorder or surveillance footage, eyewitness testimonies, reconstructed scenes, and expert statements were the first for which contemporary scientists and media actually used the term "reality TV" in the public discussion. They have also applied this term for talk shows, docusoaps, and a new form, "constructed" documentaries only since the mid-1990s (Dovey, 2001, p. 135).

The earliest notable examples for this new form were the Dutch series *Nummer 28* (1991) and the very similar American *The Real World* (MTV, since 1992). Both formats entail many of the textual characteristics that are defining the current form of reality TV. For example, young adults were cast in a manner to ignite conflict and dramatic narrative development and placed in a setting filled with cameras and microphones, and the producers employed rapid editing techniques in an overall serial structure (Murray & Ouellette, 2009, pp. 4-5). All these elements reappeared some years later in *Survivor* (first as *Expedition Robinson* on SVT, Sweden, 1997) and *Big Brother* (first on Veronica, Netherlands, 1999), the two formats initiating the boom of reality TV in the beginning of the 21st century. Both programs combined the voyeuristic aspect of the reality program with the competitive element of the game show (Tincknell & Raghuram, 2002, p. 201). In spite, if not because, of controversial discussions in the media, the new shows had immediate success and were sold to many other countries. In the following years, dozens of new formats fitting the definitions of reality television mentioned above—and first of all, sold as reality formats by the producers—were introduced all over the world and led to a massive diversification of the genre, since they combined elements of other genres and introduced new elements.

Reality TV in the 21st Century—A Wide Range of Subgenres

Various typologies to classify the subgenres of reality TV have been proposed during the past years. Murray and Ouellette (2009, p. 5) identified eight established subgenres: *gamedocs, dating programs, makeover programs, docusoaps, talent contests, court programs, reality sitcoms,* and *celebrity variations of other programs.* As rather new tendencies, they name the growing importance of *charity programs* and *lifestyle games with expert guidance,* as well as the introduction of *spoof shows.* Hill, Weibull, and Nilsson (2007, p. 18) outlined *infotainment, docusoap, lifestyle, reality game shows,* and *lifestyle experiment programs* as main categories of reality TV. Nabi et al. (2006, p. 433) proposed a categorization based on six main topics: *romance, crime, informational, reality-drama, competition/ game,* and *talent.* From the industry perspective, Fitzgerald (2003) proposed a similar categorization distinguishing talent and survival competitions, personal makeover, home makeover, get-rich-quick schemes, docudramas, and "Mr. Right" programs.

Thanks to these typologies, several overlapping categories may be discovered, including dating, game/competition, and drama/soaps. But most categorizations fail to capture the full range of reality programming, since new programs are developed every season. Furthermore, simple typologies often do not articulate program characteristics defining each category, so it remains arguable which category new formats qualify for. Finally, many formats could be seen in two or more categories: For instance, there is a strong element of competition in many dating formats, and gamedocs feature elements of docusoaps (Nabi, 2007, pp. 373-374).

Nabi (2007) attempted to map the reality TV landscape more systematically. She asked the participants of her survey to rate reality TV programs along attributes such as competitive, romantic, realistic, funny, or suspenseful. As a result, she identified romance and competition as the "two characteristics most salient to audiences when thinking about reality based programming" (Nabi, 2007, p. 383) and as key dimensions distinguishing among reality programs. With the exception of dating programs, no other clearly differentiated group emerged on her two-dimensional scheme of reality TV, which means that in the viewers' eyes, the boundaries between and among subgenres are rather fluid.

Klaus and Lücke (2003, p. 199) chose a different approach to characterize various subgenres of reality TV and to bring them in a systematic order: They distinguished *"narrative"* and *"performative"* reality TV. Narrative reality TV refers to formats entertaining the viewers by an authentic or staged rendition of extraordinary, real, or close-to-reality events with non-prominent actors, whereas formats providing a stage for uncommon performances with a direct impact on the participants' lives fall into the category of performative reality TV. By this definition, the latter category includes all reality TV formats with competitive elements. Klaus and Lücke also distinguished "docusoaps" portraying people in their usual living environment and "reality soaps" bringing them in a new, uncommon environment. The following overview and characterization of the most important subgenres is based on the work by Lünenborg et al. (2011), who refined and updated Klaus and Lücke's typology.

Telling "Real" Stories: Narrative Reality TV

Narrative reality TV includes some of the early forms of reality TV such as the news magazine programs based around emergency service activities, and docusoaps about people of any professional or private background. According to Lünenborg et al. (2011, p. 21), other subgenres of narrative reality TV are *real life comedy* such as the MTV series *Jackass* (2000-2002), *court programs* (*Judge Judy*, CBS, since 1996), and *personal help shows* about people in social professions helping other people (e.g., *Die Jugendberaterin* and *Die Streetworker*, both on ProSieben, Germany, 2002-2004).

Docusoaps remained successful throughout the first decade of the 21st century. Notable American examples include the *Real Housewives* series (first as *The Real Housewives of Orange County* on Bravo, 2006), inspired by the fictional ABC series *Desperate Housewives* and following the lives of affluent housewives in American suburbs; *Jon & Kate Plus 8* (Discovery Health/TLC, 2007-2011), portraying a family with sextuplets and twins; *Laguna Beach* (MTV, 2004-2006) about teenagers in California filmed in a rather narrative than documentary style; and its spin-off *The Hills* (2006-2010). Another series dealing with young people partying on the beach became MTV's biggest reality TV success so far: *Jersey Shore*, following eight housemates—mostly of Italian-American origin—spending their summer at the Jersey Shore and on other beaches, started in December 2009 and set record ratings of up to 8.45 million viewers per show (Gorman, 2011). The series introduced new terms, acronyms, and phrases into American popular culture and caused controversies regarding the portrayal of Italian-American stereotypes. Unlike in *The Real World*, but like in some other more recent formats, the cast of *Jersey Shore* did not change with the start of a new season. As a result, the participants' notoriety does not fade after the end of a season, as is the case in many other reality TV formats, but is continuously revived. The *Jersey Shore* protagonists have thus become well established media celebrities. However, as of the end of the fourth season in autumn 2011, their celebrity status is still no issue in the show itself. In the meantime, *Jersey Shore* has become a field of academic research of its own, with universities organizing classes and conferences focusing on the series (e.g., University of Chicago, 2011; Caramanico, 2011).

Besides docusoaps about "ordinary" people possibly becoming celebrities in the course of the broadcast, the early 21st century also saw the introduction of *celebrity docusoaps,* giving an insight into the daily life of already prominent people. Sometimes these shows are made in a humorous way, using narrative conventions of the sitcom genre. *The Osbournes* (MTV, 2002-2005), depicting the life of rock star Ozzy Osbourne and his family, may thus be categorized as a docusoap (Dhoest, 2004), but also, more precisely, as a *docusitcom* or *reality sitcom* (Gillan, 2004; Murray & Ouellette, 2009, p. 5). Other MTV series documented the life of pop singer couple Jessica Simpson and Nick Lachay (*Newlyweds: Nick and Jessica*, 2003-2005) and the beginning of the musical career of Ashlee Simpson, Jessica's younger sister (*The Ashlee Simpson Show*, 2004-2005). Success of such celebrity shows is not determined by the initial celebrity status of the portrayed personality, and this status may change in the course of the series: Kim Kardashian, the main protagonist of *Keeping Up with the Kardashians* (E!, since 2007), had mainly gained notoriety for suing a pornographic film company after the publication of a private sex tape; but she developed her career as a model, actress, and businesswoman parallel to the broadcast of her show, which offered a platform to promote her commercial projects. In any case, the celebrity docusoap or docusitcom can be seen as a means for more or less prominent people to keep the attention of the media and the audience.

In contradiction to the claim to depict "real life," not every format in the field of narrative reality TV is unscripted. Producers of reality TV formats—including *The Hills* and *Jersey Shore*—are regularly accused by viewers, former participants, or former collaborators that parts of their shows are scripted, and possibly faked scenes are discussed in Internet forums and specialized blogs like *Realityblurred. com*, sometimes also in the popular press. But in several formats, the existence of a script is openly admitted: Court programs and personal help shows usually present fictional cases; what counts is that the experts are "real" (Grimm, 2010, p. 222). Since 2009, pseudo-documentaries dealing with crime suspects (*Verdachtsfälle*, RTL), families in trouble (*Familien im Brennpunkt*, RTL), young holiday makers (*X-Diaries*, RTL2), or other everyday stories, written by screenwriters, staged with non-professional actors, and respecting formal conventions of the documentary genre, reached market shares up to 30% in Germany (Lünenborg et al., 2011, p. 24). The only formal difference to conventional, unscripted docusoaps is a discrete indication of the fictionality in the end credits. For the producers, these formats have two advantages: (1) Regarding the need for more sensational and extraordinary stories, it has become easier to cast actors than to find interesting people willing and able to tell their story on television; and (2) the makers can insert statements and confessions which would hardly be made in public by real people, especially in contexts of crime (Brauck, 2009, p. 87). The success of these broadcasts proves that viewers obviously don't care much about the lack of authenticity.

Documenting an Important Change in Life: Dating and Makeover Programs

Like docusoaps, *dating and makeover programs* usually depict the participants' actual living environment, but they are intended to have a direct impact on their lives. Contrary to earlier dating shows, modern representatives of the genre such as *Blind Date* (syndication, 1999-2006), *Fifth Wheel* (syndication, 2001-2004), or *Elimidate* (syndication, 2001-2006) are considered to be more "sexualized" with dates involving plenty of drinking, competitive stripping, bumping and grinding, and making out; while these programs played well in the late evening slots, serialized dating game shows with a strong competitive element such as *The Bachelor* (ABC, since 2002) became successful on prime time TV (Gray, 2009, p. 262). Another serialized dating program is the docusoap-like *Farmer Wants a Wife*, where farmers are presented with women from the city. This format was developed by Fremantle in the United Kingdom and premiered on ITV in 2001, but the German-speaking Swiss public television had already portrayed and accompanied farmers looking for a wife much earlier—in a documentary series dating from 1983 (Beck & Jecker, 2012, p. 358).

Finding Miss Perfect or Mr. Right has not remained the only change in a person's life documented by reality TV. Along with the serialized dating shows, *lifestyle makeover shows*, in which aspects of the everyday life of ordinary people are improved with the aid of experts, have also become quite popular (Murray & Ouellette, 2009, p. 5). These shows deal with personal appearance (*What Not to Wear*, first on BBC, U.K., 2001; *The Swan*, Fox, 2004; *Extreme Makeover*, ABC, 2002-2007), homes (*Changing Rooms*, first on BBC, U.K., 1996; *Extreme Makeover: Home Edition*, ABC, 2003-2012), or vehicles (*Pimp My Ride*, MTV, 2004-2007), which makes them a field to study lifestyle ideals in different cultures or pressure to conformity in lifestyle issues (e.g., Franco, 2008; Lewis, 2010 and 2011; Palmer, 2004). *Coaching shows* follow a similar concept of documenting an improvement in life, but they focus on serious personal problems and propose positive alternatives for acting (Grimm, 2010, p. 221). Unlike in the personal help shows already mentioned, the presented cases are not fictional. The prototype of this subgenre was *Supernanny* (first on Channel 4, U.K., 2004) trying to solve parent-child conflicts; other formats such as *Raus aus den Schulden* (RTL, Germany, since 2007) concern the financial situation of families and individuals.

Getting Along in New Settings: Reality Soaps, Swap Documentaries, and Living History Programs

The *reality soap* is defined by Lünenborg et al. (2011, p. 28) as a dramatized version of the docusoap: The participants act in artificial settings under extraordinary conditions, and the plot is formed by their interactions in a new situation. They have to get along with themselves, with the other participants, and with the role of the media. In many cases, competition between the participants is a central element, which increases the probability of conflicts among them. These conflicts are extensively discussed in the show (Thornborrow & Morris, 2004). Reality soaps with competing participants thus combine the agenda of a talk show with the style of a documentary and the format of a game show (Tincknell & Raghuram, 2002, p. 205).

The Real World, bringing together different people in a new environment, can be seen as the prototypical reality soap, but the best known format of the subgenre is undoubtedly the Endemol production *Big Brother*, first broadcast in the Netherlands in 1999 and subsequently aired in more than 40 different countries. The original concept consisted of 10 to 16 competitors living together in an apartment, isolated from the outside world, continuously watched by cameras, and trying to win a cash prize by doing their best in the games proposed by the producers and thus avoiding eviction by the viewers' periodic televoting (Aslama, 2009, pp. 81-82; Tincknell & Raghuram, 2002, p. 202). This concept was refined and varied in later seasons by additional rules and elements provoking conflicts, such as the separation of the participants in "rich" and "poor" groups, the introduction of secret missions, moles, or identical twins pretending to be a single person. Other gamedoc formats focused on rather specialized settings or aspects: In *The Farm* (first on TV4, Sweden, 2001), the contestants lived and worked together on a farm, raising animals and doing agricultural work. *Survivor*, first aired two years before *Big Brother*, tested the participants' skills to get along in the wilderness of a tropical island. *Fear Factor* (first on Veronica, Netherlands, 1998) concentrated rather on game elements: The contestants had to face trials of courage testing their physical ability and stunts meant to challenge them mentally, e.g., eating vile animal parts, immersing one's head or entire body in animals considered to be disgusting or intimidating, or retrieving hidden objects in disgusting substances. *I'm a Celebrity, Get Me out of Here!* (first on ITV, UK, 2002) combined elements of *Survivor* and *Fear Factor* by bringing together participants in a jungle camp where they not only had to struggle with the limitations of living in the wilderness, but also with mentally challenging games in the style of the *Fear Factor* stunts. Another characteristic of the format, the choice of celebrities as participants, brought two advantages: Viewers may be more interested in the show because they are already familiar with the characters, and since prominent participants are presumably more aware of the role of the media and the consequences of their appearance on television than ordinary people, there are fewer objections against particularly sensational or disgusting show elements (Lünenborg et al., 2011, p. 29). *Big Brother*, *The Farm*, and other reality soaps were thus also aired as celebrity formats in many countries. However, many candidates presented as celebrities had only gained notoriety thanks to previous participation in other reality TV shows.

A variation of the reality soap with less stress on competition is the *swap documentary* or "lifestyle experiment program" (Hill, Weibull, & Nilsson, 2007, p. 24) such as *Wife Swap* (first on Channel 4, U.K., 2003), *Holiday Showdown* (first on ITV, U.K., 2003), or, as a celebrity format, *The Simple Life* with Paris Hilton and Nicole Richie (Fox, 2003-2007). Accompanied by cameras, the participants change their usual living environment for a new environment. The main idea of these formats is to confront different ways of life, which may result in funny or conflict-laden situations (Lünenborg et al., 2011, p. 30). Finally, a particular form of reality soaps are *living history formats* in which the participants act in historical settings. These formats give an insight into everyday life in former times and focus on the differences between then and now and on the problems of modern people trying to use skills which were important in the past. Due to this educational function, living history formats, unlike other modern forms of reality TV, are seen in accordance with the tasks of public service television and therefore became a domain of public service broadcasters: *Living in the Past*, a BBC documentary following the creation of an Iron Age settlement by a group of volunteers, dates back to 1978 (Duguid, 2010). More recently, living history formats were introduced by Channel 4 in the United Kingdom (*1900 House*, 1999), PBS in the U.S.A. (*Frontier House*, 2002), ARD in Germany (*Schwarzwaldhaus 1902*, 2002), France 3 in France (*Retour vers le néolithique*, 2003), and many others. The simple rural life of the 19th and early 20th century and survival in prehistoric times were particularly popular motives for these formats. Contrary to gamedocs set in a difficult living environment, there is usually no competition among the participants in living history formats (West, 2010).

Making a Dream Come True: Casting Shows

Like reality soaps, *casting shows* have proved to be a particularly successful subgenre of reality TV. Their aim is to discover new singing, acting, or other talents presenting themselves in front of a jury. In contrast to conventional talent contests, the depiction of the selection process has become much more important in modern casting shows. The programs do not only focus on the candidates' performances, but also on their behavior and emotions behind the stage, their families and their living environment, the discussions inside the jury, and the conflicts between jury and candidates. As a result, the casting show can be seen as a hybrid format merging elements of talent contest, docusoap, reality soap, and comedy (Lünenborg et al., 2011, pp. 25-27). Strong "eventization" can be observed in many casting shows: Cross-promotion for spin-off magazines and merchandizing products (e.g., CDs and DVDs), as well as extensive media coverage about the candidates and the jury are quite frequent. In addition to revenues from TV spots, sponsoring, product placement, and merchandizing, televoting may be an important source to finance a casting show, since many formats (but not all) are interactive, with the winner being elected by the viewers. From an economic point of view, casting shows are thus particularly profitable for media companies (Jenkins, 2009).

The first modern casting show was *Popstars*, developed by producer Jonathan Dowling in New Zealand and first aired there in 1999 before being franchised in more than 30 countries all over the world. The aim of the show was to cast members for an all-girl pop group. An even greater and longer-lasting international success was the *Idol* series created by Simon Fuller and produced by Fremantle, first aired as *Pop Idol* in the United Kingdom in 2001. All over the world, more than 40 adaptations of this singing contest with single artists competing against each other have been aired, including *American Idol* in the USA and transnational versions in Africa, the Arab World, and Latin America (Livio, 2010, pp. 169-170). In some countries, very similar non-licensed derivations of the *Idol* format were broadcast, such as the Austrian *Starmania* (2002-2009) and its Swiss adaptation *MusicStar* (2003-2009) (Beck & Jecker 2012, pp. 360-361). More recent casting shows for singers such as *The X-Factor* (first on ITV, U.K., 2004) and *The Voice* (first on RTL

4, Netherlands, 2010) lay more stress on the role of the jury members, who don't only evaluate the performances, but also act as coaches or mentors for the candidates.

While singing contests were the earliest and probably most typical form of casting shows, the subgenre soon diversified: The *Top Model* series, featuring young women competing for a contract with a major modeling agency, started in the U.S.A. in 2003 and became a similar international success like the *Idol* format. In the *Got Talent* series (in the U.S.A. since 2005, in the U.K., where the show was developed by Simon Cowell, since 2006), any extraordinary show talent can be presented in front of a jury. Casting shows have also been made for comedians (*Last Comic Standing*, NBC, 2003-2010), dancers (*So You Think You Can Dance*, Fox, since 2005), chefs (*Hell's Kitchen*, first on ITV, U.K., 2004), business jobs (*The Apprentice*, first on NBC, 2004), fashion designers (*Project Runway*, Bravo/Lifetime, since 2004), and even mentalists (*The Next Uri Geller*, first in Israel in 2007). Particular research has been done about the depiction of work ethic in such formats (e.g., Hendershot, 2009). *Dancing with the Stars* (first as *Strictly Come Dancing* on BBC, U.K., 2004) pairs celebrities with professional dancers competing in ballroom and Latin dances and can thus be seen as a casting show format involving celebrities as candidates. In *Hit Me, Baby, One More Time* (first on ITV, U.K., 2004), former pop stars trying to make a comeback competed against each other.

Hoaxing the Real: Spoof Shows

The boom of reality TV has also lead to the introduction of *spoof shows*. While formats such as *The Joe Schmo Show* (Spike TV, 2003-2004), a gamedoc in which all but one participant were actors playing stereotypes of common reality TV show contestants, can be seen as humorous parodies for the entertainment of savvy viewers (Hearn, 2009), some spoof shows were intended to animate the critical discussion about the reality TV genre or about a social issue. One of the best-known examples is the Dutch *Big Donor Show* about three contestants striving to receive the kidney of a supposedly terminally ill woman, produced by Endemol in 2007. The announcement of the show triggered a debate on the current state of television, and some members of the Dutch parliament considered banning the broadcast. The revelation of the hoax created even more accusations of ratings driven by sensationalism, but Endemol claimed that the goal was to cast a critical eye on the situation of patients awaiting organ transplants (Murray & Ouellette, 2009, p. 1).

Some years earlier, when *Survivor* and *Big Brother* had become an instant success on private television, most European public service channels refused to air such formats, judging them unsuitable with their mandate and their quality standards. In summer 2001, it was thus a surprise when TSR, the public service broadcaster in the French-speaking part of Switzerland, introduced *Génération 01*, a Big-Brother-like series with particularly hard conditions for the contestants. But the show was a fake: All "contestants" were in fact actors, and their actions were fully scripted. TSR wanted to reveal this in the final episode in order to start a discussion about the boundaries between reality and fiction in reality TV formats, but journalists from *Tribune de Genève*, a regional newspaper from Geneva, became suspicious, investigated, and published the facts while the series was still running. In the following discussion, TSR was harshly criticized for having fooled the audience and other media when announcing the show (Clavien, 2003, pp. 109-111).

The controversies about the Dutch and the earlier Swiss spoof show do not only illustrate the high media interest in reality TV formats, but also document how the public perception of programs between reality and fiction has changed with the viewers' growing experience with the genre. While in 2001, some media still saw a scandal in the mere fact that *Génération 01* was faked, the main controversy about the *Big Donor Show* from 2007 was caused by the provocative, taboo-touching setting of the show. Unlike these examples, more recent "scripted reality" formats, which are in fact also faked, have no longer provoked similar public discussions.

Globalization of Factual Entertainment Formats

The popularity of factual entertainment formats such as *Idol* is "more than just another trend in an industry perennially hungry for hit shows and eager to follow them" (Waisbord, 2004, p. 360). It is a trend geared by the globalization of the business model of television. Scholars (e.g., Waisbord, 2004) argue that the commercialization and homogenization of media systems served as the bases for successful exports and imports of formats across the globe. As soon as media organizations adapted principles of a market model of journalism such as private ownership and profit-oriented strategies, they became interested in reality TV to attract a wide range of viewers. For example, the success of *Pop Idol* (in the UK) and *American Idol* (in the US) did not reside in one country only. The format successfully traveled to Canada (i.e., *Canadian Idol*), Switzerland (i.e., *MusicStar*), and many more countries.

However, few viewers today suspect that their favorite shows are adaptations of foreign formats, as is the case with soaps such as the German *Gute Zeiten, Schlechte Zeiten*—an adaptation of the Australian soap, *The Restless Years* (Chalaby, 2011). This is mainly because the shows are adapted to a local culture and available to a local audience. Hence, their success rests upon their integration into a particular culture. In essence, the industry today is dominated by global television formats. That was not always the case. Before the 1990s, when television was more a protected industry with "regulatory stonewalls" (Waisbord, 2004, p. 360), producers of European public service channels often imported the idea or elements, but not the format of American shows. In many cases, the concepts of U.S. game shows were "dissolved" in long-lasting variety shows made to appeal to the whole family (Bourdon, 2004, p. 296). For example, *Teleboy* in Switzerland (1974-1981) and *Verstehen Sie Spass?* in Germany (since 1980) were Saturday night prime time shows combining hidden camera clips in the style of *Candid Camera*, games, and entertaining show elements.

The hesitation of European producers to integrate foreign formats in their own programming reflects the importance of cultural and system level influences on TV programming (Shoemaker & Vos, 2009). In other words, the success and the integration of factual entertainment formats still remain tied to local and national cultures.

One of the contemporary paradigms in comparative media research results from such a paradoxical co-existence of the differences and the universal (i.e., the West and the Global) in media structures and content across the globe (Wahl-Jorgensen & Hanitzsch, 2009): National borders may no longer draw distinctions between one media culture and another, but diversities in media cultures might be based more on cultural, linguistic, or ethnic criteria, which may cross national borders.

Media system analyses resonate well with such an approach. Distinctive media traditions developed because of the dependencies of the media field on economic and political pressures (Benson & Hallin, 2007; Hanitzsch & Mellado, 2011). Hallin and Mancini (2004) provide ample evidence that different philosophies have lead to different concepts of *media systems*. Contrary to the US, western European countries have long been skeptical of a free media market and seek to improve diversity by assigning a specific role to the state as a regulative force to enhance the media's role as a social institution. Such media system differences are mirrored in media freedom rankings, which are annually published by non-governmental organizations such as Freedom House, for example. On the other hand, endogenous and exogenous forces of change are also at play. Privatization of television and convergence toward the US model are affecting media systems, which has led scholars to conclude that distinctions have disappeared while a global ideal is appearing (Benson & Hallin, 2007).

Without a doubt, the success of television formats was dependent on the globalization of the economics of the television industry (Waisbord, 2004). After media systems were commercialized, economic interests stimulated an appeal to increase financial resources—an attractive move for media corporations to position themselves in a global market. Revenues no longer depended on a single market, but expanded to global markets. Furthermore, as soon as commercial principles dominated a wide global market, formatted programs could be adopted elsewhere. For example, Britain's Pearson Television's hit *Who Wants to Be a Millionaire?* has been sold to over 100 countries including Afghanistan, Russia, and Saudi Arabia (BBC online, 2006). On the other hand, a number of non-Western companies also became important producers and exporters of television programming. For example, Latin America started exporting products to Europe and the United States. But the US influence remains strong. And, with new entrants participating in the global exchange of audiovisual products, enormous inequalities still exist on a global scale (Waisbord, 2004).

Global Market Logic—Cultural Adaptation?

Global market logics consist of the aim of selling audiences to advertisers. The higher their audience share, the more attractive is their programming to advertisers, which eventually determines the organizations' position in comparisons to its competitors. If television stations buy a format, they, on the other hand, also save money as game shows or other reality TV formats do not require the acquisition of professional actors. For example, NBC's game show *Twenty one* costs three times less than an episode of *Law and Order* (Waisbord, 2004). And they provide low risks for a media company since in a way they provide a history of success and knowledge because of their experiences with adaptation processes in other countries. Furthermore, they draw a lot of their fans onto their website, which increases audience engagement and attracts advertisers in the long run.

Because media organizations are embedded in a particular culture, the standardization and adaptation processes of TV formats are also a battle among competing ideas to what extent a format should be adapted to a local culture or whether a global product should be part of a certain media culture at all. In fact, some European countries indeed have quotas that primarily aim to curb the import of Hollywood programs (Tunstall & Machin, 1999). Hence, similarities and differences that come with a globalization of TV formatting have to be looked at in their interplay, rather than deciding whether global or local trumps in a particular case. As Waisbord (2004) argues, global media trends and the national are not antithetical, but integrated.

How can a global product then be integrated in a local culture and attract local viewers? This bears on the underlining question whether a global economy may transform a local culture into a globalized television culture. On the other hand, the local and national cultures may still pull the economy of TV formatting in an opposite direction by influencing its success in a local market. Such a discussion reflects internal struggles of a media industry of how "the globalization of the business model of television and the efforts of international and domestic companies deal with the resilience of national cultures" (Waisbord, 2004, p. 360).

While economic global successes of TV formats are discussed widely, discussions on cultural adaptations seem to be more complex. To begin with, culture is defined as networks of knowledge (Hong, 2009). As a knowledge tradition, culture is shared among a collection of interconnected individuals (often demarcated by race, ethnicity, or nationality) to form a common ground for communication. Culture is transmitted from one generation to the next while undergoing continuous modifications by newer social orders. Such a definition prevents conflating culture with racial, ethnic, or national groups. While those groups are agents of culture, the causal potential does not reside in them. Rather "networks of shared knowledge are activated in a probabilistic manner in certain social contexts" (Hong, 2009, p. 4).

Indeed, factual entertainment represents networks of shared knowledge and functions as a cultural transmitter, as a binding force in certain social contexts. In other words, embedded in a meaning, which may be understood only to members of a certain social context (particularly evident in humor used in such shows), their content offers representation of cultural values, beliefs, and processes of perception for a particular culture.

Research into intercultural communication has revealed that perceptions of cultural similarity affect with whom people initiate and maintain communication (King, 1976; McCroskey, 1966; McCroskey & Young, 1981; Neuliep, Hintz, & McCroskey, 2005; Wheeless, 1974). Furthermore, research shows that consumers respond to advertising messages congruent with their culture and with people who reflect its values (e.g., Paek, 2005). In a cultural context, a celebrity for example, functions as a cultural hero. Viewers identify with reality stars because such stars represent a high amount of culturally shared norms and values like national celebrities or heroes (de Mooij, 2010; Shearman, 2008; Ting-Toomey & Chung, 2005). For example, Roger Federer represents such a prototype Swiss celebrity. He embodies values like modesty, being natural, and cultural diversity (by speaking a variety of languages), which are values praised and recognized in a Swiss culture.

Do Global Products Travel to Local Viewers?

Following the shared-meaning of culture argument above, it seems not surprising that viewers still prefer domestic and regional content to foreign programs and that the cultural adaptation to foreign product is rather slow (Langdale, 1997). However, in line with the cultural argument, the distinction whether formats are successful or not bears on the question whether formats are imported from countries that share "cultural proximity" (i.e., similar values) or come from countries that share less cultural proximity (i.e., dissimilar values).

Because of the complexity, globalization phenomena linked with localization forces have long called for a better term to reflect global-local encounters. More than 10 years ago, Kraidy (1999) argued that "the term 'glocalization' obtained by telescoping 'globalization' and 'localization' is a more heuristic concept that takes into account the local, national, regional, and global contexts of intercultural communicative processes" (p. 472). The intersection of globalization and localization is thus conceptualized as a hybridity, which becomes the rule rather than the exception. Distinctions based on the two poles—local audiences and global media—foremost serve heuristic categorization in understanding a global TV market. However, practical inquiries preserve a *glocalization* logic, i.e., an understanding of global products embedded in a local culture.

In recent years, scholars followed glocalization claims to analyze how global narratives are operating in a local context to established discourses of national identities (e.g., Price, 2010; Baltruschat, 2009). For example, Price (2010) looked at popular Australian myth in reality formats and argued that reality TV serves as a means to construct Australian identity; it reinforces "dominant ideas of culture and values with televisual conventions of factuality and entertainment" (Price, 2010, p. 458).

In a Canadian case, Baltruschat (2009) discusses how glocalization processes led to the production of *Canadian Idol*—an adaptation of the international success of *Idol*. The combination of the UK and the U.S. versions was adapted to a Canadian market with the addition of Canadian contestants and cultural references. Depiction of local stories, references to national symbols and cultural signifiers worked well in adapting to a Canadian culture. Such cultural signifiers include "opening shots of historic Canadian sites, performing the national anthem as part of televised auditions, and staging media events, as well as a variety of online interactive elements" (Baltruschat, 2009, p. 54).

Different cultural nuances can also be accommodated by content factors. For example, Hetsroni and Tukachinsky (2003) compared the themes of questions asked in the quiz show *Who Wants to Be a Millionaire?* in America, Russia, and

Saudi Arabia. Results showed that questions mirrored cultural differences between the countries: In the U.S. case, questions focused on popular culture, whereas the Saudi quiz overemphasized national identity. Hence, we observe key elements being standardized among formats such as narratives of formats. But more in-depth, formats are also embedded into a culture by overemphasizing dominant cultural values, manifested in "cultural signifiers."

In conclusion, global formats may well succeed because they are flexible to cultural differences. In essence, standardized narratives of factual entertainment formats provide the opportunity to accommodate local cultural frames by adapting its content to a local culture, which echoes *glocalization* claims—integrating global formats for local audiences.

Reality TV from the Audience Perspective

Why do reality TV formats attract a wide range of audiences? They claim to depict real people and real events, but their "reality" is manipulated for dramaturgical reasons by edited and reconstructed scenes, by careful selection of cast and settings, and sometimes by scripted elements. Our overview of studies dealing with reality TV from the audience perspective thus starts with findings on how viewers perceive and judge the authenticity of reality TV programs. Another important research field is the viewers' motivation for watching these programs; numerous analyses have been made about the appeal of reality TV for viewers in general or concerning particular subgenres. Many of these studies are still exploratory, limited to specific social groups (often students or adolescents) or regions. Lots of research still has to be done, especially in the field of intercultural differences in the reception of reality TV formats. Yet the existing studies provide a first overview of which gratifications may be obtained by watching reality TV. The final section of this part will focus on the role of reality TV programs in imparting particular values to their audience: Various scholars have discussed how the settings of these programs reflect and promote the principles of neoliberalism.

Perception of Authenticity, Criticism, and Concerns about Reality TV

It is often assumed that regular viewers of reality TV have become quite savvy and skeptical when judging how much is actually "real" in these programs (Murray & Ouellette, 2009, p. 6). Although authenticity is desired by the viewers and earnestly promoted by the producers, various scholars argue that in the "postdocumentary context" (Corner, 2009, p. 53) of reality TV, consumers are not so much interested in absolute truth, but enjoy "the ironic mixture of the factitious and the spontaneous" (Rose & Wood, 2005, p. 286). Empirical support for this position is provided by an Associated Press/TV Guide poll from 2005: The participants indicated that "they did not believe reality TV was real, but they also didn't care that much" (Murray & Ouellette, 2009, p. 8). In fact, 25% of the 1002 adults polled assumed that reality shows are totally made up, and 57% believed that they show some truth, but are mostly distorted. But only 30% said that it mattered for them whether the shows were truthful or not (Bauder, 2005).

Alice Hall (2003, 2006, 2009) conducted focus group interviews in order to analyze the perception of the authenticity of reality TV programs more in-depth. Among the various criteria contributing to audiences' perceptions of realism, she considered two as particularly relevant to reality programs: typicality, i.e., the perception that a media text portrays events or characteristics that are representative of a particular population, and factuality, i.e., the perception that a media text accurately represents a specific real-world event or person. In the discussion of typicality of reality programs, many respondents argued that the cast members and situations they represent were strikingly unrepresentative. They were more likely to accept the factuality of the programs, tending to expect nonactors in unscripted situations, but acknowledging that these situations were often contrived and that the presence of the camera may have influenced the cast's behavior (Hall, 2009, p. 209).

In their study based on in-depth interviews with 15 adult reality TV viewers, Rose and Wood (2005) found that the programs are seen as a mix of authentic and fictional elements. In order to consider the programs as authentic, the viewers have to negotiate the paradoxes and contradictions inherent in the genre and to reconcile the tensions between what is subjectively real and fictional. The highest satisfaction with the authenticity of a program is reached if these contradictions are experienced as resonant and engaging rather than as bewildering or confusing (p. 294). But the perception of the authenticity of a particular format can change in the course of time. In group discussions with college students, Lundy, Ruth, and Park (2008) found that situations and characters in reality TV programs were considered as more and more unreal and exaggerated over the years. The participants explained this development as a strategy of the broadcasters to attract more viewers, but criticized that the original premise of reality TV was distorted. Still, they thought that "reality TV is set up to make people believe that these things on the reality shows can actually happen" (p. 217).

While these findings show that adult viewers seem to have a rather savvy and reflexive approach towards the authenticity of reality TV, a German survey focusing on children and adolescents came to a different conclusion: Götz (2012) interviewed pupils from 6 to 18 years old about the scripted docusoap *Familien im Brennpunkt*, a format presenting fictitious cases of family troubles in documentary style. Thirty percent of the 294 respondents familiar with the series believed that real families were filmed in their everyday life, 48% thought that real cases were staged with actors, and only 22% gave the correct answer that the stories were entirely fictional. The detailed analysis showed that only among the respondents older than 16 years, a majority was aware of the way the show was produced (p. 6). The stories in *Familien im Brennpunkt* are highly dramatized, with conflicts between "good" and "evil" persons, and concentrate on particular social milieus. Due to the documentary style, they may have a higher impact on the children's perception of reality than openly fictional entertainment. As an example, 60% of the 6- to 14-year-olds agreed to the statement: "Since I watch *Familien im Brennpunkt*, I know that many people are really mean" (p. 7).

Effects of reality TV such as a distorted perception of reality may be a concern for producers, but also for viewers and scholars alike. Regarding the concerns over the effects of reality TV often discussed in public, Cohen and Weimann (2008, p. 285) also mentioned the power of reality TV to invade privacy, considering that viewers enjoy watching other people's highly personal experiences, the commercial nature of the shows serving as marketing vehicles and attracting the audience to advertisers, and the "escape from reality" that such shows provide. In their survey of television viewers in Israel, the authors found that the more people watched reality TV shows, the more they thought that these shows have an impact and should be regulated and limited. However, criticism of the shows was not related to the intensity of watching. The main criticisms were that the shows are faked, voyeuristic, and exploitative (Cohen & Weimann, 2008, pp. 392-394).

All in all, adult reality TV viewers can be seen as a rather "active" audience reflecting on the authenticity of the programs and expressing criticism and concerns. As already mentioned in Part 2, the consumers are also "active" due to the interactivity of many reality TV shows, participating in televoting, and discussing the latest developments in online forums and on social media platforms. The authenticity of characters and situations is a widely discussed topic. Viewers' activities on the Internet may also influence the general perception and the outcomes of a show, which makes the show less predictable for the producers. As an example, Enli (2009) mentioned the case of singer Susan Boyle in the second season of *Britain's Got Talent*. Boyle's fame was largely based on viewers' distributing the video of her stunning performance on social media platforms. She gained celebrity status even outside the United Kingdom, but soon some people questioned her status as a true amateur, and stories about prima donna behavior ruined her image. This may have been a reason why, in spite of all praise for her talent, she ended up being only second in the final competition; the audience preferred to award the members of a dance group who, after the media hype around Boyle, were obviously seen as more authentic representatives of ordinary people with an extraordinary talent (p. 488).

Motives for Watching Factual Entertainment Content

The appeal of reality TV programs to viewers has been explored by various researchers on the theoretical basis of the *uses and gratifications approach* (Katz, Blumler, & Gurevitch, 1974; Palmgreen, Wenner, & Rosengren, 1985), which assumes that viewers are frequently, but not always, actively engaged in the selection of media content. Their use of media programs can be either instrumental, i.e., in order to obtain gratifications meeting cognitive, affective, or social needs, or ritualized, i.e., out of habit. In an exploratory survey with 157 college students, Papacharissi and Mendelson (2007) found that habitually passing time was the most important motive for watching reality TV programs—this activity had become a ritual in the daily routine of many respondents. So in many cases, the mode of engagement with reality TV was rather passive, and designed to fill time when no other activities are available. The second most salient motive was capturing the appeal of reality content and reality characters in opposition to fictional programs, followed by relaxation and social interaction (pp. 365-367). Another general survey about the motives of watching reality TV programs was conducted by Ebersole and Woods (2007), who surveyed 530 college and university students in the United States and Canada and identified five factors that explained program choice preference: personal identification with real characters, entertainment, mood change, passing time, and vicarious participation. The authors also found that the most popular programs were watched by the viewers because they found them "humorous," i.e., they were amused, or humored, by the "stupidity" of the characters and their actions (pp. 34-36).

Other studies also imply that superiority motives may drive the appeal of reality TV. Reiss and Wiltz (2004) centered their analysis on 16 basic needs and found that in comparison to non-viewers, reality TV viewers are in general more status-oriented, i.e., they have an over-average need to feel self-important. This need may be gratified by the feeling that they are more important than the ordinary people portrayed in reality TV shows, and they can fantasize that they could also gain celebrity status when they see people like themselves on TV. Furthermore, reality TV viewers are more motivated by vengeance than are non-viewers, a desire that is closely associated with enjoyment of competition (pp. 373-374). In a more recent study focusing on teens and pre-teens, Patino, Kaltcheva, and Smith (2011, p. 293) noted that adolescents striving for popularity and physical attractiveness are particularly likely to feel connected to reality TV, which leads to the assumption that satiating social and personal integrative needs may be an important motivation to watch reality-based programs, at least for this group.

Regarding the lay hypothesis that reality TV is popular because it appeals to the voyeuristic nature of the population, Papacharissi and Mendelson (2007) and Nabi et al. (2003) in a similar study showed that voyeurism is present as a motive to watch these programs, but that it is not the key motive. This may be partly caused by respondents who are reluctant to report voyeuristic tendencies for fear that it might be perceived as socially undesirable, but Nabi et al. (2003, pp. 324-325) explained four reasons why voyeurism may in fact be less important than other motives: First, viewers watch with some knowledge that the targets are generally aware of their presence; second, the potential of fulfilling a voyeur's sense of illicit pleasure is limited by constraints on TV stations regarding the broadcast of explicit sexual material; third, the data of the survey indicate that people watch not to see sexual behavior per se, but to watch interpersonal interaction and because they are curious about other people's lives; and fourth, regular viewers often watch for motivations based on personal identity, which seems inconsistent with motives of voyeurs. However, the measure of voyeurism used for these studies emphasized sexual gratifications that viewers may derive from consuming reality programs and, as Andrejevic (2009, p. 321) argued, there may be "much more revealing scenes of love and rage" in fictional formats. If a different conceptualization of voyeurism is applied, one that defines it not as a sexual deviance, but as a commonly occurring fascination with access to private details of other people's lives, a "non-pathological" voyeurism is likely to be an important gratification for reality TV viewers (Baruh, 2009, p. 207). As a result of a study combining a survey administered to television viewers and a content analysis of 15 different reality TV formats, Baruh (2009, p. 190) suggested that scenes which adopt a "fly on the wall" perspective, take place in private settings, contain nudity, and/or include gossip contribute to the voyeuristic appeal of a reality TV program.

A differentiation between regular and casual viewers has to be made, since gratifications obtained from reality TV depend on the amount of TV watching. The more people watch TV for entertainment, relaxation, as a habitual pastime and as a basis for social interactions with others, the more likely they are to develop a greater affinity for reality TV programs. In other words, the reality genre is rather unlikely to attract new audiences or lead to high consumption of TV unless those tendencies are already pronounced (Papacharissi & Mendelson, 2007, pp. 367-368). In comparison to casual viewers, regular reality TV viewers receive stronger and more varied gratifications; not surprisingly, parasocial interaction is a particularly important motive for regular viewers who have the possibility to develop parasocial relationships with participants in serialized shows (Nabi et al., 2003, p. 320-322). An important condition for positive parasocial ties is the ability to name a favorite reality TV character. Ho (2006, p. 20) found in her survey that respondents who had chosen a favorite character developed quite strong ties and found the shows much more appealing than people who didn't name a favorite character. The latter group scored higher in their beliefs that reality TV contestants are motivated by selfish goals, such as acquiring fame and winning prize money. Viewers who do not watch reality TV regularly enough to have favorite characters thus often have a stereotyped perception of the protagonists in these shows, which may explain why they are not interested in the genre.

The appeal of reality TV shows also depends on how realistic they are judged by the viewers. People enjoying reality TV for its entertaining and relaxing value tend to perceive the content of reality shows as more realistic than people with less affinity to the genre. This implies that in order to obtain the gratification of entertainment by watching reality TV, people first have to accept the realism of its content (Papacharissi & Mendelson, 2007, p. 367). Although most consumers do not believe that the programs are entirely real, they likely find them more real than other types of programming (Nabi et al., 2003, p. 327).

The uses and gratifications paradigm can be linked to another construct explaining the appeal of entertainment programs: the notion of enjoyment. In their study comparing viewers' enjoyment of fictional and reality programs, Nabi et al. (2006, p. 425) considered not only a set of gratifications previously sought or obtained from TV programming, such as parasocial relationships or learning, but also other factors that might associate with the enjoyment of entertainment programs. Program interest and enjoyment may be caused by perceptions of drama and suspense, as well as by emotional reactions as suggested by the mood management theory (e.g., Zillmann, 1988). On this basis, the researchers depict a differentiated view of emotional and cognitive assessments predicting enjoyment. While for fiction, suspense and pensiveness enhanced, and surprise detracted from enjoyment, for reality TV in general voyeurism, happiness, surprise, and relief positively associated with, and anger detracted from enjoyment (Nabi et al., 2006, p. 431). A more detailed analysis however revealed that each reality TV subgenre evinced different patterns of gratification, and that reality programs may differ as much from one another as they may differ from fiction. For instance, suspense is positively related to enjoyment of casting shows where viewers can guess the winner, but it is negatively associated with enjoyment of crime programs such as *America's Most Wanted*, in which it may be upsetting to see that the portrayed criminals are still on the loose. Voyeurism was identified as a significant predictor of enjoyment for several reality TV subgenres (reality-drama, romance, and game), but not for fictional programs, so the attraction of watching real people may still be a key feature for viewers preferring reality TV to fictional contents (pp. 440-442).

Case Studies for Various Subgenres

The diversity of the genre and different predictors of enjoyment for various subgenres have led to a wide range of more specific studies about the appeal of particular reality TV programs for their viewers. Only a few examples can be presented in this context. In a comparative study, Barton (2009) analyzed a corporate-themed casting show (*The Apprentice*), a serialized dating game show (*The Bachelor*), and a gamedoc with contestants battling extreme conditions (*Survivor*) by examining the differences between gratifications sought and gratifications obtained by the viewers. The results show that personal utility (relaxation, escapism, uniqueness of the program) is seen as a more important gratification for all three formats than social utility (keeping up with others who watch the show, talking about it), which may reflect the fact that reality shows have become more and more individualized and specific with the ongoing diversification of the genre (pp. 473-474). Perceived realism does not determine the appeal of each analyzed show to the same extent. While this factor is rather important in *Survivor*, this is not the case in *The Bachelor*, which features a highly unlikely plot (25 women competing over one man). Conversely, the romantic elements in this show result in a higher level of obtained gratifications in terms of social utility than the minimalist conditions in *Survivor* (pp. 469-470).

Due to their high audience ratings and their combination of elements from various other genres, casting shows are a particularly popular research field. Several German researchers have analyzed how adolescents as a very important target group (Hackenberg & Hajok, 2010, p. 60; Hajok & Selg, 2010, p. 61) perceive these shows. According to Klaus and O'Connor (2010), the main functions of casting shows for adolescents are providing topics for conversation, providing topics for discussions about ethical questions, and satiating integrative needs in cultural and social fields such as nation, race, class, or gender. Seeking entertainment, fun and thrill, and avoiding boredom are the main motives for watching the shows; while girls have a stronger interest in the outcomes of the competition (Götz & Gather, 2010, p. 53), boys like to watch the candidates' behavior and to trash talk about them (Hajok & Selg, 2010, p. 61). Most 12- to 17-year-old viewers are aware of the commercial intentions of casting shows; pupils on a lower education level are more likely to believe that the producers want to organize a fair competition and to give the candidates "a real chance" (Götz & Gather, 2010, pp. 54-58).

Dover and Hill (2007) analyzed lifestyle and makeover programs by looking at their production and reception. Viewers associated such programs rather with light entertainment than with factual information and a didactic approach: "Those who enjoy makeover shows do so because of the programs' emotional and entertaining content; they do not tend to have high expectations of watching informative or true-to-life content" (p. 24). In the reception of coaching shows such as *Supernanny*, cognitive motives seem to play a more important role. Viewers compare the protagonists' everyday life with their own, feel relieved to see that other people have similar, or more serious, problems, and like to know how other people can solve their problems. Voyeurism and experiencing superiority over the helpless protagonists portrayed in these shows are also present as motives, but are less important (Grimm, 2010, p. 245; Lauber & Würfel, 2010, p. 68).

Supernanny was also the topic of a study comparing the reception of a reality TV program in various countries. Grimm (2010) found that the recommendations given by the nannies did not represent the same parenting style in all analyzed countries and that the success of the format varied. The British original, propagating an authoritarian parenting style, and the German program with medium authoritarian and democratic tendencies were very successful, as well as the Spanish and Brazilian versions boosting rather democratic-permissive recommendations. In contrast, audience ratings of the Austrian program, recommending a distinctly more democratic parenting style than the program of the German neighbors, stayed below expectations, and the show was cancelled after three seasons. Viewers' expectations regarding the recommendations given by the nanny may thus depend on specific educational traditions in their country (pp. 229-235).

Reality TV, Neoliberalism, and "Technologies of the Self"

Sociologist David Grazian argued that "the narrative conventions of reality TV echo the most central policymaking paradigm in America in the past decade: the neoliberal agenda" (2010, p. 68). In this context, various scholars have discussed the role of reality TV in communicating and supporting neoliberal values. Neoliberalism can be defined as a range of discourses absolutely legitimating the market, but delegitimizing institutional forces seeking to counter the market, such as the state and the social (Couldry, 2008, p. 4). This worldview has generated specific trends which have accelerated globally since the 1980s, such as spending cuts on public services, economic deregulation, privatization of state-owned institutions in the name of efficiency, and the elimination of the concept of public good or community, replacing it with individual responsibility (Ouellette, 2009, p. 225). The importance of entrepreneurial liberty leads to an organization of social resources and human labor, which requires of its participants continuous loyalty and the acceptance of permanent surveillance in order to optimize products and to allow closely targeted marketing. For example, it may affect an individual's personal life in a way that employees have to be flexible in their working hours and "always available" for the company. But the system also demands accepting the fragility and impermanence of the opportunities it provides (Couldry, 2008, p. 3).

In fact, similarities between these characteristics and the settings of competitive reality TV shows are obvious: Contestants are provided with tasks, which they must fulfill on their own, and for which they have to take full responsibility for success or failure. At the same time, they are under constant surveillance, and even in cases of a good performance, they can be easily expelled from the show. In his analysis of *Big Brother*, Couldry (2008, p. 9-11) stated that the show legitimates the concept of constant surveillance, since this concept is the precondition for the viewers' pleasure to see the candidates in intimate situations. Furthermore, he argued that the performance "values" of *Big Brother* are striking for their fit with the demands imposed by neoliberal practice on workers. First, candidates have to obey an absolute and unquestionable external authority, the media producers; second, team conformity is also demanded, since the acceptance of compulsory teamwork is a basic rule of the game; third, candidates have to be "passionate" and to show a positive attitude, but must remain "authentic" to have success in the game—which reminds one of guidelines for employees as made, for example, by the British supermarket chain Asda, requiring emotional investment and demanding that every smile must be "a real smile" (*The Observer*, July 11, 2004); finally, in spite of all social dimensions of the show, the contestants are judged against each other as individuals.

Constant self-improvement is often suggested as the only reliable protection from the uncertainty about employment stability and opportunities in a neoliberal economy demanding flexibility, ongoing corporate reinvention, and a shift from production to branding (McGee, 2005, p. 13; Ouellette & Hay, 2008, pp. 99-100). The boom of the self-help industry with specialized literature, as well as contributions in magazines, the tabloid press, and TV broadcasts in the early 21st century contributed to that trend. For example, in the field of reality TV, makeover and casting shows present work on the self as a prerequisite for personal and professional success. The most obvious examples of self-fashioning on television are beauty and style makeover programs. Sender (2006), in her study about *Queer Eye for a Straight Guy*, as well as Ouellette and Hay (2008) in a more comprehensive analysis, discussed the role of these formats promoting "technologies of the self" with which candidates should be able to engineer better, more fulfilling lives.

In a similar way, coaching formats such as *Supernanny* or *Honey We're Killing the Kids* represent an entrepreneurial ethic of self-care, using a combination of disciplinary and self-help strategies to enable individuals to overcome their problems (Ouellette & Hay, 2008, p. 6). Another form of crisis intervention by television is the subgenre of charity programs (*Extreme Makeover: Home Edition, Three Wishes, Miracle Workers*), where private resources (money, volunteerism, skills) are mobilized in order to remedy personal hardship without state assistance. Reality TV may thus adopt functions of public welfare programs that have been cut back. However, only the most "deserving" cases of need, as determined by casting departments, are assisted (pp. 5-6).

Conclusion and Discussion

Reality TV as a research field is foremost complex and dynamic, as it has undergone an enormous diversification since the 1990s. Dozens of new formats were introduced every year. With this essay, we attempted to conceptualize reality TV as a meta-genre that includes various subgenres. Hence, examining the meta-genre's components, which may also apply to subgenres, most often serves the purpose to provide a theoretical definition of reality TV. Such components include, for example, featuring ordinary people who are engaged in unscripted actions. In the viewers' perception, there is also more or less consensus about which formats are reality TV, but the boundaries between the subgenres are rather fluid. Nabi (2007) suggests mapping the reality TV landscape along the dimensions "romance" and "competition," whereas Klaus and Lücke (2003) distinguish between "narrative" and "performative" reality TV.

It seems important that reality TV's primary intent is to entertain an audience. The shows are less concerned about providing a journalistic function such as stimulating a political debate or to educate. It may well be that these are secondary goals, but reality TV's main goal is to engage their audiences to attract advertisers. Interestingly, research shows that personal utility (relaxation, escapism, uniqueness of the program) is perceived as more important gratification than social utility (keeping up with others who watch the show, talking about it). Diversifications of the genre may have led to a more individualized approach of reality TV and to it being less a matter of social utility.

Our analysis of a worldwide boom and diversification of reality TV since the 1990s has revealed a complex interplay of factors that paved the way for the success of reality TV, locally and globally. First of all, technological developments allowed a multiplication of the available TV programs in the last two decades of the 20th century. This was caused by the development of cable and satellite TV, then by the introduction of digital channels. In countries where public-service channels previously were in a monopoly or predominant position, new commercial broadcasters could now enter the market. In order to conquer a good position in this market, the new players required popular and remarkable, but also comparatively cheap, programs to fill the additional program space. Reality TV formats fulfilled these needs: They are entertaining, they can be marketed as unique due to the authenticity of the participants, and they allow new forms of advertisement, merchandising, and audience participation in order to finance the production costs. At the same time, production costs are rather low since no scriptwriters and professional actors are needed, and the footage can be filmed with a new generation of compact and inexpensive cameras.

The overview of the genre further shows that modern reality TV formats are usually hybrids of existing genres: The docusoap as the prototypical reality TV genre, which is itself a mixture of documentary and fictional soap opera, is combined with game and talk show elements in reality soaps such as *Big Brother* or *Survivor*, with the classical talent contest and the variety show in casting shows, or with the traditional dating show in modern dating programs. In order to maintain high viewer interest, new combinations and variations are permanently developed: Mixing genres is seen as a strategy to reach audiences as large as possible (Lünenborg et al., 2011, p. 14).

Tendencies of the past years included the introduction of new settings and the increasing importance of celebrities as participants or coaches in reality TV programs. The settings in most newer formats tend to be much less artificial than in *Big Brother* or *Survivor*, and the success of makeover and coaching shows, as well as the more extensive use of coaching elements in recent casting shows, may reflect a growing importance of expert guidance and authoritative recommendations for the public (Grimm, 2010, p. 222). Public interest is particularly raised by dramatization of the content, e.g., by the choice of settings and the casting of participants in a conflict-provoking manner. A new stage of dramatization has been reached with scripted reality formats telling fictional stories but pretending for them to be "real." But the diversification of the genre has also left space for countertendencies, for example, spoof shows parodying extreme developments or formats intending to go "back to the essentials" such as casting shows with a stronger focus on the candidates' talents than on their looks or their behavior behind the stage. This may be illustrated for instance by the introduction of blind auditions in *The Voice*.

But essentially, global success and diversification of reality TV have only become possible thanks to new production routines in the television industry. Unlike fictional TV series, reality TV formats are just "global program frameworks that can be adopted on a national level in order to fit into different cultures" (Bondebjerg, 2002, p. 159). Most of them are not produced by the TV stations themselves, but by independent production companies developing the concepts and selling them to interested broadcasters all over the world. This new model allowed broadcasters to adopt formats, which have proven to be successful elsewhere instead of taking the risk to develop them on their own, which may be an essential advantage in a highly competitive market. As Andrejevic (2004, p. 12) concisely explains, "reality TV fits well the dictates of global media production insofar as it combines a local cast and local viewer participation with a customizable transnational format. What is exported is not the content itself but a recipe for creating a local version of an internationally successful TV show."

As our investigation shows, narratives of reality TV shows are not perceived as "real" in any case. In fact, 25% of an adult poll suggests perception of reality TV as made-up shows. A total of 57% believed that they show some truth, but are mostly distorted. But only 30% said that it mattered whether the shows are real or not (Bauder 2005). On the other hand, voyeurism is put forward as a significant predictor of enjoyment for several reality TV subgenres.

Hence, it may well be that viewers enjoy watching "real" people and not actors even though they believe the narratives are made-up. Viewers may identify more with reality TV participants because they embody similar lifestyles. In other words, such exposure experiences may be more easily integrated into their own lives than fictional programs based on more escape motives. Hence, we suggest further study particularly on such differences between fictional and reality TV based programs to better understand what motives drive audiences to watch such shows and how media concepts and theories such as parasocial interaction, parasocial relationships, or social identification may differ between the two. Interestingly, as outlined in this review, cognitive development, age, and education influence how viewers perceive and conceptualize reality TV programs. Hence, we may well be much more prepared to understand audience's reaction to such programs by studying individual differences and how they influence the motives of exposure, the perception of the content, and the effects of watching reality TV programs.

References

Andrejevic, M. (2004). *Reality TV: The work of being watched.* Lanham, MD: Rowman & Littlefield Publishers.

Andrejevic, M. (2008). Watching television without pity: The productivity of online fans. *Television & New Media, 9*(1), 24-46.

Andrejevic, M. (2009). Visceral literacy: Reality-TV, savvy viewers, and auto-spies. In S. Murray & L. Ouellette (eds.), *Reality TV. Remaking television culture* (pp. 321-342). 2nd edition, New York and London: New York University Press.

Aslama, M. (2009). Playing house: Participants' experiences of Big Brother Finland. *International Journal of Cultural Studies, 12*(1), 81-96.

Baltruschat, D. (2009). Reality TV formats: The case of Canadian Idol. *Canadian Journal of Communication, 34*(1), 41-59.

Barton, K. M. (2009). Reality television programming and diverging gratifications: The influence of content on gratifications obtained. *Journal of Broadcasting & Electronic Media, 53*(3), 460-476.

Baruh, L. (2009). Publicized intimacies on reality television: An analysis of voyeuristic content and its contribution to the appeal of reality programming. *Journal of Broadcasting & Electronic Media, 53*(2), 190-210.

Bauder, D. (2005). Poll: Viewers beginning to tire from reality TV. *The Spokesman-Review,* September 18th, 2005.

BBC online (2006, December 1): £106m deal for Millionaire rights. Retrieved May 22, 2012, from http://news.bbc .co.uk/2/hi/entertainment/6198424.stm

Beck, D., & Jecker, C. (2012). Gestaltung der Programme—zzwischen Tradition und Innovation. In T. Mäusli, A. Steigmeier & F. Vallotton (eds.), *Radio und Fernsehen in der Schweiz. Geschichte der Schweizerischen Radio-und Fernsehgesellschaft SRG 1983-2011* (pp. 337-383). Baden: hier+jetzt.

Benson, R., & Hallin, D. C. (2007). How states, markets and globalization shape the news: The French and US national press, 1965-97. *European Journal of Communication, 22*(1), 27-48.

Bilstereyst, D. (2004). Media audiences and the game of controversy: On Reality TV, moral panic and controversial media stories. *Journal of Media Practice, 5*(1), 7-24.

Boddy, W. (2001). Quiz shows. In G. Creeber (ed.), *The television genre book* (pp. 79-81). London: British Film Institute.

Bondebjerg, I. (2002). The mediation of everyday life: Genre, discourse and spectacle in reality TV. In A. Jerslev (ed.), *Realism and "reality" in film and media* (pp. 159-192). Copenhagen: Museum Tusculanum Press.

Bourdon, J. (2004). Old and new ghosts: Public service television and the popular—A history. *European Journal of Cultural Studies, 7*(3), 283-304.

Brauck, M. (2009). TV-Formate: Die Reality-Falle. *Der Spiegel,* (43), 86-88.

Bruzzi, S. (2000). *New documentary: A critical introduction.* New York: Routledge.

Bruzzi, S. (2001a). Docusoaps. In G. Creeber (ed.), *The television genre book* (pp. 132-134). London: British Film Institute.

Bruzzi, S. (2001b). Observational ("fly-on-the-wall") documentary. In G. Creeber (ed.), *The television genre book* (pp. 129-132). London: British Film Institute.

Caramanico, J. (2011, October 30). 'Jersey Shore' arrives in academia. Discuss. *New York Times*. October 30th, 2011. Retrieved May 22, 2012, from http://www .nytimes.com/2011/10/31/arts/television/jersey-shorehas-its-day-at-university-of-chicago.html?_r=3&ref =arts. CBS (2012). CBS casting. Retrieved May 22, 2012 from http://www.cbs.com/casting.

Chalaby, J. K. (2011). The making of an entertainment revolution: How the TV format trade became a global industry. *European Journal of Communication, 26*(4), 293-309.

Clavien, G. (2003). La réplique du service public en Suisse romande. *Média-Morphoses (Spécial Big Brother)*, HS1, 109–111.

Clissold, B. D. (2004). *Candid Camera* and the origins of reality TV: Contextualising a historical precedent. In S. Holmes & D. Jermyn (eds.), *Understanding reality television* (pp. 33-53). London and New York: Routledge.

Cohen, J., & Weimann, G. (2008). Who's afraid of reality shows? Exploring the effects of perceived influence of reality shows and the concern over their social effects on willingness to censor. *Communication Research, 35*(3), 382-397.

Cooper-Chen, A. (2005). A world of "millionaires": Global, local and "glocal" TV game shows. In A. Cooper-Chen (ed.), *Global entertainment media. Content, audiences, issues* (pp. 237-251). Mahwah, NJ: Lawrence Erlbaum Associates.

Corner, J. (2009). Performing the real: Documentary diversions. In S. Murray & L. Ouellette (eds.), *Reality TV. Remaking television culture* (pp. 44-64). 2nd edition, New York and London: New York University Press.

Couldry, N. (2008). Reality TV, or the secret theater of neoliberalism. *The Review of Education, Pedagogy, and Cultural Studies, 30*(3), 3-13.

de Mooij, M. (2010). *Global marketing and advertising. Understanding cultural paradoxes.* 3rd ed., Los Angeles, London, New Delhi, Singapore and Washington DC: Sage.

Dhoest, A. (2004). "The Pfaffs are not like the Osbournes": National inflections of the celebrity docusoap. *Television & New Media, 6*(2), 224-245.

Djang, J. (2010, May 2). President Obama trades jokes with Jay Leno. The White House blog. Retrieved May 22, 2012, from http://www.whitehouse.gov/blog/2010/ 05/02/president-obama-trades-jokes-with-jay-leno.

Dover, C., & Hill, A. (2007). *Mapping genres: Broadcaster and audience perceptions of makeover television.* In D. Heller (ed.), *Makeover television: Realities remodelled* (pp. 23-38). London: I. B. Taurus.

Dovey, J. (2001). Reality TV. In G. Creeber (ed.), *The television genre book* (pp. 134-137). London: British Film Institute.

Duguid, M. (2010). Living in the past (1978). BFI Screenonline. Retrieved May 22, 2012 from http://www.screenonline.org.uk/tv/id/583427.

Ebersole, S. & Woods, R. (2007). Motivations for Viewing Reality Television: A Uses and Gratifications Analysis. *Southwestern Mass Communication Journal, 23*(1), 23-42.

EBU – (European Broadcasting Union) (2012). Eurovision Song Contest history. Facts & trivia. Retrieved May 22, 2012 from http://www.eurovision.tv/page/history/ facts-figures.

Enli, G. S. (2009). Mass communication Tapping into participatory culture exploring *Strictly Come Dancing* and *Britain's Got Talent*. *European Journal of Communication, 24*(4), 481-493.

Fitzgerald, K. (2003, May 12). So many realities, so few slots. *Advertising Age, 74*(19). Retrieved May 22, 2012 from http://adage.com/article/news/realitiesslots/ 49114.

Foster, D. (2004). "Jump in the pool": The competitive culture of *Survivor* fan networks. In S. Holmes & D. Jermin (eds.), *Understanding reality television* (pp. 270-289). London and New York: Routledge.

Franco, J. (2008). *Extreme Makeover*: The politics of gender, class, and cultural identity. *Television & New Media, 9*(6), 471-486.

Ganz-Blättler, U. (2005, June 15). Genres zwischen Fiktion und Dokumentation. Versuch einer Neubestimmung. *Medienheft,* (23). Retrieved May 22, 2012, from http://www.medienheft.ch/dossier/bibliothek/d23_Ga nz-BlaettlerUrsula.pdf.

Gillan, J. (2004). From Ozzie Nelson to Ozzy Osbourne: The genesis and the development of the reality (star) sitcom. In S. Holmes & D. Jermyn (eds.), *Understanding reality television* (pp. 54-70). London and New York: Routledge.

Gorman, B. (2011, January 7). "Jersey Shore" season premiere draws record 8.45 million viewers. TV by the Numbers. Retrieved May 22, 2012 from http://tv-bythenumbers.zap2it.com/2011/01/07/jerseyshore-season-premiere-draws-8-4-million-sets-mtvall-time-series-high/77688.

Götz, M. (2012). Wie Kinder und Jugendliche Familien im Brennpunkt verstehen. *TelevIZIon, 25*(1), 2-8.

Götz, M., & Gather, J. (2010). Wer bleibt drin, wer fliegt raus? Was Kinder und Jugendliche aus Deutschland sucht den Superstar und Germany's Next Topmodel mitnehmen. *TelevIZIon, 23*(1), 56-63.

Gray, J. (2009). Cinderella burps: Gender, performativity, and the dating show. In S. Murray & L. Ouellette (eds.), *Reality TV: Remaking television culture* (pp. 260-277). 2nd ed., New York and London: New York University Press.

Grazian, D. (2010). Neoliberalism and the realities of reality TV. *Contexts, 9*(2), 68-71.

Griffen-Foley, B. (2004). From *Tit-Bits* to *Big Brother*: A century of audience participation in the media. *Media, Culture & Society, 26*(4), 533-548.

Grimm, J. (2010). From reality TV to coaching TV: Elements of theory and empirical findings towards understanding the genre. In A. Hetsroni (ed.), *Reality TV: Merging the global and the local* (pp. 211-258). New York: Nova.

Grindstaff, L. (2011). Just be yourself—only more so: Ordinary celebrity. In M. M. Kraidy & K. Sender (eds.), *The politics of reality television: Global perspectives* (pp. 44-58). London and New York: Routledge.

Hackenberg, A., & Hajok, D. (2010). Castingshows und Coachingsendungen im Fernsehen: Eine Untersuchung zur Nutzung und Bewertung durch Jugendliche und junge Erwachsene. *tv diskurs,* (51), 58-60.

Hajok, D., & Selg, O. (2010). Castingshows im Urteil ihrer Nutzer. *tv diskurs,* (51), 61-65.

Hall, A. (2003). Reading realism: Audiences' evaluation of the reality of media texts. *Journal of Communication, 53*(4), 624-641.

Hall, A. (2006). Viewers' perceptions of reality programs. *Communication Quarterly, 54*(2), 191-211.

Hall, A. (2009). Perceptions of the authenticity of reality programs and their relationships to audience involvement, enjoyment, and perceived learning. *Journal of Broadcasting & Electronic Media, 53*(4), 515-531.

Hallin, D. C., & Mancini, P. (2004). *Comparing media systems: Three models of media and politics.* Cambridge, UK: Cambridge University Press.

Hanitzsch, T., & Mellado, C. (2011). What shapes the news around the world? How journalists in eighteen countries perceive influences on their work. *The International Journal of Press/Politics, 16,* 404-426.

Hearn, A. (2009). Hoaxing the "real": On the metanarrative of reality television. In S. Murray & L. Ouellette (eds.), *Reality TV: Remaking television culture* (pp. 165-178). 2nd ed., New York and London: New York University Press.

Hellmueller, L. C., & Aeschbacher, N. (2010). Media and celebrity: Production and consumption of "well-Knownness." *Communication Research Trends, 29*(4), 3-35.

Hendershot, H. (2009). Belabored reality: Making it work on *The Simple Life* and *Project Runway.* In S. Murray & L. Ouellette (eds.), *Reality TV: Remaking television culture* (pp. 243-259). 2nd ed., New York and London: New York University Press.

Hetsroni, A., & Tukachinsky, R. H. (2003). *Who Wants to Be a Millionaire* in America, Russia, and Saudi Arabia: A celebration of differences or a unified global culture? *The Communication Review, 6*(2), 165-178.

Hill, A., Weibull, L., & Nilsson, A. (2007). Public and popular: British and Swedish audience trends in factual and reality television. *Cultural Trends, 16*(1), 17-41.

Ho, H. (2006, June 16). *Parasocial identification, reality television, and viewer self-worth.* Paper presented at the 56th annual meeting of the International Communication Association, Dresden International Congress Centre, Dresden, Germany. Retrieved March 14, 2011 from http://www.allacademic.com/meta / p93143_index.html.

Holmes, S (2004)."But this time you choose!" Approaching the "interactive" audience in reality TV. *International Journal of Cultural Studies, 7*(2), 213-231

Holmes, S., & Jermyn, D. (2004). Introduction: Understanding reality TV. In S. Holmes & D. Jermyn (eds.), *Understanding reality television* (pp. 1-32). London and New York: Routledge.

Hong, Y.-Y. (2009). A dynamic constructivist approach to culture: Moving from describing culture to explaining culture. In R. S. Wyer, C.-Y. Chiu & Y.-Y. Hong (eds.), *Understanding culture: Theory, research, and application* (pp. 3-25). New York: Taylor & Francis Group.

James, C. (2003, January 26). Bachelor No.1 and the birth of reality TV. *The New York Times.* Retrieved May 22, 2012, from http://www.nytimes.com/2003/01/26 /movies/television-radio-bachelor-no-1-and-the-birthof-reality-tv.html.

Jenkins, H. (2009). Buying into American Idol: How we are being sold on reality television. In S. Murray & L. Ouellette (eds.), *Reality TV: Remaking television culture* (pp. 343-362). 2nd edition, New York and London: New York University Press.

Jermyn, D. (2004). "This *is* about real people!" Video technologies, actuality and affect in the television crime appeal. In S. Holmes & D. Jermyn, (eds.), *Understanding reality television* (pp. 71-90). London and New York: Routledge.

Katz, E., Blumler, J. G., & Gurevitch, M. (1974). Uses and gratifications research. *Public Opinion Quarterly, 37*(4), 509-523.

Kilborn, R. M. (2003). *Staging the real. Factual TV programming in the age of Big Brother.* Manchester and New York: Manchester University Press.

King, S. W. (1976). Reconstructing the concept of source perceptions: Toward a paradigm of source appropriateness. *Western Speech Communication, 40*(4), 216-225.

Klaus, E., & Lücke, S. (2003). Reality TV: Definition und Merkmale einer erfolgreichen Genrefamilie am Beispiel von Reality Soap und Docu Soap. *Medien & Kommunikationswissenschaft, 51*(2), 195-212.

Klaus, E., & O'Connor, B. (2010). Aushandlungsprozess im Alltag: Jugendliche Fans von Castingshows. In J. Röser, T. Thomas & C. Peil (eds.), *Alltag in den Medien—Medien im Alltag* (pp. 48-72). Wiesbaden: VS Verlag für Sozialwissenschaften.

Kompare, D. (2009). Extraordinarily ordinary: The Osbournes as "An American Family." In S. Murray & L. Ouellette (eds.), *Reality TV: Remaking television culture* (pp. 100-119). 2nd ed., New York and London: New York University Press.

Kraidy, M. M. (1999). The global, the local, and the hybrid: A native ethnography of glocalization. *Critical Studies in Mass Communication, 16*(4), 456-476.

Krüger, U. M. (2010). Factual entertainment—Fernsehunterhaltung im Wandel. Programmanalyse 2009 – Teil 1: Sparten und Formen. *Media Perspektiven,* (4), 158-181.

Langdale, J. V. (1997). East Asian broadcasting industries: Global, regional, and national perspectives. *Economic Geography, 73*, 305-321.

Lauber, A., & Würfel, M. (2010). Coachingsendungen im Urteil ihrer Nutzer. *tv diskurs,* (51), 66-71.

Lewis, T. (2010). Mobile makeovers: Global and local lifestyles and identities in reality formats. In A. Hetsroni (ed.), *Reality TV: Merging the global and the local* (pp. 189-210). New York: Nova.

Lewis, T. (2011). Globalizing lifestyles? Makeover television in Singapore. In M. M. Kraidy & K. Sender (eds.), *The politics of reality television: Global perspectives* (pp. 78-92). London and New York: Routledge.

Livio, O. (2010). Performing the nation: A cross-cultural comparison of Idol shows in four countries. In A. Hetsroni (ed.), *Reality TV: Merging the global and the local* (pp. 165-188). New York: Nova.

Lundy, L. K., Ruth, A. M., & Park, T. D. (2008). Simply irresistible: Reality TV consumption patterns. *Communication Quarterly, 56*(2), 208-225.

Lünenborg, M., Martens, D., Köhler, T., & Töpper, C. (2011): *Skandalisierung im Fernsehen. Strategien, Erscheinungsformen und Rezeption von Reality TV Formaten.* Berlin: Vistas.

McCarthy, A. (2009). "Stanley Milgram, Allen Funt and Me": Postwar social science and the first wave of reality TV. In S. Murray & L. Ouellette (eds.), *Reality TV: Remaking television culture* (pp. 23-43). 2nd ed., New York and London: New York University Press.

McCroskey, J. C. (1966). Scales for the measurement of ethos. *Speech Monographs, 33,* 65-72.

McCroskey, J. C., & Young, T. J. (1981). Ethos and credibility: The construct and its measurement after three decades. *Central States Speech Journal, 32*(1), 24-34.

McGee, M. (2005). *Self-help Inc.: Makeover culture in American life.* Oxford/New York: Oxford University Press.

Murray, S. (2009). "I think we need a new name for it": The meeting of documentary and reality TV. In S. Murray & L. Ouellette (eds.), *Reality TV: Remaking television culture* (pp. 65-81). 2nd ed., New York and London: New York University Press.

Murray, S., & Ouellette, L. (2009). Introduction. In S. Murray & L. Ouellette (eds.), *Reality TV: Remaking television culture* (pp. 1-20). 2nd ed., New York and London: New York University Press.

Nabi, R. L. (2007). Determining dimensions of reality: A concept mapping of the reality TV landscape. *Journal of Broadcasting & Electronic Media, 51*(2), 371-390.

Nabi, R. L., Biely, E. N., Morgan, S. J., & Stitt, C. R. (2003): Reality-based television programming and the psychology of its appeal. *Media Psychology, 5,* 303-330.

Nabi, R. L., Stitt, C. R., Halford, J., & Finnerty, K. L. (2006). Emotional and cognitive predictors of the enjoyment of reality-based and fictional television programming: An elaboration of the uses and gratifications perspective. *Media Psychology, 8,* 421-447.

Neuliep, J., Hintz, S., & McCroskey, J. C. (2005). The influence of ethnocentrism in organizational contexts: Perceptions of interviewee and managerial attractiveness, credibility, and effectiveness. *Communication Quarterly, 53*(1), 41-56.

The Observer. (2004, July 11): Where it Asda be a real smile. Retrieved May 22, 2012, from http://www.guardian .co.uk/business/2004/jul/11/supermarkets.

Ouellette, L. (2009). "Take responsibility for yourself": *Judge Judy* and the neoliberal citizen. In S. Murray & L. Ouellette (eds.), *Reality TV: Remaking television culture* (pp. 223-242). 2nd ed., New York and London: New York University Press.

Ouellette, L., & Hay, J. (2008). *Better living through reality TV.* Malden, MA: Blackwell Publishing.

Paek, H.-J. (2005). Understanding celebrity endorsers in cross-cultural contexts: A content analysis of South Korean and US newspaper advertising. *Asian Journal of Communication, 15*(2), 133-153.

Palmer, G. (2004). 'The new you': Class and transformation in lifestyle television. In S. Holmes & D. Jermyn (eds.), *Understanding reality television* (pp. 173-190). London and New York: Routledge.

Palmgreen, P., Wenner, L. A., & Rosengren, K. E. (1985). Uses and gratifications research: The past ten years. In K. E. Rosengren, L. A. Wenner, & P. Palmgreen (eds.), *Media gratifications research: Current perspectives* (pp. 11-37). Beverly Hills, CA: Sage.

Papacharissi, Z., & Mendelson, A. L. (2007). An exploratory study of reality appeal: Uses and gratifications of reality TV shows. *Journal of Broadcasting & Electronic Media, 51*(2), 355-370.

Patino, A., Kaltcheva, V. D., & Smith, M. F. (2011). The appeal of reality television for teen and pre-teen audiences: The power of "connectedness" and psycho demographics. *Journal of Advertising Research, 51*(1), 288-297.

Popular Mechanics (2008, March 28). The 10 most prophetic sci-fi movies ever. Retrieved May 22, 2012, from http://www.popularmechanics.com/technology/digital/fact-vs-fiction/4256186.

Price, E. (2010). Reinforcing the myth: Constructing Australian identity in 'reality TV'. *Continuum: Journal Of Media & Cultural Studies, 24*(3), 451-459.

Reiss, S., & Wiltz, J. (2004). Why people watch reality TV. *Media Psychology, 6,* 363-378.

Riley, S. G. (2010). Temporary celebrity. In S. G. Riley (ed.), *Star struck: An encyclopedia of celebrity culture* (pp. 294-299). Santa Barbara, CA: Greenwood Press.

Riverol, A. R. (1992). *Live from Atlantic City: A history of the Miss America Pageant.* Bowling Green, OH: Bowling Green State University Popular Press.

Rose, R. L., & Wood, S. L. (2005). Paradox and the consumption of authenticity through reality television. *Journal of Consumer Research, 32,* 284-296.

Sender, K. (2006). Queens for a day: *Queer Eye for a Straight Guy* and the neoliberal project. *Critical Studies in Media Communication, 23*(2), 131-151.

Shattuc, J. (2001). Confessional talk shows. In G. Creeber (ed.), *The television genre book* (pp. 84-87). London: British Film Institute.

Shearman, S. M. (2008). *Culture, values, and cultural variability: Hofstede, Inglehart, and Schwartz's approach.* Paper presented at the International Communication Association.

Shoemaker, P. J., & Vos, T. P. (2009). *Gatekeeping theory.* New York / Abingdon: Routledge.

Thornborrow, J., & Morris, D. (2004). Gossip as strategy: The management of talk about others on reality TV show "Big Brother." *Journal of Sociolinguistics, 8*(2), 246-271.

Tincknell, E., & Raghuram, P. (2002). Big Brother: Reconfiguring the "active" audience of cultural studies? *European Journal of Cultural Studies, 5*(2), 199-215.

Ting-Toomey, S., & Chung, L. C. (2005). *Understanding intercultural communication.* Los Angeles: Roxbury Publishing Company.

Tunstall, J., & Machin, D. (1999). *The Anglo-American media connection.* Oxford: Oxford University Press.

University of Chicago (2011, October 28): The UChicago conference on Jersey Shore studies. Retrieved May 22, 2012, from http://www.striking.ly/s/pages/jerseyshore-conference.

Vena, J. (2010, July 1). Kim Kardashian gets her own Madame Tussauds wax figure. MTV News. Retrieved May 22, 2012, from http://www.mtv.com/news/articles/1642879.

Wahl-Jorgensen, K., & Hanitzsch, T. (2009). *The handbook of journalism studies.* New York: Routledge.

Waisbord, S. (2004). Mc TV: Understanding the global popularity of television formats. *Television & New Media, 5*(4), 359-383.

Walter, T. (2010). Jade and the journalists: Media coverage of a young British celebrity dying of cancer. *Social Science & Medicine, 71*(5), 853-860.

Watts, A. (2009). Melancholy, merit, and merchandise: The postwar audience participation show. In S. Murray & L. Ouellette (eds.), *Reality TV: Remaking television culture* (pp. 301-320). 2nd ed., New York and London: New York University Press.

West, E. (2010). Reality nations: An international comparison of the historical reality genre. In A. Hetsroni (ed.), *Reality TV: Merging the global and the local* (pp. 259-277). New York: Nova.

Wheeless, L. R. (1974). The effects of attitude, credibility, and homophily on selective exposure to information. *Speech Monographs, 41*(4), 329-338.

Zillmann, D. (1988). Mood management: Using entertainment to full advantage. In L. Donohew, H. E. Sypher, & T. E. Higgins (eds.), *Communication, social cognition and affect* (pp. 147-171). Hillsdale, NJ: Lawrence Erlbaum Associates.

My Strange Addiction

By Emily Nussbaum
The New Yorker, August 13, 2012

The Sleazy Wisdom of "Big Brother"

It would be neglectful for this critic to write about the CBS reality series "Big Brother," now in its fourteenth season, without making a troubling confession: twelve years ago, I was a Web watcher. This means that I didn't merely watch "Big Brother" episodes many nights a week—an embarrassing enough revelation—but also online, via 24/7 streaming footage. Each morning, I would stumble into my living room and open my laptop, letting the characters (who were in California, three hours behind) sleep on the screen, like pets. In my defense, I was freelancing at the time. I needed the company.

This might not have been such strange behavior if "Big Brother" had been a water-cooler hit. But it was a flop: the Dutch-created game show, in which contestants spent months in isolation, was a phenomenon in Europe, but its first American season was swamped by "Survivor," a ratings bonanza and the subject of outraged op-eds. "Survivor" starred jocks and was filmed in exotic locations. "Big Brother" starred "hamsters" in sweatpants, caged in a house, forced to memorize highway routes to win treats.

Even worse, the American audience had no idea how to vote. In other countries, the viewers threw out the boring people, leaving those with mood disorders and/or sex appeal. Americans did the opposite: they expelled the troublemakers, who were, early in Season 1, a black nationalist and a bisexual stripper. As a result, the cast members became paralyzed, convinced that they'd be booted if they did anything interesting. One night, I watched enraptured as my favorite character, an introverted Asian-American lawyer named Curtis, brooded over his impending expulsion, then chatted politely with his competitor—it was a subtle emotional heroism that was hardly telegenic. Later, a Midwestern roofer nicknamed Chicken George tried to persuade the cast to stage a mass walkout; you'll have to take my word for this, but those hours of filibustering were amazing to watch live. By then the show's audience was tiny, even counting my fellow Web watchers, with whom I spent hours online analyzing these important events.

Understandably, the producers changed the rules in Season 2. Now the "Big Brother" contestants voted one another off. Alliances formed, including a cruel clique called Chilltown. The Chilltown schemers believed that they were the

---

Originally published in *The New Yorker* 88.24 (13 Aug. 2012). Reprinted by permission.

show's heroes, not its villains—and they were also, in the unedited feeds, hilariously obsessed with ratings, fomenting half-real "showmances" and strutting like roosters. The Nielsen levels spiked, but I was getting too uneasy to keep watching. (O.K., I watched Season 3—but that was it, I swear.)

For fans, the early seasons of reality TV were fuelled by cognitive dissonance: the aesthetics might be ugly and the ethics dubious, but the conversations among viewers went amazingly deep, into psychology, politics, and the nature of human intimacy—talk that was more resonant than anything triggered by the polite scripted dramas that surrounded them. This never quite justified the cruelty, so I turned away. But apparently the cookies in my Web browser's cache were baked by Proust, because twelve years later, when I reopened the feeds, all the old giddiness flooded back. Ooh, there was the miserable house! The hideous "veto" medal! There was the robotic host, Julie Chen, and the dumb competitions, with contestants jumping on spinning beds like toddlers on bath salts. Naturally, I got addicted right away.

> *Diversity has always been a mixed blessing of the reality genre, which is one of the few opportunities on network television for working-class people to appear as themselves—as caricatures on the worst shows, but with brass and nuance on the best.*

Part of the fun of watching the later seasons of a half-demonic, half-fantastic series like "Big Brother" is that the contestants are themselves fans of the show—in this season's première, one hamster tells another that he saw him on TV when he was ten years old. Four characters are past contestants, including Mike Boogie, the cretinous wingman of Chilltown, now the series' professor emeritus with highlights in his hair. A newbie arrives self-branded, announcing, "I look like your typical Southern gay. But underneath it I'm tough, I'm talented, and I'm gonna kick your booty." The show may have lost its innocence—and the drama of having at least one character who is there to make friends—but I no longer worry about the cast. To quote the movie "Airplane," "They bought their tickets. They knew what they were getting into. I say, let 'em crash."

The current crew includes a tattooed Puerto Rican punk-rock lesbian, a spray-tan technician who plans to fill the house with "great energy," a pasty-white science geek, a chef who speaks in a shout, a hot nurse who mysteriously pretends to be a hot kindergarten teacher, a few other hard-to-distinguish hot girls, and a carpenter who inspires lame "good with his hands" jokes, but who is hot. Diversity has always been a mixed blessing of the reality genre, which is one of the few opportunities on network television for working-class people to appear as themselves—as caricatures on the worst shows, but with brass and nuance on the best.

"Big Brother" is not one of the best. It's also far less diverse than it was in its early years (and not only racially: in Season 1, fewer of the characters were Hollywood wannabes). But, over time, with cameras beating down on them, even the most bogus contestants can radiate charisma, learning to fake it so real they are beyond fake, to quote Courtney Love, who would make a great hamster. The live feeds remain inexplicably hypnotic. In one, the tattooed punk frets about her enemies, while out at the pool three women languidly exchange pregnancy stories, then discuss Jeannette Walls's memoir "The Glass Castle." People talk about lunch a lot, but there are flashes of intimacy and cunning.

So far, this season has been dominated by Mike Boogie and his mop-top mentee, Frank. But the characters who stand out are Ian and Ashley, the "nerd" and the "ditz." It's obvious that these two are being groomed by the producers; they're even sent on a date, with Ian dressed in Pee-wee Hermanesque drag. (Apparently, staffers on "Big Brother" picked up a viewer's tweet noting parallels to the network's sitcom "The Big Bang Theory.") In this clouded atmosphere, the fun is in discerning what's counterfeit: Is Ashley a dope, or dopey like a fox? Is the seemingly naïve Ian in fact the ultimate manipulator? On the edited show, you'll never hear what you do on the feeds, such as the sinister voice of the producers over the loudspeakers: "Please! Do not talk about production."

Back in 2000, it seemed clear what reality TV was: the slutty, embarrassing cousin of cinéma vérité. Documentary bred with soap opera, the genre was considered a grave threat to scripted television. Instead, the two styles have moved forward together, in an aesthetic three-legged race. Reality is no longer just one thing, to be responded to in just one way: You've got your joyous singing contests and your wrenching dives into addiction. You've got shows about fashion and cooking, makeovers and dating, home renovation and weight loss—a women's magazine brought to life. You've got subcultural soaps like "Polyamory: Married & Dating," misogynist vaudeville like "The Real Housewives," and decent semi-docs like "NYMed." A series such as "Teen Mom" is exploitative, then revelatory, then exploitative. Neither quality erases the other, and neither trumps.

If you don't have it in you to watch the hamsters tan, you might prefer to spend August with "The L.A. Complex," a gem hidden in the CW's slate of teen shows. Filmed in Toronto, the Canadian series has an outsider's insight into the panicked strivers of Los Angeles, a demographic that might well audition for "Big Brother." A closeted hip-hop star, terrified of being outed, beats up his lover; the star of a "Grey's Anatomy"-type show, at once cocky and needy, is solicited for a "contract" relationship with an older actress. The newest character is a homeless Manitoban teen-ager struggling to get her kid brother a Hollywood break. There are comic plots, too, including one with a wild starlet cast on a Christian soap opera. Now entering its second season, "The L.A. Complex" is maddeningly low-rated, but it's worth seeking out: it's no masterpiece of cinematography, and can veer into melodrama, but at its sharpest moments the show has as much "Midnight Cowboy" in it as it does "Melrose Place."

Why Reality TV Doesn't Suck, and May Even Make Us Smarter

By Grant McCracken
Wired, October 4, 2012

It's easy to assume reality TV is the place where bad TV went to hide when the rest of TV got a lot better. Like that old Wild West town where criminals congregate, reality TV is often perceived as the last, "vast wasteland": uncouth, desperate, lawless.

But while some shows seem irredeemably bad (*Here Comes Honey Boo Boo*, anyone?), others offer an indication of good things to come. In fact, by turning all of us into *virtual anthropologists*, reality TV may lead to the improvement—dare I say it—of Western civilization. Reality TV may even be the next stage in the evolution of television.

In its early days, TV was confronted with a series of problems. It was a new medium struggling to find a place in the world. It had quality-control problems in sound and image. And it was talking to millions of Americans for whom English was a second language and American culture was still a mystery. TV solved these problems by relying on genre. Once you understood you were watching a "cop show" or a "Western," the rest was easy.

Genre was like a cheat sheet. It flattened every difficulty: technical, intellectual, cultural, linguistic.

Successive generations got better at TV, and when this happened genre TV became grueling. It bored us. These programs "jumped the shark" and we fled. Now, show runners were free and even forced to build in complexity. But then even this complexity began to bore us.

Writers were free of genre but they were still *forming* the narrative. They were still making a story when what we wanted was the uncontrolled, spontaneous, accident-prone, and most of all, the *unpredictable*. Because, by this time, it took a matter of seconds to divine what was going on and get there first. We needed to know that not even the producer knew where this baby was headed.

Reality TV is not straight out of genre. Even when manipulated by producers, no one quite knows where things will end up. And this makes it interesting and sometimes even, as James Poniewozik has pointed out, uncomfortable. And that keeps us watching. Reality TV is where TV has always been evolving. It just took us a century or so to get there.

The Anthropological Question: What Else Is Going on Here?

Culture is a thing of surfaces and secrets. The anthropologist is obliged to record the first and penetrate the second.

From *Wired* (4 Oct. 2012). Copyright © 2012 by Conde Nast. Reprinted with permission. All rights reserved.

Once we've figured out what people believe to be true about themselves, we can begin to figure out what's really going on in this culture. In this case, the surface says, "reality TV is a dumbing down." But the secret says "not always." Sometimes, reality TV contributes to a smartening up.

Case in point: My wife and I watch *Project Runway*. She's a graphic designer, so she has a clue about how decisions are being made by students and critics. Meanwhile, I get to test my grasp of this new world by predicting the picks and the pans. But right or wrong, I learn something. And I think I'm getting better (though my wife might demur). Incidentally, trial and error is the way anthropologists build up knowledge of other cultures, venturing opinions the world approves or scorns.

Reality TV makes anthropologists of us all.

To be sure, there are some people so emotionally stunted or disappointed by life they treasure the humiliations inflicted by reality TV, but the rest of us are learning. Consider the show *Shark Tank*, which drew its largest audience ever and premiered recently at the top of its slot. Scores of websites analyze and dissect the sharks' every move, educating budding entrepreneurs everywhere—outside rarefied tech clusters—about the difference between a product and a plan, the difference between an idea and implementation. That's when anthropology doesn't just tell us, but shows us how to act and think and grow. Reality TV forces revelation.

A key feature of anthropology is the long, observational, "ethnographic" interview. Anthropologists believe one of the advantages of this method is that no one can manage appearances, let alone lie, successfully for a long period of time.

So while the Kardashian sisters may wish to create an impression—and the producers edit to reinforce that impression—over many episodes and seasons, the truth will out. Whether they like it or not, eventually we will see into Kardashian souls. That these souls are never as beautiful as the sisters themselves is, well, one of the truths that reality TV makes available to us, and here it performs one of the functions normally dispatched by religious or moral leaders.

Some reality TV remains, of course, appalling. Reality TV has a weakness for beautiful people who are too stupid to appreciate that their limitations are better kept from public view. But the rest of us are, I think, well served. And getting smarter because of it.

> *Reality TV is not straight out of genre. Even when manipulated by producers, no one quite knows where things will end up. And this makes it interesting and sometimes even, as James Poniewozik has pointed out, uncomfortable. And that keeps us watching. Reality TV is where TV has always been evolving. It just took us a century or so to get there.*

Reality Television Sets Detestable, Harmful Example for All Viewers

By Darrington Clark
kstatecollegian.com, September 7, 2012

This world cares way too much about Kim Kardashian.

I don't keep up with the Kardashians, I'm not in love with "Love and Hip Hop," I don't know any housewives and even though I am a bachelor, I don't watch that one either. And I'm not saying that I'm better than anyone who does. A cynic could make fun of me just as much as any reality-TV-show viewer for all the "Pokemon" I've seen. (All of the movies and almost every episode, in case you were wondering.)

What I am saying is that watching reality television can have more lasting effects on viewers than "Pokemon" ever could. When I think of a college student, I think about a person striving to achieve a goal, surrounded by good friends and mentors, trying to make the most out of his or her life, relationships and money.

Reality TV showcases the opposite. In my opinion, prolonged viewing of reality TV can cause some of the problems college students try so desperately to avoid.

While surfing through the news a few weeks back, I couldn't possibly help but learn of Chad Johnson and Evelyn Lozada (a basketball wife) getting a divorce. High profile divorces aren't anything new to me (thanks again, Kim), but the amount of press the ordeal received did shock me.

After a few clicks, I felt that I knew every little thing that went wrong in their marriage. Suddenly, a frightening thought hit me. Is it possible that people may imitate these behaviors seen on television, either consciously or subconsciously?

There's been plenty of research done on people imitating what they see on TV. There are numerous, tragic examples, including in March 2008, when a boy lost his life while imitating an episode of "Naruto" with his friends. But is that example too extreme to count here? Surely nobody will go around pretending to be Evelyn or Kim. Though that may be true, we have to observe the information given to us to find out exactly what the reality TV craze is doing to us as viewers.

I couldn't find a study on people who watch reality TV and then face similar problems in their lives, because I can't imagine a scientist or psychologist bored enough to do that. I have found, though, several columns listing the most common reasons why young relationships are failing. Overarching themes that keep appearing in such lists include extreme overreactions to jealousy, commitment issues, control problems and ineffective communication. What other relationships do we see

From *kstatecollegian.com* (7 September 2012). Copyright © 2012 by CBS Interactive Inc. Reprinted with Permission. All rights reserved.

Overarching themes that keep appearing in such lists include extreme over-reactions to jealousy, commitment issues, control problems and ineffective communication. What other relationships do we see and hear about almost daily that also boast these issues?

and hear about almost daily that also boast these issues?

Of course, it's completely possible that these negative characteristics develop on their own, 100 percent independent of TV. It's hard to believe that they don't come from somewhere, though. Just because you don't look and act just like a reality starlet, doesn't mean you won't face the issues that they do. Nobody teaches how to lie, cheat or steal. You learn by watching someone else do it and seeing it work.

At this stage in our lives, we are not as vulnerable and impressionable as we once were. We are still, however, very observant and prone to refer to what we know. If what you know is what you've seen on TV, which is entirely plausible and not that ridiculous for people of our generation, then you might create a problem in your relationship, your wallet or your grades that didn't need to be there.

I don't think we can ignore reality TV as a possible cause for strife and shenanigans in the lives of people our age. In fact, the longer we continue to show such generous care and support for such unintelligent programming, the more I think we'll see similar scenarios play out among young adults in society.

The desperate-basketball-Orange-County-bachelor-housewives is a fine way to entertain yourself. Just don't entertain it by emulating the negative human behavior it highlights. It always works out in the end for the people with cameras behind them. For those of us who don't, the happy ending may require a little more reality, and a lot less TV.

Darrington Clark is a sophomore in journalism and mass communications.

The Real Effects of Reality TV

By Micki Fahner
USA Today, April 18, 2012

Fist-pumping beachgoers. Singers competing for millions. Survivors outwitting, outlasting and outplaying. Turn on the television and chances are you'll see all of these things. Whether you're watching MTV, OWN, or a main broadcast network, nearly every channel is home to reality television.

Reality TV exploded in the early 2000's, and still remains one of today's most popular genres. In 1999, the most popular shows on TV were *E.R.*, *Friends*, and *Frasier*, according to the Nielsen ratings. During the week of March 12, 2012, Nielsen's top three shows on primetime, broadcast network TV were *American Idol*—Wednesday, *American Idol*—Thursday, and *The Voice*; all reality programs.

While reality television has increased in prevalence for more than a decade, the effect it's having on viewers is still widely unknown.

Dr. Peter Christenson, a professor of rhetoric and media studies at Lewis and Clark College, said that because the medium is still new, comprehensive studies of reality television and its effects are limited.

"I don't think we know that much yet," Christenson said. "It's difficult to draw the cause and effect type of conclusion."

Christenson co-authored a study in 2006 that analyzed reality television programs with medical and health themes. He found that, while the shows did seem to inspire healthier behavior in some viewers, there was a lot of emphasis placed on superficiality—something, which over time, he said, may have an effect on viewers' body image and self-esteem.

Dr. Brad Gorham, chair of the Communications Department at the S.I. Newhouse School of Public Communications at Syracuse University, said studies have shown that television does have an effect.

"All TV shows, not just reality shows, help construct scenarios that demonstrate how some behaviors will be rewarded or punished," Gorham said. "The concern is that frequent viewers of these shows will learn these behaviors, see them as desirable and then model them in the actual real world."

Gorham said one of the reasons there are so many reality shows currently on television is because they are profitable for networks.

"Reality shows are much cheaper to produce than scripted dramas or sitcoms, so they need fewer viewers in order to become profitable for the network," Gorham said. "It all comes down to money, and reality shows are good short-term performers."

From *USA Today* (8 April 2012). Copyright © 2012 by *USA Today*. Reprinted with permission. All rights reserved.

With the focus on profit, some worry networks don't pay enough attention to the negative stereotypes reality programs can illustrate and perpetuate.

Sherri Williams, a PhD candidate and adjunct instructor at Syracuse University, said that casting decisions in reality television seem to be based on stereotypes—a notion she finds to be problematic.

"It seems that reality show directors and producers are not looking to cast whole, complete people. They're casting types, and that leads to stereotyping," Williams said.

Williams also notes that many reality programs demonstrate behavior, but never show the characters facing the results of their actions.

> **"Reality shows are much cheaper to produce than scripted dramas or sitcoms, so they need fewer viewers in order to become profitable for the network," Gorham said. "It all comes down to money, and reality shows are good short-term performers."**

"There aren't any consequences on these shows, and that's problematic."

While Williams said she does take issue with a lot of the reality programs on television, she acknowledges that it's not all bad.

Williams, whose research focuses on media diversity, said shows such as *The Family Crews* and *Being Terry Kennedy* on BET are positive programs, in that they demonstrate counter-stereotypical black male behavior. Williams also said *Mary Mary* on WETV, and *Welcome to Sweetie Pie's* on OWN are positive reality programs that combat negative stereotypes.

Jaime Riccio, a graduate student at the S.I. Newhouse School of Public Communications at Syracuse University, is in the midst of researching reality television and the effect it's having on youth culture in the United States.

In 2010, Riccio said she began conducting a series of focus groups, interviews and surveys on the subject. What she's found is that reality television is leading to more dramatic tendencies in everyday life among young adults.

"Because there is so much of that now that is being broadcast and that people are consuming, it is having an overarching effect on our youth culture," Riccio said. "It's an interesting area to look at, because it's so new, and I think it's something we're going to have to look at even further in the future."

Micki Fahner is a sophomore at Syracuse University. She is double majoring in broadcast and digital journalism and English and textual studies, with a minor in political science. On campus, Micki writes for the Daily Orange, *works at Orange Television Network, and blogs for* Zipped Magazine.

Simply Irresistible:
Reality TV Consumption Patterns

Lisa K. Lundy, Amanda M. Ruth, and Travis D. Park
Communication Quarterly, May 2008

This purpose of this study was to explore college students' consumption patterns in regard to reality television, their rationale for watching reality shows, their perceptions of the situations portrayed on these shows, and the role of social affiliation in the students' consumption of reality television. The results of focus groups indicate that while participants perceive a social stigma associated with watching reality television, they continue to watch because of the perceived escapism and social affiliation provided.

Keywords: Reality Television; Social Affiliation; Uses and Gratifications

Introduction

Extreme sports, celebrity lives, and dating shows—while the phenomenon of reality television (RT) lacks clear definition (Nabi, Biely, Morgan, & Stitt, 2003), it pervades contemporary network and cable programming. Scholars in psychology and media studies, among others, have shown interest in this genre of television and its effects on modern culture. In contrast to scripted television, reality television portrays people in their natural settings. "As a presentation of non-actors in legitimately natural settings and situations working without a script, reality TV stakes its claim with viewers to regard its depictions as unadorned and spontaneous truthful documentation of natural reality" (Bagley, 2001, p. 1).

RT began to emerge as a distinctive genre in the late 1980s (Hill & Quin, 2001). Mead (2005) defines reality programming as "an unscripted program that shows real people, not actors nor athletes, active in a specific environment" (p. 3). The assumed realistic nature of RT programming is commonly associated with the television talk-show genre. Both of these television genres are similar in that they "create audiences by breaking cultural rules, by managed shocks, by shifting our conceptions of what is acceptable, by transforming the bases for cultural judgment, by redefining deviance and appropriate reactions to it, by eroding social barriers, inhibitions and cultural distinctions" (Abt & Seesholtz, 1994, p. 171). The influence of reality television is in its ostensibly accurate depiction of social experiences (Joniak, 2001).

Contradiction surrounds this television phenomenon as "network executives say they'd be happy to be rid of it," yet "still it mutates across the airwaves like a

From *Communication Quarterly* 56.2 (May 2008). Copyright © 2008 by Eastern Communication Association. Reprinted with permission. All rights reserved.

disease, growing nastier in its new forms" (Kronke, 2004, D1). While reality shows like *Survivor* and *The Real World* struggle to maintain ratings ("Reality TV turns to race 'tribes,'" 2006), reality shows still enjoy a solid place in the line-ups of network and cable channels. Reality shows were also a reliable source of programming for the networks during the recent Hollywood writers' strike. For a phenomenon that blossomed a few years ago, reality programming is still widespread in broadcast television (Joniak, 2001; Kronke, 2004). According to Hight (2001), most assumptions about the psychology of RT viewership are derived from textual analyses of reality-based programs, rather than research involving audiences. Thus, Hight calls for investigations of reality-based programming based on the assumption that such programs may implicate a network of social, economic, and political changes in modern society.

Literature Review

Viewers have conceptualized reality programming by the approach taken to various content areas of documenting real-world events (Hall, 2006). Viewers in Hall's (2006) study further clustered reality programs by characteristics such as the show's objective or prize, the format, the level of manipulation or intervention by the producers, and the message. Hall suggests this clustering of shows reflects distinct themes, ideological messages, and content areas. According to Pecora (2002),

> Reality TV is, for me, the expression of a powerful, and increasingly unbridled, tendency within democratic society, one also embedded in academic institutions, to reveal the norms and limits of individual responsibility and group identity, however exaggerated (and commercialized) the settings that reveal such knowledge may be. In effect, television is now doing the kind of social psychological research our universities no longer permit. (p. 356)

Nabi et al. (2003) offer a definition of reality-based television programming, which excludes news programs, talk and interview shows, and nonfiction narrative programs. They refer to several characteristics of RT:

1. characters are real people (not actors),
2. programs are not filmed on a set, but in natural living or working environments,
3. programs are not scripted,
4. events are unplanned, but evolve from narrative contexts, and
5. the primary purpose is viewer entertainment.

In uncovering these characteristics, Nabi et al., conducted a study of randomly selected city residents to determine their construction of the RT genre. They found that respondents perceived some reality programs as more realistic than others. In Hall's (2006) study of viewers' perceptions of reality programs, she also found inconsistencies in participants' conceptualization of reality programs. Some participants highlighted competition as a key element of reality programs, while others emphasized unpredictability or a focus on negative circumstances or behaviors.

Following the uses and gratifications perspective that Nabi et al. (2003) offer, the present study attempts to explore the choice of RT and the gratifications sought from RT viewing. In explaining media choice and the types of gratifications that result from that choice, Lazarsfeld and Stanton (1944) developed the uses and gratifications theory. At the core of extensive communication research, uses and gratifications theory has been the focus of research on understanding audience needs and motives for using mass media. Uses and gratifications theory also aids in understanding audience consumption patterns of specific mass media channels. Considered a sub-tradition of media effects research (McQuail, 1994), Wimmer and Dominick (1994) suggest that uses and gratifications originated with the interest in audiences and why they engaged in certain forms of media behavior. Early studies of uses and gratifications include the contexts of quiz programs and the reasons people listened to soap operas (Herzog, 1942), the interest in music on radio (Suchman, 1942), the development of children's interest in comics (Wolfe & Fiske, 1949), and the functions of newspaper reading (Berelson, 1949).

Although uses and gratifications has been used in varying communication contexts, Rubin (1986) confers that uses and gratifications research is best applied when exploring specific links among attitudes, motives, behaviors, and communication effects. In a summary of Katz and Blumler's contribution to this theory, Lin (1996) suggests that

> the strength of this theory is its ability to allow researchers to study mediated communication situations via a single or multiple sets of psychological needs, psychological motives, communication channels, communications content, and psychological gratifications within a particular or cross-cultural context. (p. 574)

Katz et al. (1974) describe uses and gratifications as having three main objectives: to explain how people use media to gratify their needs, to understand motives for media behaviors, and to identify functions or consequences that follow from needs, motives, and behavior. As a major communication theory, uses and gratifications is based on five basic assumptions (Katz et al., 1974; Palmgreen, 1984; Palmgreen, Wenner, & Rosengren, 1985; Rosengren, 1974; Rubin, 1986):

1. Behavior is purposive, goal-directed, and motivated.

2. People select and use media to satisfy biological, psychological, and social needs.

3. Individuals are influenced by various social and psychological factors when selecting media.

4. Media consumers are aware of their needs and whether they are being satisfied by a given media option.

5. Different media compete for attention, selection, and use.

According to Reiss and Wiltz (2004), individuals act to satisfy one of 16 basic motives: power, curiosity, independence, status, social conflict, vengeance, honor, idealism, physical exercise, romance, family, order, eating, acceptance, tranquility, and saving. Reiss and Wiltz studied the motives for watching reality TV under the premise that these motives may be achieved vicariously through television characters. The romance motive may be achieved through watching a romantic movie. Reiss and Wiltz found status to be the most significant motive for watching reality TV. The authors infer that viewers may perceive themselves as better than the characters portrayed or feel that the portrayal of ordinary people in reality TV elevates their own status. Reiss and Wiltz also found vengeance to be a significant motive for reality TV viewers as compared to nonviewers. Vengeance is closely associated with competition (Reiss, 2000). The authors also found viewing reality TV to be negatively associated with the motive of honor or morality.

In a quantitative study in 2002, Wei and Tootle found two unique gratification dimensions for reality TV viewing: life-like format and vicarious participation. This study seeks to learn from listening and watching participants discuss their viewing of reality TV. The study adds a qualitative dimension to Wei and Tootle's findings in understanding the uses and gratifications for reality TV viewing. The purpose of this qualitative study was to explore college students' consumption of RT. This study was guided by the following research questions:

> RQ1: What are the consumption patterns of college students in regard to reality television?

> RQ2: What rationale do college students provide for watching reality television?

> RQ3: How do college students perceive the situations portrayed in reality television?

> RQ4: What role does social affiliation play in the consumption of reality television for college students?

Method

Due to the limited literature regarding consumption of RT, a qualitative research design was most appropriate for exploring the research questions posed at the outset of this study. Focus groups were used as the method of data collection for this exploratory, qualitative study, allowing for in-depth exploration into the phenomenon. Focus groups allow for rich and enlightening exchanges between participants, where ideas can build upon one another. Through the interactions of RT viewers, the researchers sought to explore and understand consumption patterns for young adults of RT.

Four focus groups were conducted, with each group ranging between six and 12 undergraduate participants. Focus group participants were recruited from a large, undergraduate, core-curriculum course offered at a southern university. College students were selected because they represent one of the most targeted viewing audiences of RT programming (Carter, 2000).

Focus groups were conducted over a four-month time period from March 2004 through July 2004. Four focus groups were chosen based on Morgan's (1997) suggestion that three to five focus groups suffice for a research project because more groups seldom provide meaningful new insights. The size of each focus group, six to twelve students, was chosen based on the characteristics of the population under study. It was the assumption of the researchers that a smaller focus group would be more manageable in terms of response and the feeling of confidentiality for the college student participants. The focus groups were conducted in a classroom environment due to its convenience and familiarity for participants.

Prior to the start of the focus group, participants were asked to complete a short survey including several demographic questions as well as basic questions about their television viewing behaviors. Once the informed consent process and a short explanation of the study's procedures and purpose were reviewed, the focus group discussion began with the participants introducing themselves by sharing their name, major, hometown, and favorite television show. A question guide was then used to facilitate participants' responses to questions regarding their opinions, perceptions, and behaviors toward RT programming. A moderator opened and guided the group discussion.

The focus groups were recorded using both audio and videotape, which complimented the observations and field notes recorded by the research team during the focus group discussions. The audio- and videotapes were transcribed; transcripts were compared with field notes, and analyzed using the inductive data analysis method outlined by Hatch (2002). Following analytic methods similar to other important inductive models (e.g., Glaser & Strauss, 1967; Miles & Huberman, 1994; Spradley, 1979), the model of analysis used in this study searches for "patterns of meaning in data so that general statements about phenomena under investigation can be made" (Hatch, 2002, p. 161).

The inductive analysis methods utilized followed the subsequent steps (Hatch, 2002):

1. read data and identify frames of analysis,
2. create domains based on semantic relationships discovered within frames of analysis,
3. identify salient domains and assign them a code,
4. refine salient domains and keep record of emerging relationships,
5. decide if domains are supported by data,
6. complete analysis within domains,
7. search for themes across domains,
8. outline relationships within and among domains, and
9. select data excerpts to support the relationships.

The three researchers analyzed the data following the inductive analysis procedures outlined above. Following the analysis, the research team discussed emerging
themes and supporting elements and identified the dominant themes that characterized the data.

Results

The purpose of this qualitative study was to explore college students' consumption
of RT. From the four focus groups conducted, data was gathered from 20 females
and 14 males, totaling 34 participants. Results from a preliminary participant survey indicated that participants watch anywhere from 3 to 30 hours of television
per week, with the average being 11.5 hours. The majority of participants, 76.4%
(n=26), indicated that they watch an RT program on a regular basis (at least two to
three times a week).

Through the preliminary participant survey administered to the students preceding the focus group discussion, students provided their responses to basic open-
ended questions regarding RT. First, participants were asked to provide their own
definition of RT and through a comparative analysis of the provided definitions, participants' confusion over the nature of RT emerged. Participants provided diverse
definitions of RT. Although varying, most definitions included characteristics like
"unscripted," "everyday people," "non-actors," "portraying some aspect of real life,"
"real people in front of cameras," and "real-life yet edited situations."

RQ1: What Are the Consumption Patterns of College Students in Regard to Reality
Television?

"Oh no ...I don't really watch reality television."

The first theme that emerged from the data was the underestimation of RT viewing. Initially, participants denied watching much RT; in fact, RT was rarely mentioned when participants were asked to describe the type of television shows that
they typically watched. Instead, shows that were typically mentioned included adult
and teenage drama, sports broadcasting, comedy sitcoms, and news shows. However, over the course of the focus group discussions, it was evident that participants
watched (or were at least familiar with) more RT shows than first indicated. Despite
the fact that participants from each focus group listed only half a dozen reality
shows at the beginning of the focus groups, at least 25 different RT shows were discussed throughout the focus groups as shows that were watched on a regular basis.
One participant realized this phenomenon in saying, "I didn't think I watched this
much or knew this much about reality television but apparently I was wrong." The
RT shows that were most commonly discussed included *The Bachelor*, *The Bachelorette*, *American Idol*, *The Real World*, *Trading Spaces*, *The Swan*, *Survivor*, *Joe
Millionaire*, *Average Joe*, *Extreme Makeover*, *The Simple Life*, and *American Chopper*. There were several occasions in which a specific RT show was not mentioned
as being watched; however, when it was referred to in conversation, the majority of
the participants were familiar enough with the show to partake in the discussion.

RQ2: What Rationale Do College Students Provide for Watching Reality Television?

"It's like a great escape." Escapism and Living Vicariously through Others.

Escapism emerged from the data citing RT as an escape from reality for participants. Participants felt that RT offered the viewer a "glimpse" into another world,
which for a moment could take the viewer away from their own reality. One participant suggested,

> I think because it is an escape from the reality of like the war and a lot of economic prob-
> lems and like political problems. I mean you have the option of watching reality television,
> which although it can be extreme, it is amusing, as opposed to watching the news about
> Martha Stewart, Michael Jackson, Kobe Bryant or even the war. Basically something that
> is depressing as opposed to something, while ridiculous, is entertaining and an escape
> from some of the negative reality that people deal with day in and day out.

This theme of escapism also emerged in the discussion of viewers living vicariously through reality shows. One participant mentioned, "You can see yourself in
the show," while another said, "I mean you put yourself in their situation and you're
watching and you think, 'Oh what would I do? Would I eat that? Would I eat whatever they are eating or do whatever they are doing?'" Eloquently stated, one participant divulged what they believed to be the secret of RT by saying, "I don't think it
is real life but that is the point. Real life is boring and you watch reality shows to
live vicariously through others." As one participant said, "reality television is reality
television because as a viewer you can see yourself in that situation or you can say
to yourself, if I was on that show this is what I would do. It is reality 'cause you can
see yourself in it."

Clearly, for most participants, RT provided an escape from reality, "a break from
the depressing stuff." It seemed as though in this situation most participants pro-
jected their lives onto the characters of the shows, trying to determine what better
decisions could have been made and what they would have done differently.

"It's like a train wreck—I just can't turn away."

For most participants, disparity existed between perceptions of RT and consumption of RT. One participant best described this phenomenon by saying,
"[I]t is like watching a train wreck—horrible, but [you] can't turn away." While Nabi
et al. (2003) hesitated to characterize viewers as voyeuristic, they stopped short of
generalizing reality viewers as innocent, which supports this finding. Although listing many reasons for watching RT, participants most commonly shared that they
watched because they were bored, it was humorous and entertaining, they liked to
see other people fail, or the shock factor. Further reasons participants provided were
that they watched RT because "it doesn't require full attention," or "it is something
that you do not have to watch every week to understand what is going on."

Candid responses from participants conveyed the voyeuristic quality of RT. For
example, one participant admitted, "It is just plain funny. It's pure entertainment and
it may not be real but it is funny." Several participants reflected on their enjoyment

Eloquently stated, one participant divulged what they believed to be the secret of RT by saying, "I don't think it is real life but that is the point. Real life is boring and you watch reality shows to live vicariously through others."

in watching RT characters exposed to uncomfortable situations outside their normal realm of experience. One participant commented, "If the show has like 20 ridiculously hot girls who are all used to being pampered and are put outside in some extraordinary situation where they have to like shovel manure or something like that, it really amuses me." Aside from the pure entertainment factor of reality television, participants also mentioned that they, or their friends, had become addicted to following the characters and situations in RT. One participant's response was, "I heard so much about it that I had to see what it was about. Now I am hooked." While another participant said, "It makes you want to turn it on week after week. I don't know, maybe because you want to see who wins or who gets picked. It just has an addictive quality." Some participants even remarked that RT feels like a "cliffhanger," making it nearly impossible to prematurely abandon the show.

RQ3: How Do College Students Perceive the Situations Portrayed in Reality Television?

"It's definitely the good, bad, and the ugly of TV." Good vs. Bad Reality TV

When discussing opinions toward RT, participants described certain elements of RT shows. From these descriptions, "good" RT materialized as being beneficial because they give the viewer useful ideas or advice; give people a second chance; are entertaining or funny; and can be applied to the viewer's actual life. Good reality shows were commonly associated with home or personal appearance improvement, like The Learning Channel's (TLC) *Trading Spaces* and *Baby Story*, HGTV's *House Hunters* and *Landscape Smart*, and ABC's *Extreme Makeover Home Edition*. From the participants' perspective, these shows provide a "happy" and "uplifting" perspective of reality. As one participant mentioned, these shows "make you feel good and they attempt to educate the viewers about something, often a skill." Other aspects of "good" RT included shows that improve participants' appearances or self-esteem, that are funny and entertaining without a personal expense to participants, and that give the viewer a positive glimpse into the lives of others. Supporting the difference in good versus bad RT programs, one participant shared,

I feel like the TLC shows or Extreme Makeover do not choose people who are supermodels .... these are people that for whatever reason want to boost their self-esteem or their lives as opposed to the shows that are all about the money or 30 seconds of fame.

Yet another participant argued that some RT programs are "okay" while others are not:

> See, I think the Real World is okay because they have a goal and it is to live together. The cut-throat stuff like where people are constantly doing stuff to screw other people, I think those are what aren't good. Like I think the Real World is fine and Road Rules and stuff like the Amazing Race . . . that's fine.

Conversely, "bad" RT was commonly linked to concepts of immorality. Bad RT, also referred to as "junk TV" by participants, though indicated as entertaining at times, included television shows that were based on deception, ridicule, contempt, and physical or emotional harm. According to the participants, RT has "gone too far" with regard to the conceptual foundation of some of the shows. One participant corroborated this stance toward RT by saying that "too much humiliation exists for participants." Focus group members characterized "bad" RT as: "unrealistic," "just plain mean," "misrepresenting reality," "obvious attempts to spur controversy," "ridiculous situations," "manipulated and exaggerated," and "driven by the shock value." Shows cited as "bad" RT typically included *Married by America, I Married a Millionaire, Married a Midget, Average Joe, My Big Fat Obnoxious Fiancé*, and several other dating shows. One participant suggested that there are certain RT programs that are bad due to the immoral concept of the show:

> My biggest moral issues come with shows like *Joe Millionaire*, like I consider almost prostitution . . . I just think these girls are like you know belittling and just making themselves look like garbage, which is obviously bad.

One participant even described "bad" RT by saying, "At first it was kind of a cool concept but now it is beyond the point of entertaining. It has really gone downhill." Another participant echoed this opinion by citing an actual show that goes too far, "this trading moms (*Wife Swap*) thing is almost at the edge of not right. 'Cause now you are messing with kids that are young . . ." Yet another participant shared that it is the physical harm that encouraged them to discontinue their consumption of some "bad" RT programs. "I used to watch a lot of the dating shows, I used to watch *Blind Date Hall of Shame* and then I watch *Cheaters* for a while and then the guy got stabbed and I thought 'this is out of control.' "

This classification between "good" and "bad" RT appeared ambiguous because participants disagreed on some of the "good" and "bad" characterizing traits. For example, the RT show *The Swan* appeared to be a show that caused disparate opinions from participants. Demonstrating this disagreement, one participant noted, "I did not watch *The Swan* because I thought it was despicable that people have to do this, like get plastic surgery and change who they are to be accepted and for people to like them." However, a different participant shared the following:

> [T]hey do perform plastic surgery and judge some on their looks but it [*The Swan*] was also on how far they came emotionally and physically and how they progressed themselves. It helped these women with what they have always wanted and dreamed of.

Other shows that seemed to provoke disagreement among participants included *Survivor, Outback Jack, American Chopper*, and various MTV RT programs like *The Ashley Simpson Show, Newlyweds*, and *Real World*. Nonetheless, it was noticeable that each participant had his/her own established notions of good versus bad RT and that each made their viewing decisions based on these notions.

"It's morally corrupt." Concerns over Portrayal of Ideals

The deception and lack of morals was a common concern expressed by participants. Even though one participant indicated that RT is "not going to affect my morals," the data collected revealed that participants believed there were moral implications of RT when judging its collective impact on society. Many participants characterized RT programming as "morally corrupt." One participant said, "I think a lot of television has gone downhill, like the morals of it. There is just not much left of it anymore."

Additionally, most participants were concerned at the concept behind many RT shows, citing them as "wrong" and "corrupt." Describing this moral corruption in association with money, one participant said,

> It all happens when you put money at the end of the road. People lose track of what is important and like their morals go out the window and that is when I have a problem with the reality issue; when people start doing things they normally wouldn't do in order to win.

Confirming the negative impact money has on the morals of reality show participants, a participant echoed, "I think reality television teaches lying and deceit ...instead of wishing goodwill and friendly competition, everybody lies and deceives just to get rid of somebody and win the money, which is wrong." Yet another participant noted that RT communicates to younger audiences that "immoral and unethical actions are OK," and that "dating 20 different guys and having sex with several of them is OK; that there are no consequences with actions like this."

As a result of the "moral corruption" demonstrated through RT programming, many participants expressed concerned about the impact the popularity of this television genre will eventually have on society. Representing the majority view, one participant conferred, "I really believe what goes in comes out, and if you are constantly watching trash you are going to get trash out . . ." While most participants agreed that they believed RT can have a negative impact on viewers' behaviors, another interesting finding from one of the focus groups was that RT was more of a "reflection of society than an influence on society," implying that maybe RT was only exemplifying our "morally corrupt" world.

"The real truth and nothing but the truth, I don't think so."

Throughout the focus group discussions, participants frequently referred to the "truth" of RT. One of the largest discrepancies in participant opinions was the realism of specific RT shows. Participants shared their strong opinions toward the realistic nature of RT by referring to it as "drawing the line," which insinuated distorting the premise of RT. Basically, most of the participants indicated that many of the shows do not reflect reality anymore. Specific to the reality dating shows, one participant observed that it is "not realistic to find love with 50 people around you."

Participants also felt that many of the shows have gone "overboard" in order to attract viewers. One participant communicated, "[A]t first it was kind of cool but now it is beyond the point of entertaining, it is sickening what they will call reality television just to increase ratings." Resonating with another participant, one respondent noted, "Because the networks are making so much money on this genre, they are willing to go as far as they can." Overall, participants believed that RT is set up to make people "believe that these things on the reality shows can actually happen." Manifest in the data was the opinion that the shows and characters become exaggerated over time, to the point that "characters are reacting to unreal situations."

Coupled with this exaggeration or "drawing the line" quality of RT, the discussions also focused on the accurate portrayal of reality due to the excessive amount of editing that was believed to occur in the development of the shows. Respondents in Nabi et al.'s (2003) study voiced similar frustrations. Several participants mentioned watching television programs that provided behind-the-scenes views of the RT show production. Participants indicated that these behind-the-scenes shows provided proof of the large amount of editing that takes place during the final production phases for an RT show. A common belief was that the program's producers "don't show everything," but rather only what they want the audience to see. In addition to the editing process, many participants believed RT is "staged," "contrived," "exaggerated," and "fake." One participant summarized the realism debate in saying,

> I think it has always been staged because I mean, who do you know that would get up in
> front of a TV and really act as if they were not in front of a camera, comfortable. I think
> it has always been fake to a point, but we are now beginning to notice it more 'cause
> there are so many television stations and so many reality shows out there to watch.

As such, it can be assumed that, for these focus group participants, RT does not represent reality. Overall, RT was perceived as a "misrepresentation of reality," which participants suspected was becoming more scripted and contrived in an effort to boost ratings and derive profit for the producers and networks.

RQ4: What Role Does Social Affiliation Play in the Consumption of Reality Television for College Students?

"Social"ity TV: –Social Affiliation

The social connection that RT provides for participants is indicated in several different ways, including the way in which participants watch RT shows, the conversations that result from RT viewing, and the involvement that participants experience while watching RT.

Participants rarely watched RT alone. Participants revealed that they watch RT programming in groups, with roommates, friends, and family. It is important to note that many of the participants called watching RT "our time," alluding to the scheduled time every week that siblings or groups of friends spend together. Most of the participants indicated this social component as a rationale for watching RT. One participant exemplified this theme saying, "The reason I like it [reality television] is for the social value." Another participant described their viewing behavior saying, "When there are like more people, you get more excited. You just feed off the tension and the anticipation together." Several participants even referred to watching the same reality show every week with friends as a "routine"; conveyed by one participant, "I have friends that will get together to watch Real World like every week." This routine was echoed by another participant:

> I mainly watch with my roommates, I mean it is just a time when we all get together and kind of watch a show that is funny to watch because people can make fools of the characters on the show. And then we can kind of relate to it and discuss it from there.

In Hall's (2006) study, participants referred to groups watching reality shows to guess the outcome together, noting the unpredictability of reality programs as an attractive attribute. The social connections provided by RT also include the conversations that RT motivates between viewers. One participant mentioned the social value of RT in that it is not age-specific, allowing the topic of RT to establish common ground between any two people in a conversation. For example, one participant described their behavior by saying,

> When I meet people I am like, "Hey, do you watch reality TV?" 'cause pretty much everyone has at least one show that they can relate to or they know something about. It is always a good common ground when you are talking to a person for the first or second time.

Another participant mentioned watching RT in order to feel familiar with what others were talking about and to be able to participate in the conversation. The feeling of being left out in an RT conversation was mentioned by one participant: "Some of my friends would sit and talk to each other about certain reality characters and I would just sit there like I have no idea what was going on, like they talk about these people like they know them or something." Most participants referred to these conversations about RT as "shallow," "just in passing, or "nothing in-depth"; however, all participants indicated at least having one discussion about "a memorable episode," the "stupidity of the characters," or "what was going to happen next week" on the show.

While most participants admitted to discussing RT on a regular basis, they also insinuated an element of shame associated with such conversations. One participant said,

> I feel really stupid, I mean I am in college I should be smarter than that. I mean, I am 20 and I know I have a lot to learn but I usually like talking about something a little more intellectual than something like that.

In agreement, another participant said, "It makes me feel kind of silly, to actually be discussing reality television."

Respondents also referred to their involvement and interaction with the characters of reality shows and the show themselves. Several participants indicated that being able to make decisions affecting the show's outcome, like voting, gives the viewer a connection, a feeling of belonging and importance to the show. Additionally, participants indicated that the "real" context of some reality shows makes it possible for them to participate and get involved with the characters and situations on the show. For example, one participant conferred,

> I don't personally have time to vote. Although I did talk to my cousin and they were so hooked on American Idol that they voted every night. She was talking about how she got on the land phone, her Mom got on the cell phone, and her brother got on another cell phone and they all called like three or four times . . . they were that into it.

Another participant summarized this sub-theme by saying,

> I voted on Nashville Star once. So yeah, I think the interactivity of [reality television] gives people a connection to the show, they are more involved because they have some kind of say with its outcome.

Discussion

College students' consumption of RT appears to be a complex phenomenon that offers many opportunities for further study. In this exploratory study, focus-group participants progressed from initial denial, or underestimation, of RT consumption to the shocking realization of the actual amount of RT they consume. While reticent to characterize themselves as RT viewers, participants appeared to be watching a great deal of RT. Throughout the focus groups, the modesty over RT consumption appeared to be caused by the social stigma that surrounds RT. For example, participants seemed hesitant, as well as embarrassed, when they revealed the amount of RT that they consumed; their reactions of guilt coupled with their responses insinuated that it is bad to enjoy watching RT.

The researchers attribute one of three possible explanations for the underestimation of RT viewing. First, it is plausible that the participants did not realize that the shows they watch are considered RT; for example, there was an in-depth discussion in two of the focus groups as to whether certain shows were "reality television shows." In fact, Mead (2005) suggests that RT is different from other genres of television due to the numerous subgenres that exist, making the genre diverse and sometimes difficult to define and/or classify. Second, it is plausible that participants were embarrassed or hesitant in disclosing the actual amount of RT that they watch in the beginning of the focus group because of the social stigma associated with RT. This explanation would be consistent with the findings from research investigating the soap opera genre of television. Blumenthal's (1997) focus on the "social devaluation" of soap opera viewership explains this notion of female viewers being embarrassed or apologetic about the pleasure they find in watching soap operas; moreover, Whetmore and Kielwasser (1983) found that these feelings were commonly caused by the social stigma of soap opera programming being "silly" and "inconsequential." Similarly, Lemish (1985) investigated college students and their consumption of soap opera programming and found that their "awareness of publicly held opinions about soap operas" is what caused their feelings of embarrassment and, thus, their caution in revealing their viewing habits. Finally, another possible explanation is students simply forgot or had a hard time recalling all the RT shows that they watched throughout the year, implying that they did not omit the information on purpose. Regardless of reasoning, the underestimation of time spent watching RT programming is not unique to the RT genre in that numerous studies suggest that individuals tend to underestimate the amount of television they consume (Seiter, 1999).

Regarding their rationale for watching RT, participants referred to the "great escape" provided by RT. They felt that RT offered an opportunity to sample other lifestyles and realities than their own. Participants discussed living vicariously through the characters in reality programs. For these college students, RT seemed to offer an opportunity for them to contemplate and discuss how they would respond or behave in the situations portrayed in the programs. Many of the situations characters face in reality programs—dating, family issues, racial tension, and moral decisions—are particularly relevant for college students. Therefore, it would be valuable to investigate the reality television phenomenon through the lens of social learning theory to determine how the decisions or actions of RT characters are impacting the decisions or actions of viewers.

Another rationale given by participants for watching RT is their perception of the discrete nature of each episode. Participants felt they could watch a given episode at their convenience and out-of-sequence. They also felt watching RT did not require their full attention, unlike scripted television dramas where they fall behind if they miss an episode; therefore, the RT genre seems to fit well with the changing schedules and active lifestyles of college students. The convenience of reality television programming appeared to be a major gratification of reality television consumption.

Focus-group participants articulated two perceived types of RT, "good" and "bad" RT. They characterized "good" RT as giving viewers useful ideas or advice, giving characters a second chance, and providing entertainment or humor. They also included in "good" RT shows that improve participant's appearances or self-esteem, shows that are funny and entertaining without a personal expense to participants, and shows that give the viewer a positive glimpse into the lives of others. In contrast, participants characterized "bad" RT as shows based on deception, ridicule, contempt, and physical or emotional harm. While participants disagreed on some of the "good" and "bad" characterizing traits, it was clear that each participant had his/her own established notions of "good" versus "bad" RT, and that these perceptions influenced their viewing decisions. Participants also expressed concern regarding morality in RT. They expressed a shared sentiment that RT's collective moral impact on society was negative. Interestingly, these findings of "good" and "bad" television are consistent with the findings of Ang (1985) in studying the pleasure derived from watching the soap opera, *Dallas*. Ang found that many viewers classified the soap opera program as "bad television" in regard to quality but still found an attraction, while other viewers gave numerous reasons for why the show was "good" television and thus deserved their attention.

The college students in this study do not watch RT alone. Social affiliation appears to play a significant role in RT viewing for the participants in this study.

Participants watch RT with their roommates, friends, and family members. Television is sometimes criticized for breaking down social connections where people watch television rather than spend time developing interpersonal relationships (McKenna & Bargh, 2000). Reality television, for the college students in this study, seemed to have the opposite influence. RT appeared to bring students together, not only for watching the shows, but in conversations resulting from RT viewing. In fact, participants even acknowledged watching RT shows they do not particularly enjoy because of the social affiliation of RT viewership. They do not want to be "left out" of conversations about RT, which coincides with the findings of Babrow (1987) that suggest one of the many motives for college students in watching soap opera programming is the social interaction it provides: interaction in the form of watching the programs together but also the interaction of conversing about the program at a later time.

Participants also discussed the realism of RT. Overall, they did not perceive RT as real, feeling that RT shows go overboard in order to maintain ratings. They were also skeptical of the editing process in RT. However, participants did seem to associate their feelings about the realism of RT to their consumption patterns. Although this study was guided by the theoretical framework of uses and gratifications, to further investigate the argument over RT's realism, it may be valuable to examine RT programming through the theoretical perspective of Hall's reception theory. Hall (1980) posits that in the encoding and decoding process of media discourse, the meaning of the text is located between the producer and the reader, or in this case the viewer. According to this theory, the producer (encoder) frames the text by giving it a certain meaning based on their personal background and cultural perspective, while the viewer (decoder) will adapt the textual meaning by decoding a different version of the text based on their personal background, various social situations, and frames of reference (McQuail, 1994). This perspective on audience theory and research is especially useful in determining how individual circumstances like gender, age, ethnicity, and cultural affiliations affect the way a reader or viewer receives and interprets text. Clearly, in this case, defining characteristics of the college-aged population could have some affect on the way they receive and interpret the meaning, specifically the realism, of RT programming. For example, Brasch (2006) suggested that unique to young adults is the appeal of content involving relationship issues and their ability to identify with the no-name stars that appeared on the programs. In addition, reasons cited for the appeal to young adults have been the high volume of interactivity that attracts a generation absorbed in a multimedia world and the structure of RT programming that compliments the shortened attention span and lack of patience of the young adult audience (Hiltbrand, 2004). Finally, the view that the reception and interpretation of RT programming in this study is unique to young adults is supported by the original proposal of Katz, Blumler, and Gurevitch (1974) that media uses and gratifications differ across age, gender, and lifestyle.

Throughout the focus groups, evidence of a possible third-person effect was observed in participant responses. For example, in describing the effect RT may have on behaviors as well as in explaining the popularity of RT, participants commonly exemplified the "I don't watch but I know someone who does" syndrome. This also provides an interesting area for future inquiry.

Overall, the findings from this study indicate that RT is and will continue to be a significant part of the young adult television appetite. Although students are generally confused about what constitutes RT programming, they are absolute in their opinions and perceptions toward this growing genre of television. Due to the amount of RT consumption by these viewers, there are implications for advertising and product placement, sitcoms and traditional television programming, and extreme RT consumption on morals and behaviors, especially among younger viewers. Through the uses and gratifications perspective, RT programming provides a unique genre of television to study. Not only does RT have the attention of television networks and viewers alike, but as Oullette and Murray (2004) suggest, it provides the gratifications that viewers seek. "What ties together all the various formats of the reality TV genre is their professed abilities to more fully provide viewers an unmediated, voyeuristic, yet often playful look into what might be called the 'entertaining real'" (p. 4).

Although the findings of this study are similar to other studies that investigate the gratifications sought from young adults through RT programming (Brasch, 2006; Frisby, 2004; Hiltbrand, 2004; Mead, 2005), these studies can be used as a foundation for future research on college students and RT. Future research should investigate its influence on decision making, perceptions of reality, reactions toward specific programs and program content, exploration of good versus bad RT and association with viewing behaviors, exploration of the third person effect in RT viewers, and comparison of perceptions toward RT of high vs. low-consumption viewers. Because RT can be considered a popular culture phenomenon, future research in this area can significantly contribute to the growing and diverse field of cultural studies by uncovering how different audiences, in this case young adults, receive, interpret, and consume cultural texts.

References

Abt, V., & Seesholtz, M. (1994). The shameless world of Phil, Sally, and Oprah: Television talk shows and the deconstructing of society. *Journal of Popular Culture*, 28(1), 171–191.

Ang, I. (1985). *Watching Dallas: Soap opera and the melodramatic imagination*. London: Methuen & Co. Ltd.

Babrow, A. S. (1987). Student motives for watching soap operas. *Journal of Broadcasting & Electronic Media*, 31(3), 309–321.

Bagley, G. (2001). A mixed bag: Negotiating claims in MTV's the Real World. *Journal of Film and Video*, 53(2/3), 61–77.

Berelson, B. (1949). What "missing the newspaper" means. In P. F. Lazarfeld & F. N. Stanton (Eds.), *Communications research*, 1948–1949 (pp. 111–128). New York: Harper & Brothers.

Blumenthal, D. (1997). *Women and soap opera: A cultural feminist perspective*. Westport, Conn.: Praeger Publishers.

Brasch, W. M. (2006). *Sex and the single beer can: Probing the media and American culture* (2nd ed.). Spokane, Wash.: Marquette Books.

Carter, B. (2000). CBS is unexpected winner in ratings contest. *The New York Times*. Retrieved August 25, 2000, from http://nytimes.com/library/arts/082400survivor. html

Frisby, C. M. (2004, August). *America's top model meets the bachelor on an un-real world: Examining viewer fascination with reality TV*. Paper presented at the Association for Education in Journalism and Mass Communication Convention, Toronto, Canada.

Glaser, B., & Strauss, A. (1967). *The discovery of grounded theory: Strategies for qualitative research*. New York: Aldine.

Hall, A. (2006). Viewers' perceptions of reality programs. *Communication Quarterly*, 54(2), 191–211.

Hall, S. (1980). Encoding/decoding. In S. Hall, D. Hobson, A. Lowe, & P. Willis (Eds.) *Culture, media, language: Working papers in cultural studies, 1972–1979* (pp. 128–138). London: Hutchinson, in association with the Center for Contemporary Cultural Studies, University of Birmingham, 1980.

Hatch, A. (2002). *Doing qualitative research in education settings*. Albany, NY: Albany State University of New York Press.

Herzog, H. (1942). Professor quiz: A gratification study. In P. F. Lazarsfeld & F. N. Stanton (Eds.), *Radio research*, 1941 (pp. 64–93). New York: Duell, Sloan, and Pearce.

Hight, C. (2001). Debating reality-TV. *Continuum: Journal of Media and Cultural Studies*, 15(3), 299–395.

Hill, L., & Quin, R. (2001). Live from the ministry of truth: How real are reality soaps? *Australian Screen Education*, 30, 50–55.

Hiltbrand, D. (2004). Teenagers identify with the issues presented in reality TV shows. In K. F. Balkin (Ed.), *Reality TV*. Farmington Hills, Mich.: Greenhaven Press.

Joniak, L. (2001). *Understanding reality television: A triangulated analysis of the development, production techniques, characteristics and ontology of reality television programming*. Unpublished dissertation, University of Florida.

Katz, E., Blumler, J., & Gurevitch, M. (1974). Utilization of mass communication by the individual. In J. G. Blumler & E. Katz (Eds.), *The uses of mass communications: Current perspectives on gratifications research*. Beverly Hills, Calif.: Sage.

Kronke, D. (2004). A new batch of reality. *The Gainesville Sun*, 1D.

Lemish, D. (1985). Soap opera viewing in college: A naturalistic inquiry. *Journal of Broadcasting & Electronic Media*, 29(3), 275–293.

Lin, C. A. (1996). Looking back: The contribution of Blumler and Katz's *Uses of Mass Communication* to communication research. *Journal of Broadcasting & Electronic Media*, 40(4), 574–581.

McKenna, K., & Bargh, J. (2000). Plan 9 from Cyberspace: The implications of the Internet for personality and social psychology. *Personality and Social Psychology Review*, 4(1), 57–75.

McQuail, D. (1994). *Mass communication theory: An introduction* (3rd ed.). London: Sage.

Mead, J. (2005, August). *Fascination of reality television with the college student audience: The uses and gratifications perspective on the program genre*. Paper presented at the Association for Education in Journalism and Mass Communication Conference, San Antonio.

Miles, M. B., & Huberman, A. M. (1994). *Qualitative data analysis*. Thousand Oaks, Calif.: Sage.

Morgan, D. L. (1997). *Focus groups as qualitative research* (2nd ed.). Thousand Oaks, Calif.: Sage.

Nabi, R. L., Biely, E. N., Morgan, S. J., & Stitt, C. R. (2003). Reality-based television programming and the psychology of its appeal. *Media Psychology, 5*(4), 303–330.

Palmgreen, P. (1984). Uses and gratifications: A theoretical perspective. *Communication Yearbook*, 8, 20–55.

Palmgreen, P. C., Wenner, L. A., & Rosengren, K. E. (1985). Uses and gratifications research: The past ten years. In K. E. Rosengren, L. A. Wenner, & P. C. Palmgreen (Eds.), *Uses and gratifications research: Current perspectives* (pp. 11–37). Beverly Hills, Calif.: Sage.

Pecora, V. P. (2002). The culture of surveillance. *Qualitative Sociology, 25*(3), 345–358.

Reality TV turns to race 'tribes' to survive ratings war. New US Survivor show to pick teams on racial lines: Critics alarmed decision could deepen divide. (2006, August 25). *The Guardian*.

Reiss, S. (2000). *Who am I? The 16 basic desires that motivate our actions and define our personalities*. New York: Tarcher/Putnam.

Reiss, S., & Wiltz, J. (2004). Why people watch reality TV. *Media Psychology, 6*(4), 363–378.

Rosengren, K. E. (1974). Uses and gratifications: A paradigm outlined. In J. G. Blumler & E. Katz (Eds.), *The uses of mass communication: Current perspectives of gratifications research* (pp. 269–286). Beverly Hills, Calif.: Sage.

Rubin, A. M. (1986), Uses, gratifications, and media effects research. In J. Bryant & D. Zillmann (Eds.), *Perspectives on media effects* (pp. 281–301). Hillsdale, NJ: Lawrence Erlbaum Associates.

Seiter, E. (1999). *Television and new media audiences*. New York: Oxford University Press.

Spradley, J. (1979). *The ethnographic interview*. New York: Holt, Rinehart and Winston.

Suchman, E. (1942). Invitation to music. In P. F. Lazarsfled & F. N. Stanton (Eds.), *Radio research* (pp. 140–188). New York: Duell, Sloan, & Pierce.

Wei, R., & Tootle, C. (2002, August). *Gratifications of reality show viewing: Antecedents and consensuses*. Paper presented to the Association for Education in Journalism and Mass Communication, Miami Beach, Fla.

Whetmore, E. J., & Kielwasser, K. P. (1983). The soap opera audience speaks: A preliminary report. *Journal of American Culture*, 6, 110–116.

Wimmer, R. D., & Dominick, J. R. (1994). Mass media research: *An introduction.* Belmont, Calif.: Wadsworth Publishing Company.

Wolfe, M., & Fiske, K. (1949). Children talk about comics. *Communication Research*, 1948–1949, pp. 3–50.

4

The Play on Realism

(AP Photo)

In this photo taken Monday, September 10, 2012, seven-year-old beauty pageant regular and reality show star, Alana "Honey Boo Boo" Thompson, plays with her mother June Shannon during an interview in her home in McIntyre, Georgia. "This is who she is," Shannon said as her daughter interrupted her with silly jokes and giggles. "This is her everyday life. She's got her own little personality, especially like when the cameras come on and when she's got attention."

Rough-Cut Reality

Reality television has a reputation for not being what it claims to be. Over the years, stories of fabricated fights, faux romances, and deceptive editing have leaked to the public, resulting in a general distrust of the format.

On Discovery Channel's *Man vs. Wild*, survival specialist Bear Grylls teaches viewers how to survive in the wild with little more than a pocket knife and bandana. But in 2008, it was revealed that Grylls and crew would often stay in motels on nights they were supposedly roughing it in the wilderness. On TLC's *Breaking Amish*, five Amish teenagers leave their religious communities for New York City, where they try to navigate life in the outside world. Soon after the show's premier in 2012, news reports pointed out that many of the cast members' background stories as presented in the first few episodes were misleading, and that in fact, many of the cast members had left their Amish communities years before the show's inception. It is thus easy to understand why many people are suspicious of reality television. Labeling the whole format "fake," however, isn't exactly justified either. In fact, but for the stray fibbing survivalist, the majority of reality television is quite real.

Detractors have good reason to be suspicious. Conversations between reality cast members are frequently clunky and forced, plot-thickening events often occur at questionably convenient moments, and outrageous incidents of apparently unconscionable betrayal happen with striking regularity. With so much over-the-top drama and bawdy behavior, reality television is bound to come off as contrived. But the air of spuriousness is part and parcel of the format. Viewers expect their television shows to have a beginning, a middle, and an end. In reality television, plot points don't always occur in a linear fashion. Sometimes footage needs to be manipulated. It's not intentional deceit on the part of producers; the medium necessitates some narrative sleight of hand.

Any well-informed consumer of visual media knows it's a long way from the slate to the screen. Even scripted television shows starring professional actors working in controlled environments require extensive post-production work. Reality shows take the inherent difficulties of television production and add the element of unpredictability that comes with stepping back and letting the action happen on its own. But along with the unpredictable comes the mundane. Compelling narrative action doesn't happen so fluidly or frequently in an unscripted world. The notoriously rambunctious cast of *Jersey Shore* spent much of their inaugural summer working in a boardwalk t-shirt shop in which very little of the show's trademark drama occurred. And while shooting can often yield minimal forward action, diligence often pays off with television gold, like when *Jersey Shore*'s Snooki took a punch to the face from a random male reveler after hours of filming in a loud, poorly-lit dance club.

Left with hundreds of hours of footage capturing nonactors doing mostly nothing, producers feel they have little choice but to massage reality a bit. Showrunners shape the story using strategic and unabashedly manipulative editing, often taking creative liberties with the chronology and context of footage. This after-the-fact storyboarding is one of the most integral differences between reality television and scripted formats. Reality shows take the traditional narrative-crafting process and reverse it.

The production hierarchy of reality television is a bit abstract. The roles of producer, writer, and director are all interchangeable. Because a cast member's individual personality is such a crucial element in the reality format, even pre-production casting is considered part of the "writing" process. In a piece for the Writers Guild of America, reality producer David Rupel explains that in the course of filming, every decision is made in pursuit of a compelling storyline. Producers act as social engineers, manufacturing tension, romance, and conflict from a combination of situation and personality. "When I produced *Temptation Island*, I chose room assignments based on how I thought people would affect each other," Rupel writes. Producers nudge reality in the direction they need it to go.

Reality show cast members—with the exception of celebrity-themed programming—aren't trained actors. Some may be aspiring, but most are far from being professionals. This can prove problematic if they have difficulty adjusting to being in front of the camera. One of the primary arguments used to dispute the authenticity of reality television is based on the extent to which the mere presence of a camera crew affects the behavior of cast members. Critics claim audiences don't get a genuine version of the people on screen—audiences get the version that knows they're being watched.

Some reality cast members don't do well being watched. While their personalities might be television-ready, their composure often isn't camera-ready. During production, action sometimes occurs off screen that is necessary to move the story forward—the demise of a friendship over lunch à la *The Hills*, for example. To fill in the resulting gaps in plot, producers sometimes ask cast members to recreate events integral to the story. So the midday quarrel that played out so naturally away from the cameras is reenacted in awkwardly phrased, semi-scripted dialogue by nonactors, unschooled in the art of line delivery. To compensate for a lack of emoting, producers often use auditory cues to imbue lifeless dialogue with the desired sentiment. It could be a hardly detectable ding, or a kitschy sound effect—the scratching record is a favorite of producers seeking to convey an abrupt, unpleasant twist in conversation. The sounds and music used in reality shows play one of the biggest roles in crafting the narrative. Without the accompanying musical score, a casual comment from one of *The Real Housewives* about another's party-planning abilities is harmless. But add a dramatic bass hit followed by several seconds of tense silence, and that innocuous observation becomes fighting words.

The reaction shot is another staple of reality TV storytelling. Producers will often keep a stockpile of footage that captures a cast member's full range of facial expressions. That way, if the producers of *Keeping Up with the Kardashians* want Khloé to take offense to something Kim said, they can just drop in an expression of disgust, and just like that, you have a moment of faux conflict. But since a certain reaction shot may be pulled from a different scene, location, or time of day, editors must often manipulate footage—flipping the frame so the subject reacts in the right direction, zooming in to hide continuity giveaways, and so on.

But before any of that can be done, reality producers must sift through days of footage to find a plotline worth following in the first place. They have to identify points of conflict, find the key players, and then—from a set of footage that could potentially span days—pull together a coherent story line. Action surrounding a certain subject is often made to appear as if it occurred in the same afternoon, even if the related incidents occurred several days apart.

It's not uncommon for former reality cast members to cry foul, claiming that producers of the show cast them in a negative light, or didn't accurately capture their personality. "I'm not as mean as they made me seem," goes the mantra. In the early hours of a reality show's life, producers must establish characters. Who is the villain? Who is the outcast? Which two cast members will be this season's Will They or Won't They? So if the bad guy isn't living up to villainy standards, producers will employ tricks to make him seem meaner. It could be as simple as cutting out all of the cast member's nice moments, leaving only the footage that shows him at his worst. Or more subversively, producers could pepper a scene with interview footage with another cast member who doesn't particularly like said bad guy. If the audience is consistently told that a certain cast member is combative or prone to inappropriate behavior, then they'll start to believe it.

Partially fabricating the lives, experiences, and personalities of a group of people and presenting it as reality can prove ethically problematic. Critics argue that reality stars who, through the magic of editing, are portrayed as perpetually bombastic and reckless give impressionable viewers the notion that such a level of excess and mayhem is sustainable for any one person. Young audiences might see Snooki and her spray-tanned compatriots going out to the clubs with astounding regularity, and—not knowing that back-to-back nights of partying could have occurred days apart—assume that that's a reasonable or healthy lifestyle to lead. But reality television has never been conducive to developing positive role models. Bad behavior and social belligerence are the bread and butter of the format. To think that the youth of the world are looking up to people who routinely drink to blackout on national television is certainly alarming. But if reality stars were less like their onscreen personas, and more like their pre-show selves, it seems highly unlikely that anybody would pay attention.

It's the process of separating the outrageous from the mundane and stringing it all together that makes the format work. Because after the last snippet of raw reality falls to the cutting room floor, producers are left with a series that has defined characters, clear plot points, and a linear narrative progression—a polished, dynamic story culled from source material that is more or less real. It's a thinly veiled con, but at least it's watchable.

Unreality TV: How the Ubiquitous Genre Actually Misrepresents Life

By Eric Miller
Christian Today, February 2006

It's Thanksgiving night 2005, and millions of American eyes strain toward the TV to watch...a football game? A *Waltons* reunion show? Some Capraesque tale trying valiantly to return us to our moral roots?

Try *Survivor: Guatemala,* first in its time slot and number ten for the week in the Nielsen ratings, with an estimated 19 million viewers. From its opening footage of barely clad women crawling through mud to its ritualized closing line, *"Gary, the tribe has spoken,"* it underscores with oomph the nature of our national moment, when cathedrals have morphed into malls and sanctuaries into screens.

We've lived with the current burst of reality TV for five years now. With approximately half of all American television shows falling into the genre, according to Nielsen Media Research, how much more reality can we take?

It's the law of the jungle that has grabbed us, curiously, here at the end of history. We thrill to shows like *Survivor* and *The Apprentice* as they, frothing with animosity, sex, and intrigue, dare virtue to intrude in any meaningful way. Call this the anti-community wing of reality TV. Here there are no adults, only overgrown kids doing whatever it takes to "have it all" (the supposed reward for *The Apprentice's* champion) or to win "immunity" (the weekly hope of *Survivor* contestants). Their conversations, taped for all the world to hear, reveal a remarkably banal form of moral poverty. "It's the Weaverbutts. They suck at driving," we hear one of the *Amazing Racers* declare, as families cavort around Utah competing in an elaborate scavenger hunt. "Marcus—he's useless! He's a nuisance," an *Apprentice* contestant complains about one of his teammates.

This is immaturity by design. Reality TV's stock technique, the private aside to the camera, incites by intention the very opposite of Christian confession. It's not repentance of sin that takes place behind this curtain, but rather the mere unveiling of sin—not self-mortification, but self-inflation, or what an older, wiser generation termed "vainglory." And it is this, pitifully, that drives the competitors on.

If the anti-community reality shows make virtue impossible, the super-community shows make it inevitable. The *Pittsburgh Post-Gazette* reports that at a recent taping of *Extreme Makeover: Home Edition.* Footage of screaming crowds cheering on a family about to receive a new home was taped well before the family arrived, "as production crew members hopped up and down to stir the growing throng into a frenzy." Such is "reality."

From *Christianity Today* 50.2 (February 2006). Reprinted with permission. Copyright © 2006 by Christianity Today International. Reprinted with permission. All rights reserved.

NBC ventured in this direction this past fall with *Three Wishes,* featuring evangelical superstar Amy Grant as the emcee. Its premise was as simple as Santa Claus: The network comes to town and begins to entertain wishes, winnowing them quickly down to three. One week later, all kinds of corporate-sponsored miracles have taken place, including, so far, a costly surgery for a young girl with a fractured skull, a rent-free house in South Dakota for a hurricane-stricken family from New Orleans, a professional-quality football field for a high school in California, and even the reuniting of an adult adoptee with her birth mother.

The needy are fed and the deserving rewarded in the super-community shows. Great gifts are given by great folk. And the jungle is far, far away.

If only it were true.

> *It's not repentance of sin that takes place behind this curtain, but rather the mere unveiling of sin—not self-mortification, but self-inflation, or what an older, wiser generation termed "vainglory." And it is this, pitifully, that drives the competitors on.*

The Danger of Self-Diminishment

The awful, beautiful complexity of human experience—including our own moment in time—requires richly textured rendering for true self-understanding. Without art of this quality, our inevitable misrepresentations of our experience end up diminishing us in our own eyes; we seem more shallow or simple or happy or wholesome than we truly are. And virtue—the realizing of our divinely designed moral shape—becomes just a mirage. Or it is simply forgotten.

A novel three years in the making, a painting slowly achieved after years of study, even a long-running television series—these may possibly possess the power to take us more deeply into the mysteries of the condition in which we find ourselves, and may, most crucially, cast a vision of what we might yet become. But "reality TV"? Its tacky melodrama, *deus ex machina* plots, unending musical manipulations, and pseudo-heroic corporate saviors only undercut what it pretends to be about. Instead of showing us our truest selves, it plays to our worst impulses and misperceptions, making, in the end, a spectacle of our inner lives. Like other forms of voyeurism, it actually diminishes our taste for reality.

There is a reality out there: grand, awful, mysterious, and threatening. The truth, though, is that we postmoderns usually want reality packaged for us. Keep it titillating. Keep it shallow. Keep it safe. But the God of life is neither titillating, nor shallow, nor safe. Nor is he captured well by the screen, big or small. The more we evade him and a lively participation in his world, the less real we become. That's a fate only a network could love.

Eric Miller is associate professor of history at Geneva College.

Living on Camera

By Tim Stack, Jennifer Armstrong, and Lindsay Soll
Entertainment Weekly, August 8, 2008

Read on for three stories examining what it means to be a citizen of our ever-growing Reality Nation.

If Socrates were around these days, he might say that the unfilmed life is not worth living. For today's teens and twenty-somethings, an event simply hasn't happened until it's been documented—texted, blogged, logged in a Facebook status update, or, preferably, filmed, edited, and set to a killer soundtrack of up-and-coming artists. This generation was raised by *The Real World* to believe that you can behave any way you want—as long as you explain yourself in a confessional shot later. That your life is noteworthy if you're willing to eat a pig rectum, throw a tantrum on camera, or let America choose your husband. Prying parents must stay away, but the voyeuristic masses can totally come on in! In this special report, we look at what the Reality Era has yielded, from *American Teen*, an angsty new documentary feature that follows the unvarnished (but still rivetingly photogenic) lives of five real Indiana kids, to *The Hills*, MTV's sparkling take on one L.A. girl's life that couldn't be more of a fantasy if a unicorn galloped through the front yard of her lavish California home. We also ask survivors (not Survivors) of the genre who became overnight stars (or at least "stars") why they put themselves through a reality show, only to land back in the cold, harsh, unflatteringly lit real world (not *The Real World*) again. But don't worry, they'll always have videotaped proof that for a little while, they experienced "reality."

Once upon a time, a pretty California girl agreed to let cameras film her life. Now 'Hills' star Lauren Conrad is a millionaire whose life as a celebrity bears little resemblance to what viewers see on TV. Still, fans can't get enough, of MTV's (virtual) reality empire.

They Shoot. She Scores.

The Kress, a four-story Asian-inspired L.A. club, has barely been open one week, but tonight it's hosting the nightclub equivalent of a meeting with the Pope—that is, a visit from the cast and crew of MTV's reality hit *The Hills*. With stars Lauren Conrad and Audrina Patridge due to arrive at 8:30 p.m. for their standard videotaped girl talk over cocktails, the crew is busy prepping the space for the cameras. Two seats at the corner of the bar are reserved, and a production assistant laps around the room handing out forms asking bystanders to agree to appear on camera. If they

From *Entertainment Weekly* 1005 (8 Aug. 2008): 25–31. Copyright © 2008 by Time, Inc. Reprinted with permission. All rights reserved.

don't, production will ask them to move, or shoot around them. Most comply easily, unimpressed by the fact that MTV's highest-rated series will be shooting a scene mere feet from their plates of lobster sashimi and beef carpaccio. Clearly, they don't know that roommates Lauren and Audrina are having major tension at home, and this could be, like, a totally important conversation.

Finally, Lauren and Audrina coast into the restaurant and take their seats at the bar. No direction. No rehearsals. They just start talking. Upstairs, the director and four producers, including creator and executive producer Adam DiVello, huddle around three portable monitors. Lauren and Audrina segue into a conversation about tomorrow's barbecue at the house of Lauren's ex-boyfriend Doug. Will it be awkward, Audrina wonders, since Doug recently went on a date with Lauren's friend Stephanie? Lauren admits, "Tomorrow, I'm gonna need to drink." DiVello, catching a shot of Lauren laughing that he thinks will work well for this season's updated opening-credits montage, runs over to the story editor to have him jot down the time code. When the girls prepare to depart, the director sends one of the cameras across the street to capture them leaving. Strolling down the boulevard, Lauren, who has been living her life on television for four years and knows how to end a scene, turns to Audrina and smiles. "Tomorrow," she says, "is gonna be a crazy, fun day."

It's a wrap. And that, ladies and gentlemen, is how you make one of the most addictive, hated, beloved, vapid, influential, successful shows on television.

The phenomenon of *The Hills*—which returns for season 4 on Aug. 18 at 10 p.m.—has gone beyond the weekly tabloid covers (mostly chronicling Lauren's feud with her former BFF Heidi Montag), the endless spoofs (see Mila Kunis and James Franco's dead-on Audrina/Justin Bobby on FunnyOrDie.com), or even its place in the current presidential campaign. (After Heidi endorsed John McCain, he joked that he never "misses an episode of *The Hills*"; Barack Obama promised David Letterman, "My first act as president will be to stop the fighting between Lauren and Heidi.") The series has also transformed an ordinary California girl into a West Coast reincarnation of Carrie Bradshaw (if Carrie were a millionaire), while giving MTV its biggest success in years. Season 3 averaged 3.9 million viewers, making it MTV's highest-rated show since 2004's *Real World: San Diego*, and its May 12 finale topped even the broadcast networks in the 12-to-34 demographic. "I would go out on a limb and say this is probably the biggest show we've ever had," says MTV Networks' president of entertainment, Brian Graden. "With Lauren Conrad, a whole generation of women see themselves in her." Says Tony DiSanto, MTV's exec VP of series programming and development, "It's almost becoming like a novel at this point, like this generation's *A Tale of Two Cities* or *Oliver Twist*."

Whether or not you equate drunken nights at Hyde and Les Deux to the classic literary works of Dickens, the show's success is undeniable. And no one has reaped more benefits than Lauren. While she has yet to graduate from L.A.'s Fashion Institute of Design & Merchandising, where she majors in product development, she's already launched her own eponymous clothing line (in partnership with MTV), which is sold in 500 boutiques across the country. Forbes estimated her 2007-08 income to be $1.5 million—and Lauren says she used her own money to purchase

> *As with most scenes on **The Hills**, the cast knew ahead of time that cameras would be present at the barbecue. Almost everything is planned in advance, which is why production of **The Hills** has always faced tremendous skepticism—is it contrived? Is it fake? The answer is... to a point. The Hills **is**, essentially, scheduled reality.*

the reported $2.3 million home she lives in on *The Hills*. "I see her as a global brand," says Max Stubblefield, Lauren's agent at UTA. "Fashion and beauty are the drivers, but we've had a lot of interest from a lot of different categories." Since *The Hills* premiered in 2006, Lauren has landed endorsement deals with Mark cosmetics and AT&T, has a book proposal in the works, and wants to launch her own television and film production company. "It's about empowering girls," says Lauren, when asked to describe what she represents as a brand. "You're gonna have bad boyfriends and best-friends-turned-enemies. You need to be yourself, you need to work hard, and you'll get there." And if you can get someone to give you a reality show along the way, it can't hurt.

Up in a posh stretch of the Hollywood Hills—the same neighborhood where Jennifer Aniston lives—*The Hills* gang has gathered for the barbecue hosted by Lauren's ex Doug Reinhardt, whose dad lays claim to inventing the frozen burrito. Most of the show's main players are gathered around the backyard pool: Lauren, her roommate Lo Bosworth, Whitney Port, Frankie Delgado, and Stephanie Pratt. Audrina and her on-again, off-again boyfriend Justin "Bobby" Brescia will arrive later, after being chased up the hill by paparazzi. (Alas, Aniston never does drift over for a beer.) Four cameras prowl around the house; the producers have turned Doug's guest room into a makeshift production base. The command center is tense when a partygoer says that Brody Jenner, Lauren's ex-turned-best friend, will be bringing Heidi's boyfriend, Spencer Pratt—who Lauren believes started a sex-tape rumor about her last year. Doug goes to greet Brody at the door, and Lauren warns, "Don't let him in." But it's a false alarm—Brody arrives sans the toothy blond villain. Doug, Brody, and Frankie hover on one side of the pool, the girls on the other. Lauren watches as the fratty guys laugh and joke. "That's really gross," she says. "I've kissed two out of three of those."

As with most scenes on *The Hills*, the cast knew ahead of time that cameras would be present at the barbecue. Almost everything is planned in advance, which is why production of *The Hills* has always faced tremendous skepticism—is it contrived? Is it fake? The answer is...to a point. *The Hills* is, essentially, scheduled reality. A typical week begins with producers calling the core cast members on Sunday and getting intel on what's happened to them over the weekend. An e-mail update is sent to the staff that night so everyone can prepare for Monday's "story meeting," in which the producers and story editors sit around and dissect the *Hills* girls' personal and social lives. From that, they determine whom to film during the week.

(On average, it takes editors four to six weeks to cull through the footage and put together an episode.) Lauren and her costars are forbidden to attend these meetings. "I would love to sit through one of those," says Lauren, "because it's really them being like, 'Yo, did you hear what this person said?'"

Plotting out the shooting schedule is an elaborate process: Depending on where the girls are going and whom they'll be with, production will call ahead and clear the locations—restaurants, cafés, retail outlets—for the crews to come in. Once everything is set up, Lauren gets her shooting schedule e-mailed to her, usually the night before. If the idea of coordinating your real life with a film crew sounds surreal, it's even more so now that Lauren—thanks to *The Hills* and *Laguna Beach* before it—is too famous to have anything resembling a real life. Her schedule is packed with photo shoots, fashion shows, and red-carpet events like the *Dark Knight* premiere or the White House Correspondents' Dinner (her highlight of the evening was meeting the Jonas Brothers—sorry, Mr. President!). All that glitz seems perfect fodder for reality TV, but producers insist on keeping the celebrity side off camera. The series' original premise—and the stories that made it successful in the first place—are all about the relatable aspects of Lauren's life, like dating, heartbreak, and friendship. "We have a hard line because we really enjoy the world of *The Hills* we've created," says DiSanto. "But you never say never, because as they get more and more famous, their non-fame lives get smaller and smaller." Adds exec producer Liz Gateley, "We give people the access that they're not getting in the tabloids. They're getting their private life."

Keeping things private is tricky, given that the cast is hounded daily by L.A.'s paparazzi. "Anywhere between 6 and 12 are out there [during filming]," says DiVello. Adds Lauren, "We'll be filming at a restaurant and it will be us at a table, three cameras, and then a row of photographers behind the cameras." Out of necessity, DiVello and his crew have formed a tentative We'll get our shots, then you'll get yours alliance with the paparazzi. "We don't want to [shoot] in the back of a restaurant so people can't see us," says DiVello. "You want them on the patios. The paparazzi really work with us. They stay behind the cameras."

Still, the hovering shutterbugs are occasionally to blame for inciting rumors that the show is heavily manipulated. According to Lauren, many times the paps and their incessant flashbulbs will ruin establishing shots of the girls entering, say, a restaurant, so production will ask Lauren and her friends to do another take. Explains DiVello, "If we lose something, or there's no audio and we need them to talk about something [again], we'll ask them to talk about it. Anyone that's making a reality television show that tells you they aren't doing [the same thing] is probably lying." Lauren says she understands why fans cry foul about scenes that reek of "take 2" awkwardness. "I get that there are certain scenes where someone's like, 'Sooo, last night was weird....' And then there are people on the show who really don't help, because they are very fake. We know who we're talking about—like, you need to stop rehearsing your breakfast." Lauren won't name names, but we're guessing she's referring to series villains Heidi and Spencer. The duo did tell EW last year that they had faked arguments for the cameras, which DiVello admits he can't control.

"We work with what they're giving us," he says. "I don't think any of these kids are making up stuff, but I don't know." (Heidi and Spencer declined to be interviewed for this story once they learned Lauren was on the [Entertainment Weekly] cover.)

Feuding will continue to fuel the story lines on season 4 of *The Hills*: Lauren will attend Stephanie's birthday party—even though it means being in the same room as Heidi and Spencer—but DiVello says she doesn't stay too long in the presence of her enemies. The tension between Lauren, Audrina, and Lo will culminate in a teary blowout that had even producers crying. There will be trips to New York and Vegas—in the latter, Brody ends up in casino jail, which we're guessing is somewhere near the slots. And DiVello promises lots of dating for the ladies, including male model dating!

If it were up to MTV, *The Hills* would keep rolling indefinitely, but Lauren is ready for a break. "Every season, I think it's the last," she admits. "Right now, I think this is the last season." After all, being the subject of a never-ending home video takes its toll on a girl. "I go through phases when I've been filming where I wake up in the middle of the night and I think I'm being filmed," says Lauren. "That's when I have to take a vacation." (Lauren's nightmare served as inspiration for [Entertainment Weekly's] cover photo.) DiVello says he can see the show going at least one more season, but ideally, "I'd love to stay with it until Lauren gets married."

Unless she elopes with a busboy at Crown Bar next week, MTV knows DiVello's dream is unlikely to become their reality, so they're busy readying spin-offs for her costars. Brody will star in his own reality series, *Bromance* (scheduled for this winter), in which alpha males compete to join his posse. "It'll be like *Swingers*," says Brody. "Not your typical elimination show like Tila Tequila—it's very loose." Meanwhile, rumors persist that Whitney—the statuesque blonde Lauren befriended while interning at *Teen Vogue*—will be getting her own spin-off, focusing on her job at fashion PR firm People's Revolution in New York City. (MTV won't confirm the plans.) "There are rumors that I've heard from people at MTV, but nothing is set in stone yet," says Whitney. "It's definitely something I'm willing to do." As for Lauren, she's not entirely sure what's in her future, which makes her dad nervous. "He's like, 'Let's talk about your five-year plan'," she says. "I go, 'Let's talk about my five-day plan. I don't even know that.'" It's safe to say, though, that at least three of those five days will be on camera.

Real or Rigged? *American Idol,* Jonathan Antoine, and Fake Reality TV

By Jennifer Grassman
Washington Times, April 27, 2012

Many reality TV viewers are experiencing déjà vu. In 2009, the cocky and cute, but definitely-not-sexy Susan Boyle astonished millions with her beautiful voice. Now, just a few years later, Jonathan Antoine is inciting the same brand of shock and awe. The 280 lb. teenager may not look like Michael Bublé, but he's got a voice that would make the ghost of Le Fantôme de l'Opéra get goosebumps.

Supposedly, even the judges of *Britain's Got Talent* were shocked by Antoine's pitch perfect performance and veritable vibrato. But is that really possible? Are the judges completely unaware of the pending programming on their own show? It's hard to imagine that's the case, particularly in Cowell's position as the creator of the series, and since he's credited as script "writer" on IMDB.

Even in the case that the judges are genuinely shocked when a true talent graces their stage, surely they are not unaware that just because someone isn't hot and sexy doesn't mean they don't have skills that would inspire a Vulcan to tear up. To make an avian analogy, the very plainest of the songbirds, the nightingale, is mythical for also having the most melodic voice.

In August, 2011, *American Idol* hopefuls descended upon Reliant Park in Houston, Texas. The heat was unbearable, water was four dollars a bottle, and the portable toilets smelled and looked like they hadn't been cleaned since the Texans went up against the Saints the previous Saturday. At least one person passed out from heat stroke and was carted away by on-site medics. Nevertheless, the intrepid singing wannabes sat in the Texas sun for hours upon hours before being herded like cattle indoors.

Once inside, vocalists were processed, sorted into groups, and told to sit in the stands and wait some more. In the middle of the field below were a line of tables, at which sat two judges each.

No. Simon Cowell was not there. These were preliminary rounds. The judges were your average Joes and Janes, and they look bored to tears, if not downright crabby. Small groups of competitors were led out onto the field to their assigned judging tables, where they sang for the judges, who either nodded ascent or—more commonly—gave them the proverbial boot.

Every so often, a roar went up from the crowd as some ecstatic tryout did cartwheels, danced a jig, or threw their shoes in the air to celebrate their making it past

From *Washington Times* (27 April 2012). Copyright © 2012 by Washington Times LLC. Reprinted with permission. All rights reserved.

the first round. Curiously, most of these elated selectees were very oddly dressed. One gentleman in particular, wore a brightly colored unitard. Rumors began to circulate among the hundreds of competitors still waiting to sing that *American Idol* had already picked the "good" singers, possibly before the tour event got to Houston, and now they were only looking for "freaks."

The point is that whether you're talking about *American Idol*, Britain's *Got Talent*, *The X Factor*, or any other reality rendition Cowell may dream up next, contestants have already gone through multiple judging rounds before gaining an audience with the notoriously snarky Englishman.

> *In all likelihood, the expression of surprise on Simon Cowell's smirking face is merely a pretense. Even if Cowell is in the dark regarding who is about to audition on his live filmed television show, he is certainly not ignorant of the fact that many of the greatest vocalists of all time are also the least attractive.*

Each singer, whether talented or completely tone deaf, is carefully scrutinized, analyzed, and categorized by a team of highly trained television producers who know exactly how to make a reality TV show sensational, funny, and entertaining. There are no surprises, nothing is left to chance, and there are no wild cards. Everything is carefully orchestrated and fine-tuned to maximize television ratings and mass appeal.

When singers like Jonathan Antoine make their live on-stage debuts, the audience (both onscreen and at home), often thinks it's his debut audition. Not so. Sure, it's the first time the public has caught a glimpse of the competitor. But show producers have already heard him audition numerous times, filmed interviews with him, booked him a hotel room, and asked what brand of bottled water he prefers. In fact, they've probably even told him what song to sing, or suggested a selection for him to pick from.

In all likelihood, the expression of surprise on Simon Cowell's smirking face is merely a pretense. Even if Cowell is in the dark regarding who is about to audition on his live filmed television show, he is certainly not ignorant of the fact that many of the greatest vocalists of all time are also the least attractive. Many opera greats look more like Jason Alexander from *Seinfeld* than Beyonce, and they're arguably the most talented vocalists in existence.

Susan Boyle was commonly compared to The Ugly Duckling, the main character of a same-titled novelette by Hans Christian Anderson. In the story, an awkward little chick who is mistaken for a baby duck, grows up to be a beautiful swan. But The Ugly Duckling started out ugly and later became beautiful. Boyle, on the other hand, was beautiful long before she showcased for reality TV. In fact, she was probably singing her heart out long before Simon Cowell made it big. She may not be the kind of hot babe you look twice at when you pass her in the street, but Boyle has an inner beauty that is substantial and highly cultivated.

Until we as a culture learn what true beauty really is, people like Susan Boyle and Jonathan Antoine will be undervalued, except of course by wily TV producers looking for a ratings boost. Sadly, it is the mainstream assumption that sexually attractive people are gifted and multifaceted, while those with less gaudy physiques are inept and boring. This ignorant and bigoted misconception is the bread and butter of reality TV, because it opens the door wide for cliche publicity stunts.

How sublimely simple it must be to unearth a gawky vocal talent—an awkward teen or middle aged misfit desperate for long overdue recognition—and use them as a trick pony to launch ratings into the stratosphere.

Perhaps this is why the entertainment industry leaves a bad taste in the mouth of many disillusioned artists and professionals. True talent is often skipped over while mediocrity is celebrated, unless of course the true talent is somehow packaged (or packageable) in such a way that money grubbers can take advantage of it.

Is this unethical? Maybe. Is it unfair? Certainly. Is it real? Yep. That's why it's called "reality television."

Singer, songwriter and pianist, Jennifer Grassman is an award-winning recording artist and founder of SeeTalkGrow, a 100% online music, film, technology, and communications conference.

Live from the Ministry of Truth: How 'Real' Are Reality Soaps?

By Lawrence Hill and Robyn Quin
Metro Magazine, Winter 2003

Reporting from the Recent MIP Trade Show in Cannes, *Variety* quoted the Paris-based Eurodata TV research organization on the 'huge impact' that reality programming is having on television schedules around the world, with *Survivor* and *Big Brother* among the top ten shows in five out of the fifty-five countries surveyed last year.[1]

Part gladiatorial combat, part soap opera, part 'fly-on-the-wall' documentary, the new reality format employs the principle of elimination (either by voting or according to the contestants' performances) to provoke socio-emotional dramas and betrayals between people that are 'real', even if everything else is highly contrived. Analysts at Eurodata TV have described these shows as 'psycho-games' or 'reality soaps'.[2]

Big Brother, Popstars, Temptation Island and *Survivor* mark a return to one of the earliest paradigms of broadcast television—'liveness' and this is a primary reason for their success. Live television promises participation—somewhere else (but also in your lounge room), something is happening … and we can all feel part of it. These programs, like quiz shows, offer the viewer dual status: at the same time removed observer and involved participant, the latter through the process of identification with one or other participant. This position is superior to that of a member of a live audience because he/she has access to the close-ups, the cut-aways and the 'best angle' on the action.

Reality programming is clearly not 'live' in any technical sense. However, these programs offer the same enticements as live television. They promise unpredictability, spontaneity (through a supposed lack of editorial control), and audiences which choose to consume them do so as if they were indeed live (i.e. when broadcast, or with only a short delay if taped at home.) This pattern of immediate consumption is determined by the programs' location within a broader discursive formation which includes lively post-mortem discussions on the Internet, newspaper articles about the program and its participants, other related television programs and chat while at work or at leisure-based meeting places around the country. Watching the actual show is only part of the enjoyment and engagement in the discourses surrounding it provides other pleasures.

From *Metro Magazine 31* (Winter 2003). Copyright © 2003 by ATOM Publishing. Reprinted with Permission. All rights reserved.

Origins

Reality television began to appear as a distinctive genre in the late 1980s. Poster argues a link between particular technologies, historical change and modes of representation.[3] Reality television was made possible by the development of lightweight video recording equipment capable of producing broadcast quality images in low-lighting conditions and digital editing, which provides for rapid editing. These technologies have made it possible to capture events in the lives of individuals or groups that can then be edited and repackaged into a television program 'which can be promoted on the strength of its "reality" credentials'.[4] On occasion the cameras are in the hands of amateurs (as with *Australia's Funniest Home Videos*) but 'the control over what gets shown and how it is presented resides firmly in the hands of professional television personnel'.[5] This control is employed to tell stories in such a way that 'tensions are built and climaxes reached in a manner that is more akin to the narratives of popular TV drama ... fast editing, pulsating mood music and other tension-building devices ... all calculated to heighten the sense of dramatic involvement'.[6] Kilborn argues that the entertainment value of these shows is an overriding concern for their producers, and the need to generate excitement by ensuring visual interest, pace, and even an element of voyeurism in some programs has given rise to the charge that this is a form of 'tabloid television'.

A widely anticipated writers and actors strike has seen Hollywood producers rushing to complete existing projects while TV networks are looking to get more reality shows into production because they are unscripted and use non-actors. Some writers have argued that reality programming was largely the result of economic pressures. Raphael argued that the proliferation of reality television programming was a response to economic restructuring in US television.[7] Rapidly rising production costs associated with conventional production practices were squeezed by declining per-show revenues arising from changing patterns of distribution with the spread of cable, VCRs, the Fox network and local independent stations. The pressure on production budgets made reality television programming attractive because the genre largely did away with the need for expensive, professional and unionized acting talent. Furthermore, the wholehearted embrace of low-end production values such as handheld cameras and the use of available lighting could reduce production costs. In some cases the sets, props and costumes were provided by the agencies profiled in the program, further minimizing costs to the producers. As a result, 'Reali-TV is the only primetime programming category which is not deficit-financed'.[8]

The Question of Realism

Arguing that modern viewers are aware that what is usually seen on television is in every sense a constructed reality, Kilborn sees a key attraction of this new kind of programming coming from its apparent ability to capture 'the vibrancy and spontaneity of real-life events'.[9] The authenticity of what the audience is seeing is often 'guaranteed' by some of the technical difficulties associated with handheld camerawork such as framing problems and temporary loss of focus.

In this aspect, the genre appears to be drawing on some of the earliest traditions of *cinema verité*. Examining the history of ethnographic documentary, Hassard traces the first developments in theory and practice to the Russian film-maker Dziga Vertov, who argued that sets, scripts and actors should be dispensed with in order to present 'realistic' images of everyday lives.[10] This style of film making tried to avoid 'judgment' and 'subjectivity', with the role of the film-maker limited to revealing 'reality'. In its purest form there should be no direction, no plot, no questions posed or answered, with the only permissible tools being lightweight cameras and portable sound recorders. 'Decisions concerning action should rest with the subject: the film-maker merely decides whether or not to film a particular piece of action.'[11]

This view considers the camera operator to be the most important crew member, with the success of the film resting on his or her ability to keep pace with the action. Long takes are characteristic of the style in order to give the viewer a feeling for the character and atmosphere. When it came to editing, sequences were to be cut close to the way they were actually shot, in order that the process should '... as far as possible, be "true to life", rather than footage being manipulated by the editor to create a "new" and essentially "different" reality ...'[12]

In this respect, *Survivor* seems to go out of its way to draw attention to the fact that it is an edited construct by employing the 1990s cliché of speededup vision at every possible opportunity. Clouds race across the sky, aerial shots of mazes twist onto the screen with the speed of computer graphics—on no account must the audience experience the slow passage of time characteristic of life in the outback or on a deserted island, for fear that they might become bored and the ratings drop.

In fact, the reality soaps depart from *cinema verité* in a number of ways. Certainly, it appears that the editors in this new genre of reality soaps highlight certain aspects of people's behavior for entertainment value, as part of the process of character construction. A frequent comment from ex-contestants is 'I'm not really like that' because a series of individual incidents have been strung together with exaggerated effect. In this context a comment from Richard, the 'villain' who won *Survivor I* is illuminating:

> Richard said that even though the episodes had been "edited somewhat" to portray her (Jerri) in a bad light, she deserved her reputation. "You do all of those things that you're edited to do," he said, "and she was evil to people."[13]

Contestants are questioned, and drawn into soliloquising to the camera in ways that are reminiscent of Francis Urquehardt in the BBC drama *House of Cards*. This privileges the audience with some fascinating discontinuities between each contestant's view of the action, in a manner similar to *Blind Date* or *Perfect Match*. In episode nine of *Survivor II*, Jerri and Colby spent a day on the Barrier reef:

> I couldn't have come out here with a better person," declared Jerri. "We are having a great time and we are getting to know each other. This is basically the perfect honeymoon without the sex.

> Colby had different thoughts: "I was just looking for some down time away from the game, and that's exactly what I got."[14]

Earlier in the show the audience had been made privy to Colby's resentment at the thought of sharing this prize with Jerri, whom he was clearly beginning to dislike, and so was placed in the same kind of privileged position often occupied by consumers of fictional narratives. In part, the format allows audiences access to the subject's inner thoughts and then have their insights validated or otherwise by subsequent events. When the tribe subsequently voted off Jerri, the audience had been given the clues (like a whodunit) to deduce the likelihood of Colby's betrayal.

In Ang's study of the highly popular television drama *Dallas,* she used data from a viewer survey to postulate that an attribution of realism was a key principle in the popular aesthetic. She discussed both 'empirical realism' (likeness of setting, social action, themes) and 'classical realism' (continuity editing, classic montage, etc.) before dismissing them as inadequate explanations. Ang concluded that an 'emotional realism' which links the actions of the characters with the viewer's own experiences as being the most likely explanation of audience pleasure. It was, she said '... produced by the construction of a *psychological* reality ... an "inner realism" ... combined with an "external unrealism"'.[15]

Thus despite the external unrealism of shows such as *Survivor* and *Big Brother,* which are every bit as fantastic as the Ewing family's circumstances, it seems likely that the viewers are responding to what *is* 'real' in the situation—the contestants themselves, their inter-relationships and the interpersonal drama. That audiences are responding to reality soaps on a psychosocial level seems to be confirmed by the importance attached to the interactive possibilities offered by the genre:

> Ever since millions of fans religiously scoured cyberspace for the last scintilla of information about the original Survivor series, Web sites have become a must-have for all new reality shows. [16]

The evidence suggests that the audience has an intense curiosity about the contestants themselves, according to a report on the second *Survivor* series posted recently to cnn.com:

> In a separate analysis prepared [by] Nielsen NetRatings (NTRT), Amber ... led the pack, with 22.9 percent of the audience scoping her out ... the highest-ranking male was Jeff ... who came in behind six women, with 17.1 percent of the audience visiting his bio page. David Katz, CBS VP of strategic planning and interactive ventures, said that he is 'bowled over' by how well-trafficked the Survivor site has been, citing (from internal CBS-tracked stats) 30 million page views during the past week.[17]

To achieve this level of interest, the producers of reality soaps undertake an exhaustive 'casting' process, in order to give viewers a cross-section of society. Regardless of a viewer's demographic he/she can find someone with whom to identify. Over the course of a series, television audiences come to know the contestants as individuals, as characters. The emotions and inter-relationships between them as they make friends and enemies are a primary focus of reality soaps, framed within a larger narrative which requires them to compete/co-operate with each other in order to win.

In reality soaps it is arguably the contestant selector rather than the camera operator who is the most important crew member.

Reality Soaps and Voyeurism

The dependence of this kind of programming upon non-actors raises some significant issues about the morality and ethics of putting ordinary people into situations where they reveal private, personal behaviors for the vicarious pleasure of a television audience. Placed in an unreal situation, motivated by money or fame, it defies belief that the individuals would not act in ways that might be quite different from their ordinary behaviors in daily life.

The executive producer of *Survivor I*, in constructing a television entertainment that has all the elements of a sociological study, shows some disturbing similarities to the amoral director in Peter Weir's *The Truman Show* (Peter Weir, 1999). Quoted on CNN's web site, Mark Burnett even refers to it as such:

> *The producer created the rules governing people's behavior on the island, and by requiring the castaways themselves to determine who would be the ultimate winner, it could be argued that the rules were designed to maximize the potential for conflicts to arise.*

> What a great experiment: Take a diverse group in race and age and job background, put them on an island and see how they get along.[18]

Establishing a utopian society in the wilderness is a foundational concept within American ideology. Some of the *Survivor* castaways approached life on their island with such ideals. This idyllic fantasy was soon shipwrecked by the need for drama, conflict and ratings. Those contestants who naively believed themselves to be surrounded by characters as winsome and charming as those appearing in a 1960s sitcom were gradually eliminated by party politics. The game show element required participants to achieve a complex blend of competition and co-operation to succeed, and it seems that *Survivor I* explicitly set out to mirror contemporary American capitalist/corporate society:

> Survivor executive producer Mark Burnett told me the island culture on Pulau Tiga was no different from the bedrooms and boardrooms of American society. That is, we have to learn to get along with people we like and people we dislike and, to survive, we have to keep trying.[19]

The enormous prize money and the fact that it was 'only a game' were repeatedly used by the 'final four' castaways as justifications for their Machiavellian intrigues in *Survivor I*. These were a major part of the storyline, and considerable screen time on the show was devoted to the machinations of the contestants. The producer created the rules governing people's behavior on the island, and by requiring the castaways themselves to determine who would be the ultimate winner, it could be argued that the rules were designed to maximize the potential for conflicts to arise.

Ostracism is an old, sometimes brutal instrument of social punishment. When carried out in front of a viewing audience numbered in the millions, there is a great potential for people to become seriously hurt psychologically. Two years ago in a Swedish version of *Survivor*, the first member to be ejected from a group committed suicide. His widow told a Swedish newspaper that:

> her husband had become deeply depressed ... he felt degraded and didn't see any meaning in life, worrying about having to wait to see his failure on the air. 'He was a glad and stable person when he went away,' Savija says, 'and when he came back he told me, "They are going to cut away the good things I did and make me look like a fool, only to show I was the worst, and that I was the one that had to go"'.[20]

Some commentators have noted disturbing parallels between *Survivor* and experiments by sociologists after World War II involving a simulated prison camp, which showed that, given the opportunity, ordinary respondents could become brutalized. The most famous of these was the Milgram experiment, where so-called 'teachers' (in fact the unknowing subjects of the experiment) were directed to administer electric shocks of increasing intensity to a 'learner'.

> When Milgram conducted the study, he found that with a little bit of coaxing, the majority (60 per cent) of subjects would administer shocks right through to 450 volts ... interviews with his subjects tended to confirm the view that ordinary, everyday people can cause pain and suffering to another person under the right set of circumstances.[21]

The Milgram experiment was exploring the issue of obedience to authority. It reached the disturbing conclusion that most people would continue to obey directives (albeit, in some cases, with extreme personal distress) even when those directives were clearly causing harm to another person.

The authority of *Survivor's* producer over production crews operating in isolated locations must be considerable. If some on the production team have reservations about the consequences of their actions for the well-being of the castaways, it is unlikely that they feel able to challenge his authority. The CBS production appeared to be well-resourced, and presumably operated within the ethical constraints imposed by a major television network. Yet, despite this, there were two incidents in the second series that caused considerable controversy. One involved the illegal removal of coral from a national park and the second was a heavily edited sequence that showed Michael Skupin hunting and killing a pig:

> one contestant clumsily stabs to death a small wild pig for—let's be clear about this—entertainment ... Remember, this really happened. The pig really is dead. Its killer really is a sick bastard. The CBS network really should be ashamed of itself.[22]

In some shows there is even an element of danger, and contestants place themselves in hazardous situations. As with many sporting events, the possibility of injury may be part of the thrill for the audience. In *Survivor II*, viewers witnessed Michael

Skupin being evacuated by helicopter after being badly burnt and the effect that this had upon the other contestants. The presence of crocodiles on the same location with the contestants was clearly established by the cameras, and even highlighted in attendant publicity. In the same interview the host, Jeff Probst, also played up the possibility of injury in the next series:

> I think there is a chance that somebody could die or be seriously hurt. Nobody wants it to happen, but you can't go and fence off people from the outside world in a program like this … you can take precautions, but you can't take the risk out of it.[23]

Reality Soaps and 'Liveness'

When television began, anything seen by the audience was either live or telecined from film. With the introduction of videotape in the 1970s the amount of live content declined rapidly and the current trend amongst television theorists is to reduce its importance. A contrary view is argued by Bourdon, who maintains that the technical possibility of live broadcasting remains important to audiences because:

> From the top, major institutions have all used news, then radio and television liveness, to create a connection between the masses and events … at the base, the need to connect oneself, with others, to the world's events, is central to the development of the modern nation … [24]

Even though live broadcasts are now comparatively rare, television remains deeply influenced by its possibility. This is because 'liveness' is more than just a technical phenomenon. Audiences may deliberately choose to consume a television product in such a way that it feels 'live', as a way of connecting with others in their society.

Bourdon suggests the following typology for degrees of 'liveness' in television sequences:

- *Fully live*—major media events such as election night specials or Princess Diana's funeral, which break into the normal run of programming; other examples are news shows or channels such as CNN where the viewer 'knows' the broadcast to be happening 'now', particularly where these might involve live crosses to an OB unit on location.

- *Continuity*—has the appearance of being live but may not be—sporting matches, game shows, variety programs; the viewer cannot really tell from cues within the program if the show is coming to them live or off tape. In some circumstances, viewers enhance their viewing experience by preserving the 'liveness' (for example, by avoiding news bulletins on radio about a sporting event which they intend viewing as a delayed telecast—it's 'live' to me).

- *Edited*—non-fictional television such as news stories within the evening bulletin, or documentaries; these may use 'stand-ups' to indicate 'presentness'; or cover jump cuts in the interviews by cutaways to the journalist ('noddies') but despite this the viewer almost certainly does not believe them to be live.

- *Fiction*—programs that have been recorded live before an audience such as sitcoms, followed by most forms of fiction such as series or soap operas, which in today's television are no longer broadcast live. Films have minimal 'liveness'.

In this typology, reality soap programs would appear to fall somewhere between *edited* and *fiction*. The possibility of truly live broadcasts barely exists in most of these shows because the participants tend to spend a great deal of their time waiting around for something exciting to happen. In order to make this interesting for a television audience the editors must take on a role similar to that played by the writers of a fictional series. They construct a narrative from the raw material that both compresses time and highlights the inter-relationships between members of the 'cast'. The application of new editing technologies to this process should not go without comment. The sheer volume of material generated by these shows could not be cut (and presumably re-cut in the light of later events) without the speed and flexibility offered by nonlinear computer-based editing systems, which became a common feature of the television industry only in the mid to late 1990s.

However, the game show element injects a kind of uncertainty which is reminiscent of live television. The audience is aware that non-actors are competing in situations that are unscripted, where the outcomes have not been predetermined by the producers. This element of uncertainty provides a sensation of 'immediacy', by allowing audiences to have the expectation that 'anything might happen'—one of the characteristics of live television. The elimination of contestants is a common feature, and the producers go to inordinate lengths to ensure that audiences do not know in advance of viewing who wins or loses, recognizing that uncertainty of outcome (as with most game shows or sports events) is a key element of viewing pleasure. Occasionally the reality soaps become fully live, as in *Big Brother* when the audience votes on who should be evicted, or the final episode of *Survivor II* in which the winner was revealed before a studio audience in Los Angeles. In this latter event the cast transmogrified into Barbie dolls sitting around a *Flinstones*-like recreation of the Outback Tribal Council area. Although live, it was a truly bizarre discontinuity which succeeded in being more unreal than the earlier part of the show that had been produced some weeks previously.

The ratings success of these shows (the final episode of *Survivor I* attracted in excess of 50 million viewers in America) would also indicate that viewers are choosing to consume them as if live, and once the outcome of the contest is known it seems that this kind of programming is apparently not attractive to audiences the second time around:

> 'Reality shows have a short shelf life,' one programr notes, 'they just don't seem to sell well in syndication.' Another comments that watching Reali-TV reruns is like 'reading yesterday's news.'[25]

Conclusion

Television is combining modern, lightweight digital cameras with a newfound ability to process high volumes of wild footage using non-linear techniques to produce a new form of entertainment, which has variously been described as 'reality soap' and 'psycho-games'. Instead of actors following scripts in a studio, audiences can see people very like themselves plotting and scheming for advantage in any setting imaginable. The story is driven by a game show element which forces people into situations where conflict is inevitable. The audience consumes these shows in much the same way as the live telecast of a sporting event because uncertainty is a key part of the viewing experience. However, the focus on inter-relationships between the contestants brings in elements more usually found in fiction, and suggests that this deepening of the 'live' experience resulting from a crossover between genres might account for the extraordinary successes these shows appear to have achieved. In this respect, 'reality soap' seems to hark back to the very early years of 'live' television when 'anything might happen'—and sometimes did.

An earlier version of this article appeared online at www.mediaculture.org.au/reviews/ features/realitytv/ministryc.html

Lawrence Hill is a postgraduate student in Communications at Edith Cowan University. Robyn Quin is the Professor of Media Studies at Edith Cowan University.

Endnotes

1. A. A. James, 'Reality Shows Global Impact. Sports Keeps Pace as Genre Fave', Available at www. variety.com, 2001.
2. David Lawrence, 'New on the Air: Fall 2000 TV Programming Trends', available at www.eurodatatv.com, 2001.
3. Mark Poster, *The Second Media Age,* Polity Press, Cambridge, 1995.
4. R. Kilborn, 'How Real Can You Get? Recent Developments in 'Reality' Television', in *European Journal of Communication* 9(4), 1994, p. 241.
5. ibid., p. 437.
6. ibid., p. 432.
7. C. Raphael, 'Political Economy of Reali-TV.' *Jump Cut* (41), 1997, pp. 102-109.
8. ibid., p. 105.
9. Kilborn, op. cit., p. 423.
10. J. Hassard, *Representing Reality: Cinema Verité,* Thousand Oaks, London, 1998.
11. ibid., p. 44.
12. ibid., p. 61.
13. 'Original Survivors Speak Out', Available at www.cbsnews.com, 2001.
14. *Survivor: The Australian Outback,* available at www.cbs.com

15. I. Ang, *Watching Dallas: Soap Opera and the Melodramatic Imagination*, Methuen, London, 1985, p. 47.

16. A. Donahue and T. Swanson, 'Co-op Effort Ties Web sites to Reality Shows', Available at www.variety.com, 2001.

17. C. Schultz, 'Survey: *Survivor*, a big hit for CBS.com', available at www.cnn.com, 2001.

18. G. Hillard, '*Survivor*!: Questioning Candidates—and the Game', available at cnn.com, 2000.

19. L. L. Hunter, 'After *Survivor*: A Reality TV Check', available at www.cnn.com, 2001.

20. Hillard, op.cit, p. 2.

21. G. Baxter, *Psychology: Obedience to Authority*, University of Otago, Dunedin, 2001, p. 4.

22. S. Romei, 'Brain-eating Censors Miss the Main Course', in *The Australian*, Perth, 2001, p. 17.

23. A. Newton, 'Survivor's Deadly Fear', in *The Sunday Times*. Perth, 2001, p. 35.

24. J. Bourdon, 'Live Television Is Still Alive: On Television as an Unfulfilled Promise', in *Media, Culture & Society* 22(5): p. 553.

25. C. Raphael, 'Political Economy of Reali-TV', in *Jump Cut* (41): p. 109.

Mom & Pop Culture: The Reality of Reality TV Parenting

By Avital Norman Nathman
Bitch, December 15, 2011

Okay, I'll admit it. I have a (probably somewhat unhealthy) addiction to reality television. It started in the mid '90s with MTV's *The Real World*, and only grew as shows like *Survivor, Big Brother* and almost every single thing on TLC appeared.

I've done my best to get my reality TV habit under control, and I mostly just watch shows like *Top Chef, The Voice*, and the occasional *Real Housewives of Somewhere Fancy*. However, that doesn't mean I'm immune to or unaware of the vast amount of reality television shows that supposedly depict "real" families. Shows like *Wife Swap, Supernanny*, and *Kate Plus 8*, have come and gone, only to be replaced with the newest incarnations: *Teen Mom, Toddlers & Tiaras, Sister Wives, Dance Moms, 19 Kids and Counting*, my "beloved" *Real Housewives*, and more.

I understand that reality television has to have some sort of "hook" to get you, the viewer, interested enough to stick around. For the most part, that's usually drama. Even when shows are about parenting, it's not the day-to-day rhythm that gets airtime, but rather the sensational, unbelievable, and usually questionable parenting decisions that take center stage.

So...is that really the "reality" of parenting?

I think we all know that it's not. The types of families being broadcast are hardly representative of the diversity of families in our country. These shows focus mostly on middle-class, white, heteronormative families. Very rarely will you see a non-white family (although to their credit, TLC is starting to test those waters with their new show, *All American Muslim*, and have defended it despite the controversy over various sponsors pulling their ads). LGBT people are seldom visible, or else are presented as the token family member inserted to create drama or comedic relief. Disability is only talked about when it serves as a plot point to stir up more drama, or to exploit somebody, rather than as a day-to-day reality for many people. Poverty is rarely explored, and in fact, these shows often promote consumerism. (For more on reality television and the wealth/poverty dichotomy, check out Gretchen Sisson's current guest blog series, The 99%.)

So what are these family shows portraying? Mostly they're perpetuating negative stereotypes and poor examples of parenting. I highly doubt the intention of any of these shows is to instigate a dialogue about what healthy parenting looks like. Rather, they capitalize on creating situations that usually turn out humiliating for the parents and kids alike.

From *Bitch* (15 Dec. 2011). Copyright © 2011 by Bitch Publications. Reprinted with permission. All rights reserved.

What it comes down to is that the majority of these shows are less about real situations, and more about stringing together manufactured and sensationalized moments of conflict. They're not showing real moments in parenting, just like they're not actually showing "real" families. While you can find some shows that don't follow these "rules" (i.e. *Sister Wives* and *19 Kids And Counting*), most are actually comprised of people using reality television as their first step in making entertainment their career.

Many of the Real Housewives have gone on to launch jewelry/clothing lines, write books, record "music," or sell alcohol. Eden Wood dropped out of *Toddlers & Tiaras* once she found fame, appearing on numerous talk shows and making her own music videos.

> **These shows hardly skim the surface of reality. Instead, they're made up of people who are willing to put their families and their problems (whether real or contrived) on display. What does this say, not only about them, but about a country that tunes in week after week, allowing these shows (and their participants) to be a part of a multimillion dollar enterprise?**

These shows hardly skim the surface of reality. Instead, they're made up of people who are willing to put their families and their problems (whether real or contrived) on display. What does this say, not only about them, but about a country that tunes in week after week, allowing these shows (and their participants) to be a part of a multimillion dollar enterprise?

In the backbiting *The Real Housewives of Orange County*, parenting is not off limits. One of the women, Lynne, is constantly harangued for her parenting skills (or lack there of in the eyes of the other OC housewives). Perhaps Lynne should serve as a cautionary tale, but there seem to be plenty of those...where are the "success" stories when it comes to parenting on reality TV?

A fairly new trend in reality TV focuses on parents (almost always moms) whose kids are involved in pageants or dance. Shows like *Toddlers & Tiaras* and *Dance Moms* have come under fire for promoting the sexualization of young girls, yet they continue to be produced, with record high audiences tuning in to watch. These shows end up focusing more on the drama and scandalous behind-the-scenes footage than on the actual activity the kids are performing.

In [one] *Dance Moms* clip, two mothers get into a nasty argument over dance costumes. While it starts off away from the dancers, it continues in front of them as well. The girls hear their moms flinging insults (about the kids!), and nobody seems to have the sense to take the fight away from impressionable ears. By the end of the fight, one young girl, Brooke, looks absolutely crestfallen and like she has no interest in going on to compete. She makes the point later that she knows her dancing was impacted by the costume-related argument.

The sad fact is that both of these clips pretty much exemplify how most families are portrayed by reality television. Between very occasional glimpses into happy, "normal" times, it is the loud arguing, crying, and tantrums that get the most screen time.

As somebody who rarely airs her own "dirty laundry" in anything that could be deemed a public forum, I have a hard time wrapping my head around folks who allow cameras into their homes to film theirs. These shows continue to push not only tired stereotypes about moms and families, but questionable parenting practices in general.

Maybe one day there will be a true reality show about parenting. It won't be all that glamorous, that's for sure. It might show a parent (and not necessarily the mom!) scrambling to make breakfast for everyone while simultaneously getting ready for work. Perhaps the big argument of the day revolves around who will take the trash out, or whether ice cream is an acceptable alternative for dinner. Maybe there's a soccer practice or band rehearsal, but not one where the kids are decked out in make up, wigs, spray tans, or questionable costumes.

Then again, would anyone tune in to watch that?

Reality TV Isn't Real, and Why Viewers Don't Care

By Gavin Polone
NYMag.com, July 19, 2012

Is reality real? René Descartes, *The Matrix,* and *Inception* have theorized that we can't know if what we are experiencing is fake or not. But assuming that I'm not just a brain in a vat with electrodes stimulating my synapses and creating the illusion of this world, I can make at least one claim with great certainty: Reality *TV* is pretty fake. It isn't as fake as scripted TV, but a viewer understands that a show like *The Walking Dead* isn't a documentary—even if I wish it were. The big question is one of degree: When does "producing" a reality show cross the line into the territory of fabricating character, plot, and incident as one would with a scripted show? And does the distinction even matter?

While watching June's season finale of *The Real Housewives of Orange County,* my experience in TV production told me that much of what went on during the fight-filled episode *had* to have been staged. The camera angles were too planned, the plot was too linear, the interpersonal drama too heightened. It was too unbelievably narratively convenient that Vicki and Tamara would erupt like volcanoes at the very end of the season. I called a top executive at a network with several hit docu-soaps to suggest that shows like *RHOC* are becoming too manipulated to be thought of as "reality." But she disagreed, saying that reality arcs that feel like scripted arcs aren't the producers' doing ... at least not entirely. "The reality characters *self-produce,* knowing that they need to be a heightened version of themselves," she said. "They end up over-reacting. I can't tell somebody to do things, but we know that we're putting two people together that will have conflict. Sometimes we'll leak information to them [meaning things each character wouldn't know that the other characters said or did, which may instigate a conflict] but we won't tell them what to do." When I pressed her on the practice of doing "pickups"—scenes shot after the fact, re-creating something that may have happened off-camera and placing them within the body of the show, as if they were shot contemporaneously with the other scenes—she explained that her producers won't "re-create a fight but they can re-create the setup for a fight." I asked her what she thought was going too far when it came to "producing" a scene, and she said, "One time a producer [on one of her shows] suggested to a character that he propose to his girlfriend [even though he had not previously considered doing so] and we said, 'No'! We thought it was ridiculous. If you watch *The Bachelor,* I think they are bullied into proposing. That's too far."

From *NYMAG*.com (19 July 2012). Copyright © 2012 by New York Magazine. Reprinted with permission. All rights reserved.

I went to another long-time reality producer with much experience working on multiple high-profile shows, who seemed chagrined at how the genre has been increasingly molded by producers and networks. She acknowledged that scenes in most shows are overmanipulated, explaining that "at the beginning of my career, we followed a true 'cinema verite' code and we truly let situations play out authentically ... we would never re-

> *"One time a producer [on one of her shows] suggested to a character that he propose to his girlfriend [even though he had not previously considered doing so] and we said, 'No'! We thought it was ridiculous. If you watch* **The Bachelor, I think they are bullied into proposing. That's too far."**

shoot a conversation for a second camera angle or have a couple reinvent a fight ... But these days, that would get a producer fired off a show. Additionally, we had significantly more time to produce shows ... now networks want higher drama on lesser budgets. The fact is, producers must ensure that each episode has some kind of high-level, promo-worthy drama or it will be perceived that they simply did not do their job." And, like the network executive, this producer sees how savvy the reality stars have become about delivering the needed performance. "A great cast absolutely knows that the bar is high for drama on TV," she says. "They, too, watch their smug network execs watching monitors behind the camera and they know that they better deliver lest they be uninvited back for the following season—gasp!—and never have an *US Weekly* cover again." Though she certainly seemed dismayed by the increased falseness with these shows, she also felt that "as a producer, if I found out that someone was faking their drug addiction to get on *Intervention* (or pregnancy for *Teen Mom*), I'd find that appalling and I'd be highly suspicious of not only the series but of the producers as well. However, if the Kardashians or the *Jersey Shore* cast were lying about someone they slept with or some fight they had ... I'm not sure I'd care (as a producer or viewer)."

When I was a small boy, I used to love watching professional wrestling, and I remember clearly the day my grandmother told me that this "sport"—which I thought was as legitimately competitive as other sports I watched on TV, like baseball and tennis—was in fact fake. I was crushed. More important, I stopped watching it then and there, not in protest but rather because there didn't seem to be a point to it if the situations were completely contrived and the outcome preplanned. I think that is where the line ends up for me. When it was recently revealed that participants on HGTV's *House Hunters* had already purchased one of the homes from which they were supposedly choosing and the other two possibilities were just their friends' houses and weren't for sale, I would have thought it would affect the perspective of the series' viewers in the same way I was affected when my grandmother cruelly spilled the beans about my favorite masked wrestler. And yet, the ratings didn't change after this news; that could mean most regular viewers never heard about it or, of course, that they just don't care. Maybe they would have a more negative response if there were a disclaimer at the top of the show stating that the events that follow are not real and have been staged to create drama. But maybe they would just shrug and go back to looking at people compare square footage.

I talked to someone with inside knowledge of Showtime's *Gigolos*, a "reality show" billed as "an uncensored look into the personal and professional lives of five hot guys in Vegas who like to hang out, have fun and get girls, but in their case they get paid for it." My source recounted similar stories about pickups being shot and producers suggesting ideas to the cast, but also noted that the women on the show aren't regular clients of the gigolos as the viewers are led to believe; the producers find women willing to have sex with these guys on-camera and pay them $300 to do it, because actual women who hire male prostitutes want to keep it discreet. So, in a show purported to be about men who are paid by women to have sex, the producers are actually paying women to have sex with men whom the producers are also paying. (Showtime did not respond to a request for comment.) But while I was surprised by this, I don't think the revelation would undermine *Gigolos* viewers' interest; much like those who watch *House Hunters* may be more interested in house porn than veracity, people watch *Gigolos* for the sex, not a real insight into male prostitution. I guess the answer to the question of whether or not it matters that reality TV is fake or real depends on why the viewer is watching the show. If you just want to vicariously snoop around a bunch of different houses, it doesn't matter if the people you're following aren't really in the market to buy a home; and if you're watching a show to see attractive people have sex, it doesn't really matter who's paying whom to copulate. And, most certainly, if you find it funny or interesting to watch a couple of drunk, vapid, rich women who have had a lot of freaky plastic surgery yell at each other at a social gathering, you'll still enjoy *The Real Housewives of Orange County*, no matter how "produced" the show has been.

5

Reality Identities

(© RD/Pluviose/Retna Ltd./Corbis)

The Push Girls attend the New York premiere of IFC's *Peace, Love and Misunderstanding* at the Museum of Modern Art In New York City on June 4, 2012.

We Are What We Watch

The concepts of identity and reality are both surrounded by the indeterminate issues of subjectivity and objectivity. Identity, for example, is not unequivocal, but open to interpretation and based on an individual's personal feelings, perspectives, and prejudices. For the purposes of this [essay], identity has a double sense: It pertains to a person's unique characteristics and sense of self, and it involves social categories, such as race, gender, and sexual orientation.

The construction of both personal and social identity is complex and influenced by a myriad of factors. A person's unique characteristics, for example, are influenced by his or her life experiences, family, peers, and social attributes such as religion and race. Likewise, social identity is composed of a particular group's experiences in society and their position in the larger culture. African American identity, for example, is influenced by the deep-rooted racial tensions in American society.

The issue of identity has become more complicated and amorphous in today's media-saturated society. The media, in other words, has become omnipresent in our culture, and it therefore has a profound impact on our identity. Television is the medium that most pervades our society. According to Nielson Company, approximately 96 percent of American homes have at least one television, and the average person spends 34 hours per week watching TV. This extensive exposure to television has a direct effect on our behavior, our perception of social norms, and the construction of our individual identities and the identities of various social groups.

In recent years, the phenomenon of reality television has added another layer of complexity to the construction of identity. Similar to conventional television shows, reality television is not "real" in that it is, to some extent, scripted—producers and editors mold and choreograph a reality show to appeal to a certain audience. Techniques such as voiceovers, soundtracks, and fly-on-the-wall recording all play a pivotal role in captivating, and, more importantly, entertaining an audience, which is the ultimate goal of most television programs. But reality television is not just mindless entertainment: It does reflect aspects of our reality and culture. In the process of exposing viewers to aspects of culture, reality TV is reinforcing, re-creating, and revealing social identities in today's society. The reality television programs we watch, for example, reinforce stereotypes of social groups and influence how society identifies a specific group.

It is difficult to talk about reality television without mentioning postmodern theories about media and its effect on reality and identity. Jean Baudrillard, a French sociologist and philosopher, theorized that the proliferation of media and images in our society has blurred the distinction between symbols (which he called simulacra) and reality. The omnipresent saturation of images, in other words, is replacing reality with a simulated reality. Baudrillard argued that this hyper-reality is becoming indistinguishable from actual reality. Nothing illustrates this theory better than reality television: It has combined real life with television, therefore merging reality with an artificial depiction of reality. When we watch reality television we become de-centered as actual reality merges with the reality that we experience while watching reality television. These reality programs reflect back on us our own reality, in other words, and therefore have a profound impact on our identity. Baudrillard said it best: "You no longer watch TV, it is TV that watches you (live)."

Before the introduction of reality TV, certain social groups, such as homosexuals, suffered the absence of identity—they were invisible in society and nonexistent in popular culture. But reality television shows, such as *The Real World*, *Project Runway*, and *The Amazing Race,* have regularly included homosexual cast members; consequently, openly gay people were introduced into the mainstream. Since its debut as one of the first reality TV shows in 2000, *The Real World* has included openly gay men and women who have defied conventional stereotypes of homosexuality and represented a diversity of human behavior. This milestone in television has established a more "human" and accurate identity for homosexuals, a social group that was once abstract and defined by preconceived notions of homosexuality.

A decade ago, an all-gay reality television show would not have been acceptable, but the gradual exposure of homosexuality in reality TV has led to shows such as *The A-List* and *RuPaul's Drag Race*, which have all-gay casts. The increased visibility of homosexuality on reality TV reflects the growing acceptance of homosexual identity in American culture, evidenced by the legalization of gay marriage in some states and the repeal of the "don't ask, don't tell" policy on gays in the military on September 20, 2011.

The Real World, however, does not only concern itself with homosexual identity—it deals explicitly with a cast of young people (both gay and straight) who are in the process of entering adulthood and establishing their identities. Likewise, the audience watching MTV's *The Real World* is primarily young and in a similar position. In the process of observing how others act in this situation, young viewers are exposed to a variety of identities from which they can draw and with which they can experiment as they develop their own sense of self. This is not to say that a young person's identity is solely constructed by watching reality television; it's not. Identity is complex and influenced by a number of factors, but reality television is part of the equation for those who watch it. When a teenager or young adult observes the behavior of others and how they interact in social situations, their sense of self will be influenced, because they will begin to adopt behaviors with which they identify. A gay teenager, for example, who watches an adult homosexual character on *Project Runway* or *The Real Housewives* may imitate the observed characteristics that he or she finds agreeable.

Other social groups whose identities are reflected on and therefore to some extent shaped by reality TV include African Americans, Muslims, people with disabilities, and others. Television has historically been predominately white, with African Americans not well represented on screen. If an African American character did appear on TV, they were placed in menial and often comic roles. Television has perpetuated other negative African American stereotypes: They have been depicted as "other"—criminal, unintelligent, impoverished, and invariably removed from white society.

Fortunately, the quality and quantity of African American characters on television has increased dramatically in the last decade, and reality television has contributed significantly to this advancement. An African American audience watching *The Real Housewives of Atlanta*, for example, are exposed to high-society African Americans who are not only wealthy, but have achieved celebrity status. Nene Leaks, the African American star of *The Real Housewives of Atlanta*, is the highest-paid housewife in the franchise, earning $750,000 per season. This popular reality show—and others like it, such as *Run's House*—have played a part in establishing an African American identity that defies conventional stereotypes by highlighting professional, upper-class, and successful African Americans.

American Muslims are also benefitting from reality television. *All American Muslim* is a new reality show that is helping to change the identity of American Muslims. Following 9/11, the image of American Muslims became, to some extent, synonymous with terrorism and "the enemy." This has been reinforced with their portrayal in the media as anti-American, dangerous, and extremist. Needless to say, their negative depiction has resulted in widespread discrimination. But *All-American Muslim* has contributed to a realistic and positive depiction of Muslims as devoted and peaceful Americans.

Not all reality shows, however, reinforce positive stereotypes. Many regard *Jersey Shore*, for example, as depicting Italian Americans and the residents of New Jersey in a negative light. This is an example of how a reality show can prey on preexisting identities and stereotypes and build a highly successful reality show around them. Since its debut on MTV in December of 2009, *Jersey Shore* has become the most-viewed show in the network's history—setting an MTV record with 8.87 million viewers in a single episode. The show was heavily criticized, however, and New Jersey Governor Chris Christie accused it of perpetuating a negative image of New Jersey. Moreover, UNICO, a service organization for Italian Americans, demanded the show's termination for spreading negative stereotypes that damage the Italian American identity. The opposition to *Jersey Shore* speaks to the powerful effect reality TV has on identity in the real world, for better or for worse.

In 2000, reality shows were scarce, but in the second decade of the century they are arguably the most popular programs on television. *American Idol*, for example, is one of the most-watched television shows on the air, with an average of 30 million viewers tuning in to the season finale—making it second only to the Super Bowl. On the surface, *American Idol* appears to be a lucrative singing competition with the sole intention of producing a "star" who will go on to commercial success. While this is not untrue, *Idol* is also significant in that it produces "idols" who take on an identity that resonates with the American Dream, a concept that lies at the core of American identity. This also speaks to the American belief that if you don't like your identity and who you are, you can change it and achieve success—you can achieve the American Dream.

Furthermore, in addition to appealing to different musical genres, the contestants on *American Idol* reflect the multicultural identity of America: The show specifically appeals to a broad audience by including a diverse cast of different racial, regional, and religious backgrounds. The show establishes America's identity as a melting pot and appeals to an audience composed of numerous identity groups. As a result of this mass appeal, *Idol* is the most relatable and, therefore, popular show on television. Its success has produced numerous spinoffs, including *The X-Factor*, *America's Got Talent*, and *The Voice*.

Another interesting aspect of identity is that it is often the product of rehearsal and performance. The more you practice a certain behavior or ideology, in other words, the more likely that it will become a part of your identity and ingrained behavior. This theory links identity to repeated actions that we learn, both consciously and unconsciously, from watching and imitating others. The behavior we acquire from others in our environment is then reinforced by means of social performance, or role-playing. This philosophy also applies to reality television: The more you watch a certain behavior on the screen, the more likely you will be to adopt that behavior in real life. Watching reality television, therefore, is not unlike observing other people in your environment and copying their behaviors and social characteristics, thus incorporating these traits into your own social performance—resulting in the formation of an "identity."

There is a reality show for almost every demographic and identity group. The success of these shows is due not only to their entertainment factor and the intrigues of voyeurism, but to their appeal to identity groups and to the public fascination with popular culture. When a person watches a reality show, he or she probably realizes that it is not "real," and is left to differentiate between what is real and what is a simulacrum, to use Baudrillard's term. Regardless of its authenticity, reality television's power to influence the position of social identities in today's society is becoming increasingly clear, leading to the conclusion that, to a significant extent, we are what we watch.

Reality TV Finally Gets Personal with Gay Men Again

By Jamie Maurer
AFTERELTON, December 16, 2010

Bravo's *Boy Meets Boy* was ahead of its time. The 2003 dating reality show, which had confirmed bachelor James Getzlaff choose between a bevy of available men (some of whom were secretly straight), was one of the first shows specifically geared towards the personal and romantic lives of gay men.

Alas, *BMB* didn't exactly burn up the airwaves and its first season was its one and only. Nor did it set off a stampede of similarly themed programming.

Nonetheless, reality TV has always had at least a hint of gay. Even the first reality show, *An American Family*, also gave us Lance Loud, the first openly gay person on television, and *Queer Eye for the Straight Guy*, the flagship that led Bravo into a new age of gayness and popularity, not only helped make gay judges and "experts" a staple of competitive reality TV, but put straight and gay men together in a way never seen before.

But it's been rare to see a show that gives us a deep and personal look into the lives of gay men themselves. After *Boy Meets Boy* went off the air, the only dating shows that gay men tended to appear on were about finding love for heterosexuals. Fox's 2004 show, *Playing it Straight* featured a mix of straight men and gay men all trying to convince a single woman they were all straight (and only lasted three episodes), while 2007's *Gay, Straight or Taken?* featured a gay man, a single straight man, and a partnered straight man all trying to fool a single woman into picking one of them for a date.

But reality shows that featured gay and bisexual men as more than just roadblocks to heterosexual love or as supporting players in someone else's story have been harder to find. The always gay-friendly MTV provided one of the rare exceptions with their dating show *Next*, which featured gay and straight singles seeking love via a rapid fire series of five dates.

However, as gay people on most kinds of reality shows have gradually become so commonplace as to not even be noteworthy, a new trend in reality TV has begun to develop: shows specifically about gay and bisexual men. No longer are the most visible gay people solely contestants on *The Amazing Race* and *Project Runway*, or experts passing judgment from the sidelines.

It began with small strides on existing mainstream shows. *Project Runway* gave us slightly deeper portrayals of gay contestants, like when Jack Mackenroth revealed

From *AFTERELTON* (16 Dec. 2012). Copyright © 2010 by AFTERELTON. Reprinted with permission. All rights reserved.

his HIV-positive status. Frequent appearances by Jay Manuel and J. Alexander on *America's Next Top Model* and Bruno Tonioli of *Dancing With the Stars* made audiences increasingly comfortable with gay men on TV.

This eventually evolved into shows where gays became the main event. One of the first to put a gay man front and center was Bravo's *Flipping Out,* which features Jeff Lewis and started airing in 2007. Meanwhile, 2009 saw Logo [AFTERELTON's], debut *RuPaul's Drag Race,* which featured all gay men and gave a fair bit of time to their personal lives.

And in 2010 the trend of reality programming actually about gay and bisexual men seems to be accelerating with a veritable barrage of gay-focused reality shows, like *Project Runway* spin-off *On the Road with Austin and Santino* and Logo's *Real Housewives* facsimile *The A-List: New York.* And word is that Bravo, the network that started the *Real Housewives* genre, has its own gay *Housewives* program in the works.

> **However, as gay people on most kinds of reality shows have gradually become so commonplace as to not even be noteworthy, a new trend in reality TV has begun to develop: shows specifically about gay and bisexual men. No longer are the most visible gay people solely contestants on The Amazing Race and Project Runway, or experts passing judgment from the sidelines.**

Even networks with much less history of specifically targeting gay audiences have gotten in on the action. Planet Green, a channel dedicated to environmental issues, introduced us to *The Fabulous Beekman Boys* with both a series about the couple and a Christmas special airing this month. And the Sundance Channel launched *Be Good Johnny Weir* earlier this year and just this month premiered *Girls Who Like Boys Who Like Boys* about gay men and their best female friends.

All of these shows are giving gay and straight audiences a look into the lives of gay men that go far beyond what we see in most reality shows. Folks who watched *The Fabulous Beekman Boys* got a close up look at Josh Kilmer-Purcell and Brent Ridge, a gay couple who clearly love each other, but also have a fractious relationship.

Meanwhile, *Girls Who Like Boys* features one gay man struggling to come out and integrate into the gay community (Sahil), another who is determined to become a dad (Nathan) and a third who is getting married to his partner (Joel). And *Be Good Johnny Weir* chronicled the very complicated life of the Olympic skater as he dealt with the disappointment of another Olympic failure.

Why is American reality TV suddenly so interested in the actual lives of us gays? This might be wishful thinking, but the increasing popularity of "gay reality" might just be a positive sign that American culture is truly beginning to think of gay people as being part of reality. Not that reality shows have much to do with reality in the first place. But they do have a great deal to do with our culture.

As ridiculous as it might sound, even shows like *The A-List* might actually be a sign that Americans are becoming more tolerant, more accepting, and just all-around better people.

At least, that's what I keep telling myself.

Are Reality Television Shows Good for Black America?

By John B. Landers
Regal Magazine, October 8, 2009

Most television aficionados will tell you that reality television shows started around 2000. The fact is that reality television shows have been around in some form since the invention of the media. It is television programming that is based on the lives of people who live out their real-life dramas, emotional issues and humorous circumstances in front of a television viewing audience. Many of the situations occur naturally; however, there are some circumstances that are scripted.

Come on, admit it. How many times have you gone channel surfing only to end up watching one of these programs? If only to satisfy your curiosity, and see what all the fuss is about, you settle in to watch, all the while you're kicking yourself as you partake in the latest such classless rubbish. In the eyes of many critics, Black and White, most of the present day reality television shows follow the same formula as many Black televisions shows beginning with *Amos and Andy* in the early 1950s.

In the overwhelming majority of these reality television shows, Blacks are often portrayed as monolithic, simple-minded, calculating criminals. In most instances, there is an obvious lack of intelligence or the ability to think critically. Besides butchering the English language, they are completely devoid of any semblance of morals and compassion, and, they lacked the cultural traditions or significance.

One thing you could count on is that they are very good at singing, have excellent rhythm, can run fast while bouncing a ball. Some of the reality television shows targeted toward African Americans have included: *Being Bobby Brown*, VH1's *Flavor of Love*, *Real Chance at Love*, *College Hill* and *Frankie & Neffe*.

Debuting in 2005, *Being Bobby Brown* was billed as a "documentary-style production on the private lives of R&B star Bobby Brown and his wife Whitney Houston." The show seemed to embody all of the stereotypical attributes mentioned earlier, even taking some elements to a new level. This was obviously a family unit that was dysfunctional for the entire world to see. The show jettisoned this famous couple to the front of the pack as a laughing stock around the globe.

One of the most controversial reality television shows was *Flavor of Love,* which started its first season in 2005. The show featured rapper Flavor Flav, of the music group Public Enemy, who spent three (profitable) seasons looking for love. There was Flavor Flav in all his glory, his gold grill, a gigantic clock hanging from a gold chain around his neck and the rainbow color outfits, which included a signature top

From *Regal Magazine* (8 Oct. 2009). Copyright © 2009 by *Regal Magazine*. Reprinted with permission. All rights reserved.

hat and cane. Then there were the women, mostly Black, but also White, Latino and Asian females. The women, for the most part, were loud, loose and sassy. One critic, who was obviously a fan of the show, wrote that "young girls watching the show will be able to relate to at least one of Flav's potential love interests."

Another one of the dating-related reality television shows, *Real Chance at Love*, revolved around two brothers, named Real and Chance, who were searching for their own love interests. The theme operated along the same lines as *Flavor of Love*. The actual and the contrived situations were fairly predictable.

College Hill is one of the reality television shows that is produced by Black Entertainment Television (BET) and Tracey Edmonds. It revolves around the lives of nine to 10 college students who live together for a semester while attending historically Black colleges. It shows various dynamics of young Black adults all living together, which include petty arguments, individual struggles and giving back to the community.

Frankie & Neffe is the show based on the lives of the mother and sister of singer Keyshia Cole. Her successful show (in terms of ratings), *The Way It Is*, was not renewed for a second season. So someone saw fit to spin-off a show for Keyshia's mom and big sister.

> *There seems to be a concerted effort to portray a fairly functional Black family with a loving father and mother who nurture and provide for their family. The show actually has many positive attributes.*

For those of you who are not familiar with their backgrounds, Frankie, Keyshia's mother, is trying to get her life back together after spending three years in jail for drug use.

Neffe is the single mother of five kids and is desperately trying to mend her relationship with her mother. As was the case in Keyshia's show, the two will continue to play off of their dysfunctional relationship to bring in the ratings. *Frankie & Neffe* made its debut on BET in August 2009. In an interview with the *Atlanta Constitution*, James Dubose, the show's executive producer said: "This will show their growth and independence in their personal lives."

Not all the Black reality television shows are full of the negative stereotypes. *Run's House* is based on the family of Reverend Run, of the ground-breaking rap group RUN-DMC. The reverend is the brother of music mogul Russell Simmons. The show won a 2008 NAACP Image Award for Outstanding Reality Series. There seems to be a concerted effort to portray a fairly functional Black family with a loving father and mother who nurture and provide for their family. The show actually has many positive attributes.

There is also the reality television show featuring former NFL star Deion and his wife Pilar Sanders, *Deion & Pilar Sanders: Prime Time Love*. Deion explains his show like this: "We're doing this, really, to substantiate the claim that there are many African American families that live properly and (are) not necessarily argumentative, in disarray and total chaos." This is indeed a twist from the usual plot.

Although the latter two reality television shows make a sincere effort to bring positive energy to this media, the fact is that the audience is watching people and families with lifestyles and challenges vastly different from their own lives. For example, Reverend Run drives his young children to school in a Rolls Royce. Deion and Pilar resides in a 40,000 square foot home on 112 acres of land.

When the stars of many of these reality television shows speak about their productions, the standard line seems to go something like this: "I created the show because I want to help other people so they won't have to go down the same road and make the same mistakes I did." While there may be a small element of truth to the statement, you rarely hear them mention the fact that it's an avenue to market their brand and a way to rake in a lot of money. That brings us to the facts about television reality shows and television in general: There is an overwhelming amount of data that has proven that watching too much television has negative consequences.

Initiative Media North America reports that African Americans watched almost 22 hours more television per week than other households in the United States. A Yale University study, one of hundreds conducted, suggested that Black kids, from family with incomes of more than $75,000 per year, were less likely to succeed academically due to watching more TV than White students in comparable households.

The evidence continues to mount regarding the direct connection between watching television and the level of violence among African American kids and young adults. Columbia University Medical School conducted a 17-year study that concluded that males who watched "significant" amounts of television increased the probability of violent behavior 16 to 116 percent. In this study, "significant" was defined as an hour or more each day. Black children watch more than five hours of television, on average, each day.

The health consequences of sitting and watching too much TV is also apparent. The Center for Disease Prevention and Control reports that watching a lot of television could lead to problems with obesity.

With the reams of reliable data on the effects of television, the question is not if the focus of many of reality television shows targeted toward Black viewers is harmful. The evidence clearly backs that assertion. The more appropriate question may be why that continues to be the case when the destructive capacity of television has been proven over and over. Someone once told me that many words and phrases that we take for granted are usually coded and have deeper levels of meaning and are only understood by a few, or the initiated. He took the word "television," and broke it down for me. This is what he got:

"TELL A VISION."

So what vision is the reality television shows our kids are watching telling them?

Reality Bites

By Max Berlinger
Out Magazine, September 25, 2012

When *The Real World* debuted on MTV in 1992, the premise was so simple yet promising, it's a wonder that it hadn't been done before. A blend of documentary and theater, the show promised to bring together seven strangers of different backgrounds and histories, and force them to live together while allowing cameras to capture the human spectacle, i.e. mudslinging. But an unforeseen byproduct emerged from the combination of *The Real World*'s immediate popularity and attempt at mass-market cinéma vérité: It acted as affable mediator between the gay community and the general population. It turned out that *The Real World* (and, well, the real world) were real gay.

The series' co-creator, Jonathan Murray, adapted the concept from the landmark 1973 PBS special *An American Family*, which featured Lance Loud, often credited as the first gay man to appear on television. "That had been a huge success," Murray, who is gay, says. "But nothing happened between when that aired and when we did *The Real World*." So when the network decided Murray's initial concept, a traditional soap opera, would prove too costly, he pitched the idea of an unscripted series shadowing a cast of unknowns as they transition to adulthood—and all the juicy messiness that goes along with it.

"From the beginning, the focus was diversity," Murray says. "It's about that crucial point when you're figuring out your identity, trying things on, and society doesn't judge you for it because you're young and that's what you're supposed to do."

Over the years—and 27 seasons—that has included 25 openly queer characters (an additional three have come out after doing the show). Gay cast members' stories often mirrored zeitgeisty touchstones: Pedro Zamora's struggle with AIDS (season three, 1994); Danny Roberts's (season nine, 2000) relationship with an active member of the military mid-DADT era; and Katelynn Cusanelli (season 21, 2009), who completed a sex-change operation shortly before filming.

"When *The Real World* began, the idea of reality television wasn't as bastardized as it's become today," says Jon Caramanica, a cultural critic at *The New York Times* who reports on the genre, among other topics. "It had a probative value that most people don't associate with reality television in 2012. Because they were operating outside of the accepted rules, MTV had a lot more flexibility in terms of what they could put out into the world."

From *OUT Magazine* (25 September 2012). Copyright © 2012 by Here Media, Inc. Reprinted with permission. All rights reserved.

Familiarizing audiences with LGBT issues served as a precursor to the gay-friendly bonhomie of today, and through the use of non-actors, queer cast members were tacitly allowed to defy, and at times reinforce, stereotypes under the guise of verisimilitude. Gay *Real World*ers, "haven't all been perfect people," Murray points out. "Some have been Machiavellian, or slightly villainous. We wanted to include a variety of gay people, as we did with straight people." On *The Real World*, sexuality in and of itself didn't necessarily make for engrossing television—drama and conflict still reigned supreme.

> *... we wanted to include a variety of gay people, as we did with straight people." On The Real World, sexuality in and of itself didn't necessarily make for engrossing television—drama and conflict still reigned supreme.*

Caramanica sees early seasons of the show as particularly influential. "A character like Pedro is almost transcendently important to the history of representation of gay people on television, and certainly to people living with AIDS," he says. "I think we've barely seen any characters, to this day, on mainstream network shows that are half as complex. We're living in an age of *Modern Family* where Cameron and Mitchell don't even kiss for the entire first season, and people talk about that being progress. Pedro and Sean (Zamora's partner during filming) were kissing on television and living these issues 20 years ago." So impactful was Zamora's story that when he passed away, President Bill Clinton released a public statement addressing his death, part of which read, "In his short life, Pedro educated and enlightened our nation. He taught all of us that AIDS is a disease with a human face and one that affects every American, indeed every citizen, of the world. And he taught people living with AIDS how to fight for their rights and live with dignity."

Those who lived inside the fishbowl can attest to the show's ability to shape public opinion. Former cast member Danny Roberts (he of the blurry-faced military boyfriend, Paul) says, "I'm 100% certain that the show influenced a lot of people, especially Generations X and Y and their viewpoints, on different social topics, especially toward the gay community. I think that being gay was an abstract concept to most people, but MTV showed that it was more human." In a serendipitous coup for the show's producers, Roberts had met Paul after being cast, and surprised the crew when he arrived for filming with news of an Army captain lover. "The surprises are better than anything you could have planned, anyway," Murray admits.

Today, reality television, recent seasons of *The Real World* included, has devolved into mostly lighthearted philistinism. Programs like *Jersey Shore* or Bravo's *Real Housewives* franchise—successors to *The Real World*—exist in a time where participants and viewers alike are conditioned to the tropes of the genre and agree to suspend disbelief and buy into feigned authenticity. Murray is reluctant to credit himself as a progenitor of the reality TV movement, despite it preceding the dual CBS ratings juggernauts *Big Brother* and *Survivor* by eight years. "That's not for me to judge," he says, but does concede that "we have seen a lot of what *The Real World* does reflected in television." However it has ultimately panned out, Murray's quixotic aspirations may be credited for the dissemination of queer culture into the mainstream. "It's sort of an old-fashioned, liberal idea, but Mary-Ellis Bunim (*The Real World* co-creator who died in 2004) and I believed strongly that if you live with people who are different than yourself, ultimately you'll find that you have more in common than not," he says. "That if we just get to know each other, maybe some of the craziness will go away." Just be sure the camera is rolling.

The Reality of the "All-American Muslim" Reality TV Show

By Wajahat Ali
The Guardian, November 17, 2011

The series about five American Muslim families can't represent all of us—any more than Jersey Shore *does Italian Americans*

For those constantly fretting about the inability of Muslims to integrate or assimilate into western culture, fret no more!

American Muslims finally have their own reality TV show—the Learning Channel's "All-American Muslim"—focusing on the lives of five American Muslim families in Dearborn, Michigan, who are predominantly Lebanese and Shiite. The show's premiere gave TLC huge ratings and made the show No. 2 in its time period. Mainstream critics have embraced the show citing it as "intimate and informative" and a "deeply intriguing, uncharacteristically thoughtful reality series."

Reality TV is the current zeitgeist of popular culture. Unlike the euro, it is the predominant cultural currency, whose value is skyrocketing. America is on a first-name basis with their cultural ambassadors: Snooki, Kate Plus 8, Paris, Ozzie and Kim. Could Shadia, the show's tattooed, country music-loving Lebanese American Muslim, with an Irish Catholic boyfriend, belong in the pantheon?

"[All American Muslim] is just a natural fit for us …We're always all about telling compelling stories about real families," says TLC's Alan Orstein, VP of production and development. But some have already taken deep offense to this "reality" show, which claims to portray the "real" lives of Muslims.

Within days of the show's premiere, the fear-mongering Islamphobia network complained the show is actually propaganda that promotes a "submission to Islam through the hijab" and "tries to make a religion which believes in world domination and the inferiority of women, seem normal. "The author of this article, posted on David Horowitz's inflammatory *Front Page Magazine*, also goes on to compare Muslims to Nazis: "Muslims are like us [Americans]; that's the problem. The Nazis were like us too. So were the Communists."

Apparently, TLC is a stealth-jihadist outfit with grand schemes to brainwash American women into burning their swimsuits and tank tops and replacing them with modest, traditional Islamic clothing as a gradual means towards converting them to Islam. I'll be waiting for their next reality TV show: "UV Radiation Fighters."

From *The Guardian* (17 November 2011). Copyright © 2011 by Guardian Newspapers Ltd. Reprinted with permission. All rights reserved.

Pamela Geller, founder of the shrill Atlas Shrugs blog and co-founder with blogger Robert Spencer of Stop Islamization of America, is convinced the show "is an attempt to manipulate Americans into ignoring the threat of jihad. "Who would have thought a reality TV show could have so much brainwashing potential? Instead of mounting violent campaigns, all our enemies needed to secure victory was to produce "The Real Housewives of al-Qaida."

If Geller, Spencer and Horowitz were producing their version of American Muslim reality, the episodes would focus on the families' radical stealth jihadist plots. Through eight episodes, they

> *The portrayal of Muslims living their daily lives is not only a welcome relief from the usual tawdry caricatures of Muslims as terrorists, extremists and taxi cab drivers, but it also helps defuse the deep-seated fears and bias that unfairly lumps 1.5 billion members of a faith in with the perverse criminal actions of a few.*

would attempt to turn McDonald's golden arches into minarets, transform California to Caliph-ornia, place a burqa over the Statute of Liberty, creep sharia into the Denny's breakfast menu, and spike the elementary school eggnog with sumac and lentils.

A "real Muslim" according to many is this anti-American, extremist, violent stereotype—an image often plastered over news headlines. This myth is unsurprising, perhaps, considering 60% of Americans say they don't know a Muslim. Furthermore, the No. 1 source of information about Muslims for American is the media, and often the images are negative. Yet, according to all the studies and evidence, the reality of American Muslims is that they are moderate, loyal to America, optimistic about America's future, in tune with American values, well-educated, and are the nation's most diverse religious community.

That being said, nearly half of American Muslims say they have faced discrimination. The FBI just announced anti-Muslim hate crimes have risen 50%. And a Republican presidential candidate with an alleged proclivity towards sexual harassment and unintentionally hilarious campaign videos has claimed a majority of Muslim Americans are extremists.

The portrayal of Muslims living their daily lives is not only a welcome relief from the usual tawdry caricatures of Muslims as terrorists, extremists and taxi cab drivers, but it also helps defuse the deep-seated fears and bias that unfairly lumps 1.5 billion members of a faith in with the perverse criminal actions of a few.

However, even American Muslims have voiced their criticisms with the show. The Twitterverse exploded (figuratively) with comments reflecting the diversity of the American Muslim opinions. Some said the show misleads with the title "All-American Muslim," since it solely focuses on one niche religious, ethnic community (Lebanese Shiite in Dearborn, Michigan) and leaves out the majority of American Muslim communities, such as African Americans, South Asians, Sunnis and those from the low-income middle class. Others, apparently, want their TV Muslims to be avatars of religious and moral perfection and complained about some of the characters' portrayal of Islam. (Shadia is a tattooed, partying rebel dating a white, Irish Catholic man who converts to Islam in order to marry her. Nina is a busty, dyed-blonde, opinionated business woman, with a penchant for tight dresses and ambitions to open her own club.)

Which only goes to show that representing Muslims and Islam in the mainstream is an utterly thankless job. The term "Muslim" is itself so politically and culturally loaded that it is impossible to escape controversy, no matter how trivial or manufactured. Since Muslims are a marginalized community with very few positive mainstream representations, audiences unfairly project onto these five families all their own insecurities, assumptions, fears, political ideologies, religious opinions, personal stories and other gratuitous baggage. So, if the characters do not 100% reflect the reality of certain audience members, then they cease to be authentic or valid.

The five families on "All-American Muslim" should not be asked to represent all Muslims, Arabs or Americans. Does "Jersey Shore" represent all Italians? If so, you can hear Frank Sinatra crooning in his grave. Similarly, Kim Kardashian does not represent all narcissistic, wannabe socialites with a fetish for athletes. (That may be an insult to fetishes.)

The best way to view "All-American Muslim" is simply as a show about five families doing their best to be themselves. They're just people, who happen to identify as Muslim, Arab and American. Their story isn't the wild-eyed, paranoid fantasy that is colored by the hate-filled minds of the Islamophobia network. It isn't the terrorist stereotype familiar to most American audiences thanks to mainstream Hollywood depictions and sensationalized news headlines. And it won't be the story of this nation's 3–4 million American Muslims (population estimates vary from 1.3 to 7 million), who will hopefully find more avenues to tell their unique narratives through mainstream outlets.

In the meantime, we should exhale and simply let this reality TV show succeed or fail on the merits of its ability to entertain, instead of obsessing about how "realistic" its depiction of Islam and Muslims is. If the ratings decline, TLC can always create a new talent show featuring the cast members of "The Real Housewives" and "All-American Muslim," judged by Kim Kardashian and Ozzy Osbourne, whose winner gets an opportunity to join all the previous winners from "Dancing with the Stars" in a new "Survivor" series about who lives beyond the 15th minute of fame.

That's a reality show whose authenticity cannot be denied.

A Taste for Trash:
A Conversation about Reality TV

By Eve Blazo
The College Hill Independent, April 21, 2011

This is the real world. There are no prizes for piecing together the best office-appropriate outfit or eating bugs in the wilderness. There are no expert celebrity judges determining how well we can 'smize' in photographs while being harnessed in mid-air.

The reality we watch on television is a fantasy. Yet even the most scripted reality TV shows reveal something about life—the banality, the little victories and losses, the absurdity—that fictional shows can't. Whether we watch with irony or sincerity, reality TV has seeped into our cultural consciousness—introducing words like Andre Leon Talley's 'dreckitude' and various Snooki-isms like 'kookah' or 'badonk.'

"We Are Who We Watch: Reality Television, Citizenship, Celebrity," the reality TV symposium taking place at Brown University this Friday, April 22, [2011], addresses the perverse pleasures and complexities involved in watching reality TV—how the form both entertains and moralizes, insidiously instructing its viewers on what it means to be a good or bad citizen. Professor Lynne Joyrich and MCM PhD candidate Hunter Hargraves, organizers of the symposium, spoke to the *Independent* about the necessity of interrogating the really real affects of this global phenomenon.

Indy: So why host this symposium now? Why at Brown? What can we learn from reality TV in an academic institution?

Hunter Hargraves: The genesis of this course started in the Fall… I was talking to Professor Joyrich, who said she's going to be teaching a course on Television Realities, which is a graduate seminar that's running this Spring in MCM. We were just kind of bouncing some ideas off of one another about how reality television, at least within the field of television studies, has accrued a significant weight of books and articles and scholarship as a whole, and how a lot of that [scholarship] has tended to start thinking through questions of citizenship and what sort of lessons reality TV ultimately ends up teaching the viewer, or its audiences.

Lynne Joyrich: We're trying to think about it critically from our positions as scholars and as viewers. We really tried to mix who's there—so we have internationally renowned scholars from different fields, some from a mass communications background, some emphasize more issues of political economy, and some of the other scholars come from a more MCM-ist, textual-theory background. We also

From *The College Hill Independent* (April 21, 2011). Copyright © 2011 by *The College Hill Independent*. Reprinted with permission. All rights reserved.

really wanted to mix in Brown students. So the panels are a mix of visiting scholars, Jill Zarin, star of The Real Housewives of New York City, and also presentations from Brown graduate students and one Brown undergraduate student. And, obviously, the reality TV viewers who we assume will be our audience.

And, as Hunter was saying, there is a lot of very interesting scholarship in television studies about reality television, obviously because it is such a big and important trend in TV itself—so therefore television studies is trying to analyze why is it such a big and important trend, not only in the US, but globally. There's a lot of [scholarship] on the economics behind global reality television and what lessons it teaches us on how to engage with the world, about reality television in terms of our culture's constructions of race, gender, and sexuality. And celebrity—what does it mean to live in a society of instant, real celebrity? So there are all these issues that television studies scholars are debating, and it seemed it would be useful to bring them together and take this thing that a lot of people see as the lowest of the low in some ways, and say it actually raises these very important issues for thinking about our culture. What does it mean that this is such a prevalent, dominant media form now? We have to take it seriously, we can't just dismiss it, or laugh at it, or cry about it, or whatever.

Hunter Hargraves: It's almost as if within the history of TV studies itself, there's always a kind of bad object. It used to be that TV studies would critically interrogate the soap opera and actually talk about how the soap opera is a lot more complex than just being daytime women's trash TV. And then it became the daytime talk show, the Jerry Springer, the Ricki Lake, and scholarship appeared about that. Now I feel like it's reality TV's turn to occupy the site of the trash object of TV, where people like to say, "We're smarter than that." Audiences can actually watch it with a degree of skepticism or irony. What we're trying to say [in this symposium] is that, just as much as audiences are responding to this, reality TV is sending some very curious messages back to the viewer about what it means to be a citizen, what it means to be of particular identity groups, or not.

Lynne Joyrich: I feel like people who are not in the discipline immediately think that it sounds so silly to do a whole [symposium] about reality TV. Whereas, again, I would say, TV is the world's most dominant media form, it pervades our entire society and defines the times and spaces of our lives. We can't just ignore it. TV studies is not about either approving or disapproving, it's serious analysis of what does it mean to live in a world where these are the forms that people are seeing, this is what people do in their leisure time, these are the things that they talk about. We are trying to really study this thing that is making up the fabric of our lives and talk about it critically, to produce a media literacy in people.

Indy: Where do you think reality TV fits on the high–low–brow art spectrum? What are its implications for issues of "taste" in art? Is this the death of popular art or is this creating something new?

Hunter Hargraves: High and low culture traffic with one another. Reality TV provides a funny example of that with something like *Slumdog Millionaire*. It was a reality TV show that was then exported to another country, then a book was written about that reality TV show in another country, that then became a movie. So there's this really interesting re-circulation of this reality TV text, *Who Wants to Be a Millionaire*, but that literally travels across the globe and across media, but then also across the registers of taste. Which is to say, a movie that won Best Picture at the Oscars was first something that starred Regis Philbin, which we laughed at as a primetime reality TV program.

Indy: Something that is so explicitly about making money can be translated into more of an art form as a film.

Hunter Hargraves: Exactly.

Lynne Joyrich: As opposed to wanting to argue about what is high or low, in television studies, it's better to actually ask: what's at stake in those very categories? Why do people want to categorize things like that? What does that signify, how does it let audiences make sense of other audiences or themselves? But I do think reality TV tends to be seen, as Hunter said, as the bad object. It's interesting though, given its dominance across TV, that now there are subdistinctions made within the genre, like high-class reality TV versus low-class reality TV. Actually, one of our MCM alums, Lauren Zalaznick, the head of Bravo, was interviewed in the *New York Times* about how Bravo is now seen as making high-class reality shows, like *Project Runway* and *Top Chef*.

Indy: Not *Jersey Shore*.

Lynne Joyrich: Yeah, and *The Real Housewives* series is different from *Fear Factor* or *Survivor*. So even with their attempts to create status distinctions within the genre, what's most interesting for me is to interrogate what's at stake in people even wanting to do that. What is that code for? How is it itself just a marketing term, a kind of branding, and how does that fit into today's economic world?

Hunter Hargraves: Which is also to say that celebrity culture has turned to reality TV as a fantastic, untapped reservoir of what we now know of as tabloid celebrity. So you look at any of the supermarket tabloids and they're talking about *Teen Mom*, they're talking about *The Bachelor*, and these are now the kind of sources where we get this celebrity culture that migrates into other media forms such as the Internet. This is why I think having a Real Housewife as part of the symposium makes it precisely that much more fascinating, because there is something about reality television that has now adopted celebrity as both what it produces and what it relies upon. So you need celebrities like Tyra Banks or Heidi Klum or Jennifer Lopez to serve as your judges. But [reality TV] also produces celebrities. You have people who win reality-show competitions that then get another reality show documenting their own lives. So there's a way in which the notion of celebrity has become part and parcel of the form and the genre.

Lynne Joyrich: And, as with any form, it has certain conventions. There are things you can do with it and there are limitations. So with any of these shows, I would say it's not that the form in and of itself is inherently good or bad, but it's the particular way it's articulated. I feel that you can use some of the conventions of reality TV in interesting, unique ways, and there are even artists playing with that form. Or you can use it in incredibly troubling and exploitative ways. So I feel like one has to really stand back and analyze what exactly is this form, what are the conventions, and therefore start to be able to see how could one maybe play with it, articulate it differently, explode it, or restructure it.

Hunter Hargraves: Importantly, this isn't just an American phenomenon. Many of the reality programs that are considered to be some of the more famous ones, at least in an American context, we actually poached from other areas of the globe. *Big Brother* used to be Dutch.

Lynne Joyrich: Even *American Idol* used to be *Pop Idol* in Britain. That's a great example of the ambivalence of reality TV. Because it is such a hugely popular global form, it is so easy to import and export. Instead of having to export a whole program and then subtitle it and translate it, you can just sell the format. These media conglomerates will sell the formats to different countries to remake them with their own contestants so it has that kind of local flavor. So you could say, well, it's totally part of a kind of economic media imperialism. On the other hand, it's not that simple, because when they are redone in other places, they do take on other local meanings. They're articulated differently and they read differently in different places. I think it's important to look at the different ways in which local audiences always make sense of things through their own particular social and discursive frames, so it's not just like Western culture taking over the world. They're way more complicated relations.

> *Reality television has offered many more spaces for women, queer folks, [and] African Americans than most TV, but also in very circumscribed ways. So you could ask: is it changing the notion of what it is to be American—for good or for bad?*

Indy: I'm so interested in what you said about citizenship and morality. What does reality TV do to its viewers? What is it producing, what identities or ways of being is it naturalizing, enforcing, and disrupting?

Lynne Joyrich: Reality television has offered many more spaces for women, queer folks, [and] African Americans than most TV, but also in very circumscribed ways. So you could ask: is it changing the notion of what it is to be American—for good or for bad? We have a panel that looks at reality TV as a moralizing machine, the way it suggests for people notions of good and bad, and how it enters into ethical discourses. And then we have one panel about reality TV and notions of citizenship, the way reality TV is so much about people actualizing themselves within communities. How do you think about how to literally survive in the world of business or in a social situation and what is this suggesting to people about the ways we enact the self?

Hunter Hargraves: We're also bringing in scholars such as Anna McCarthy, whose work looks at programming in the 1950s and what sort of genealogy of reality TV we can trace in television's own rich and expansive history.

Lynne Joyrich: McCarthy looks at early developments of television in which there was in an interest in using it as a tool for governance, teaching people what it meant to live in a civil society. She's interested in the way that's articulated in Golden-Age documentary on television up through today's ideas of reality TV that offer these lessons for citizenship. Laurie Ouellette's work is also about these issues of neoliberalism, governmentality, and citizenship. She's another one of our invited speakers who's co-written a book entitled *Better Living Through Reality TV: Television and Post-Welfare Citizenship*.

Hunter Hargraves: That whole book is about how makeover programs, rehabilitation programs, and court TV are very instructive in teaching individuals how to manage their own selves.

Lynne Joyrich: In very particular and historical terms, in that they teach a notion of success and citizenry as managing the self and learning how to be entrepreneurial and self-enterprising, having to both market and make use of the commodity form in our culture—but not too much. It's interesting and potentially quite troubling how that fits into today's state discourses. We're in a society that tells people to take care of themselves, sacrifice themselves, to be entrepreneurial. We have this whole cultural [rhetoric] all about self-reliance, so what does it mean that state functions of government are getting less and less support while this entertainment form based on watching people compete for their self-actualization [is getting more]?

Hunter Hargraves: In very direct cases, charity has shifted from the state to reality TV programs like *Extreme Makeover: Home Edition*.

Lynne Joyrich: And a lot of the therapy shows, where people can't get medical coverage. What does it mean that now we can turn on our TV and watch people call in and get their families into an intervention center, or a new home built for people who are established as models of their own civic duty?

Hunter Hargraves: It's always people who have lots of community involvement and volunteer.

Lynne Joyrich: Even Trump's *The Apprentice*: what does it mean to prove you're a wiz at business? It's TV as a job market. The way that reality TV fits into certain social and historical conditions is really important for people to analyze instead of just dismissing these shows. [These shows], in fact, have a real impact on our world and help construct the way people think. They're fitting in to what's going on in our society in ways we really need to interrogate.

Indy: Is it possible that resistances to, or subversions of, dominant culture emerge from this form?

Hunter Hargraves: Tyra Banks has always said about *America's Next Top Model* that this program for her is a way for her to expand the Western notion of beauty to include more women of color.

Indy: And plus-size women!

Hunter Hargraves: Now she calls them "fiercely real." This reality program is a way for her to not wage war on the fashion industry, but certainly challenge a lot of their preconceived notions of beauty. But on the other side of the coin, you also have shows that have a much more narrow focus, like a *Jersey Shore* in which it's all about a kind of repetition and circulation of what it means to be an Italian-American in your twenties.

Lynne Joyrich: Or even the ones that are broader like *The Real World*. People joke about how there's always the angry black-man role and the naive white-girl role and the fiery-Latina role. So in a way it's opened things up, but in very circumscribed ways. But also I think it's important to think about issues of reception with reality TV, that when people condemn reality TV for producing these troubling images, it's always these other viewers that they talk about, these "dumb" other viewers that model their lives on *Jersey Shore*. But one of the things that a lot of TV theorists are interested in is precisely the real complexity of the way that people engage with television shows. A lot of it is a game that people play with [reality television], knowing that it's not real life. People play with those levels of what counts as real, what doesn't count as real. When is somebody the really real or the parody of the real. There are all these different levels that are producing new understandings of what we mean by reality. Nobody puts themselves in that position of, "Oh yeah, I just fall for reality TV," but we have these patronizing discourses of those other audiences who are supposedly just so dumb that they fall for it. But everybody has a much more complicated spectator relationship, I would argue. Which doesn't mean we're also still not falling for certain things, often in ways that are more invisible.

Indy: What is the pleasure or guilty pleasure in watching reality TV? What makes it addictive, appealing, entertaining? Is this just voyeuristic pleasure? What is the fascination with watching what can often be banal, mundane things going on?

Lynne Joyrich: I think it's a mix of a lot of different kinds of pleasures, and different ones in different mixes for different shows. Certainly there is the pleasure of voyeurism, but there's also the pleasure of playing with voyeurism—imagining oneself as the object of voyeurism, the exhibitionist pleasure—taking Andy Warhol's "everybody can be famous for 15 minutes," but now it's like 15 seconds. Everybody kind of imagines the reality show of their life. It's about voyeurism but it's also the critique of voyeurism. I think often people watch precisely to say, "I can't believe those people want to be filmed." I also think part of the pleasure is moving throughout what we think of as different levels of the real. It's a form of epistemological game playing—[people want to] get a glimmer of the real-real within the reality. But everybody also knows that it's a fantasy. Many of these shows are unscripted but clearly constructed through editing, casting, etcetera. We still don't have an adequate vocabulary in our culture to talk about the complex ways in which we all live in a mass-mediated world between virtual realities, fantastic realities, gritty realities—they're all marketing terms, yet also the realities in which we live. I think that people in their daily lives are constantly making judgments about how you present and perform yourself to the world. We don't have a good language to talk about this yet, which is partly why scholarship about this is so important to get people to think about: what do we even mean by reality?

Push Girls: The Real Spokeswomen of LA

By Chet Cooper
Ability, August-September, 2012

It's happy hour in Los Angeles and cocktails are on the way as four glamorous women discuss sex, overcoming breakups and toasting life—all while being filmed for their own reality TV series called *Push Girls*. Sound familiar? Not exactly, for this is not a reality spin on *Sex and the City*, nor does it mimic the unseemly catfights of the Real Housewives, Instead, it pushes beyond. The Sundance Channel's new hit show *Push Girls* offers a refreshing perspective on women who defy stereotypes and celebrate their deep connection with each other The series, which premiered in June, invites viewers to roll through the everyday lives of this fierce foursome of BFFs who endure trials and tribulations with family, friends, lovers and life, but with ample amounts of spunk and humor

Reality-TV pioneers—Angela Rockwood, Tiphany Adams, Auti Angel and Mia Schaikewitz join *ABILITY Magazine's* V David Zimmerman and Chet Cooper for an interview. Angela is a model, actress, producer and an ambassador with the Christopher & Dana Reeve Foundation. She is described as "Buddha-like" and is the "Mother Earth" of the foursome. Tiphany, the blond bombshell of the group, has an uncensored mouth and an open, honest nature. She loves sex with her partner—man or woman—and doesn't like labels, unless they're on a new outfit. Auti is a firecracker. She heads her own dance team. Colours 'n' Motion, as well as the Save a Soul Foundation. She appeared in the film "Musical Chairs" and has danced alongside artists such as L.L. Cool J. Mia is a down-to-earth beauty and an account manager in a marketing firm. She's also a competitive swimmer and a proud, independent woman who is looking for a man to share her life. She tries to teach through both words and actions—and now, of course, reality TV.

David: Why a reality TV show about the four of you?

Angela: Why not? First of all, the name started with the Sundance Channel. It's an amazing name, especially since it represents who we are and how we overcome everything that gets thrown into our path. We just push through it, push the limits and the boundaries.

Mia: Since we have lived in LA, a lot of us have gone on auditions for certain wheelchair roles that never seem to fit, and I think it's because they've always continued to play on these stereotypes that aren't necessarily true. So, this is the perfect platform to be able to break those stereotypes. It's about us. It's about reality, about our real lives, and that's how people are going to connect with us most naturally.

From *ABILITY* (August-September 2012):40-51. Copyright © 2012 by CR Cooper. Reprinted with permission. All rights reserved.

Tiphany: What's funny is, I was just talking to my little niece, who's four, and she said, "Titi, why is the camera in your face? Why is it following you?" And I said, "You know, your Titi's in a wheelchair, and a lot of people don't understand why Titi's in a wheelchair. You know how she drives her car and you know how she goes swimming and you know how she does those things? Well, some people don't understand and don't think it's possible." The show is totally about opening people's eyes and letting them see that we live life just like they do, only we do it sitting, which is a different perspective. I call us chicks in chairs.

Angela: I had the beautiful honor and blessing of meeting Gay Rosenthal [*Push Girls* executive producer] through a mutual friend named David Horowitz. Basically, when she asked me what I wanted from the show, I said it wasn't about me. It was about my girlfriends. Being friends with these three women has been a blessing. It's been so powerful in many ways and on many levels. I shared with Gay the importance of getting this out there and showing the world what it's about, and not just to educate but also to remind others what life is truly about. We want to inspire people to do their best and push through anything.

Chet: So, were you all in acting class? How did *Push Girls* come together?

Angela: At my first Christopher & Dana Reeve Foundation benefit, in Laguna Beach, CA, I met this wonderful man, Mr. Tobias Forrest, who was actually being awarded the Reeve Foundation scholarship. He turned to me and asked, "So, what do you do?" I said, "I used to model and act." And he said, "What do you mean, used to? You can still model and act." He had a facility that he worked at where they hire people in wheelchairs to act; they're not just able-bodied people pretending to be in wheelchairs. So anyway, I was introduced to David Zimmerman. I rolled in, took his class. And that was seven years ago.

Chet: Has anything changed since the airing of the show—anything from old friends contacting you to "You're the girl on that new reality show!"

Angela: I am married to Dustin Nguyen from *21 Jump Street*, so I'm used to people coming up to him. When I was in New York, we were leaving a club and this girl came running after me. "Excuse me, excuse me!" I turned around and she says, "You're on that show *Push Girls*! You're the model!" And I said, "Yeah." With excitement she said, "Can I get a picture with you?" Then I turned to the camera and in my head I'm thinking, "Wow, all over the world, women in wheelchairs are probably going to be getting stopped and asked, "Are you on that show *Push Girls*" (laughs)

One reporter asked, "So, are you guys prepared for fame?" Without a beat I leaned into the mic and said, "Were we prepared for paralysis?" Bruce Lee said it very well. He said, "Superstar, that word is an illusion." We were doing this before, but because of the show, we're able to share our story and able to touch and inspire on a bigger platform and actually reach more people.

Chet: Where did you do the screening of your first show?

Angela: The *Push Girls* screening was held at the White House. The amount of press they had us doing was ridiculous. I did some of my interviews from my hotel bed. Tiph was in the car for one, the park for another, and another time I think she was in H&M. We did *Good Morning America*, came back to the hotel, changed and went to a Christopher & Dana Reeve luncheon. Then, we ran off to Jane Fonda's red carpet event, went back to the hotel, changed and finally ended up going to our premiere. The hotel concierge was probably thinking, "Oh my gosh, these girls just don't stop!"

Chet: Can each of you explain your injuries?

Angela: I am a quadriplegic. I was planning my wedding in San Francisco with my maid of honor. I was coming back to LA after Labor Day weekend, I was sitting in the back seat. My girlfriend lost control of the car, because we were going around a turn on I-5. She tried to correct and she overcorrected. The car spun out of control, and the impact pushed me forward. I shattered my C4-C5 vertebrae and severed the spinal cord. The car proceeded to flip four or five times and I was catapulted out of the little triangle window. I flew about 30 to 32 feet, where they found me lying on the side of the road, face down. When I woke up in the hospital, the doctors told my fiancé and dad that I had a three to five percent chance of moving or feeling anything from the neck down. I was rendered a complete quadriplegic for the rest of my life.

Of course, I didn't take that diagnosis. I didn't believe in it. I knew I was going to push forward and just try to heal as quickly as I possibly could, so I went in that direction and never looked back. I had stem cell surgery three years later. My accident was one week before 9/11. The stem cell surgery was right before 2004. Bush was running the country, and he wasn't allowing stem cell surgery here, so I went to Lisbon, Portugal, and Dr. Carlos Lima performed the surgery. I was the third American to have it done, and the 11th patient. At the time, I was in a power chair, and I'm now in a manual chair. I don't have full sensation, but a lot of sensation came back. 1 became stronger. If I could do that surgery all over again, I would.

Tiphany: I was a senior in high school and I decided to go to a wakeboarding event that eventually turned into a party. There were thousands of people there. When I left that event—

Chet: Where are you from?

Tiphany: Northern California, *born* and raised. This was in Lodi, California. I was leaving that event and there was a two-lane highway. Highway 12, which does not have a median in the middle. One of the girls who was at the event earlier in the evening had gotten a ride home because she was too intoxicated to drive, but when she got home, she then got into her car and drove back to the event. Meanwhile, we were traveling eastbound on the way home, and she was traveling westbound, when she passed a semitruck. She passed the semitruck over the double yellow lines, came into our lane and hit us head on at a 130-mile-an-hour impact. The license plates were completely melted together. There were no skid marks.

An off-duty paramedic had driven by and was on the scene. He noticed I made a slight sound and thought that my pinky moved, so they got the Jaws of Life to cut me out of the car, and took me to the nearest hospital. I was bleeding internally, and in a coma for three weeks. They told my father and family that I had a five percent chance of survival by the end of that week. I was flown to Santa Clara Valley Medical Center in San Jose, where they did the rest of my surgery, so I had over 24 hours of surgery. The accident happened on October 15, 2000. I woke up in November with a feeding tube and all that fun stuff. I left the hospital December 21 and went back to school in February. I graduated with my class in June and started college in August.

Chet: What degree did you pursue?

Tiphany: I love children, so I was going into liberal studies, child development and psychology. I earned enough units to start teaching preschool and working as a teaching assistant in classrooms. I did that up until I moved to Los Angeles. I haven't done that in LA, but I would love to do it more. I love working with kids. That's my story.

Mia: I was 15 when I got paralyzed. I was completely fine one day. Then I had a stomachache and it got bad enough so that I had to go to the hospital. At the hospital, they thought it was appendicitis. It wasn't until I was getting X-rays taken that I realized my legs felt really heavy. They continued to do tests and couldn't find anything wrong with me, and they said, "You must be nervous about your swim team physical, so it is probably psychosomatic." And it wasn't until the next morning, when they did an MRI, that they found out there was a vein in my spinal cord that had ruptured, causing paralysis. Nerves don't regenerate, and there was damage to the nerves, resulting in a spinal cord injury. So, from that point on—

Chet: I know there is a medical term for that kind of occurrence. What is it called?

Mia: It's called arteriovenous malformation—AVM. An AVM is similar to an aneurysm, but it was in my spinal cord where the blood vessel ruptured, leaving me paralyzed. I'm a T6.

Tiphany: My vertebra was fractured at TIO, but the nerves were more affected at L3, so my sensory is L3—my movement and stuff.

Auti: I was 22 years old, and I had my accident in 1992. A car clipped the front end of my car and went spinning out of control; then, we hit the center divider head on. I snapped my back and severed my spinal cord at a TIO level. So I'm T10-T12—complete, paralyzed from the waist down.

Chet: The accident, did it cause that metal thing to stick into your tongue?

Auti: Yep, scrap metal fell onto my tongue. [laughter] No, I got my tongue pierced about six or eight years ago.

Chet: When you heard that Angela elected to have stem cell surgery, did any of you think, or have you thought since, about doing some other things?

Auti: I love what it did for her, and if she wanted to continue down that road, I would support her. For me personally, if somebody offered me a million dollars to go get a study done and even if they said that I would have a 99 percent chance of walking again, I would use that million dollars to help somebody else out instead, whether in Third World countries, or our country, with accessibility or things that they might need or want.

Chet: What about two million?

Auti: I would still help others. For me, walking is overrated and I'm comfortable where I am in my life. I love who I am. I love that this is a vehicle and a tool that can touch so many lives, and I know I would not have touched as many lives if I'd never had the accident and been paralyzed. I've lived in a chair for people to see: "Wow, she's overcoming, she goes shopping, she drives."

Mia: We talk about quality of life, and that is a huge, huge aspect to independence as well as just giving back. With Ang, the stem cell surgery has been a blessing. Just to gain back anything that is going to help her quality of life—I definitely encourage it in those situations. For me personally, I don't feel like it would enhance my quality of life, to be able to walk. So I don't think about wanting to walk. In fact, I feel like it's much more of a gift to be able to inspire other people from afar. People that I don't even have to talk to or have a conversation with—they may just see me on the street and be affected by it. That's something I don't think we can necessarily do if we were back in the position that we were in before.

Tiphany: I have always been interested in stem cell research, but financially it's costly. I am very blessed and happy with the fact that I have so much mobility and consider my level of injury to be quite low. I look at it as an adventure and a challenge, something to work for. Of course, I'd love to walk again. I loved jumping. I loved doing handstands and handsprings and crazy little jumps. What's wild is I actually crossed paths with a very close friend of Dr. Lima's when I first moved to LA. That was about four years ago. Two years later, I crossed paths with his associate who bought me dinner. And then, two years later again, I ran into him at Panera Bread. He gave me the card again, so I thought, "Wow, when the time is right and if something becomes perfected in the stem cell surgery realm, I'm open to it," but there's so many different things going on with it right now. When it's meant to be, it will be.

Auti: Stem cell doesn't have to be about walking again. It can be about taking the pain away and adding to our quality of life. I think we were more or less thinking that we have quality of life. We don't need to enhance.

David: So, how did the four of you become friends?

Angela: I met Auti two or three days after I arrived at the rehab facility in Downey, CA, Los Amigos. She was visiting injured patients and I happened to be one of them that day, and she and I connected instantly. And Mia I met four years after my accident. I started this wonderful acting class at my house with this amazing man named David Zimmerman, and Mia decided to take the class, and that's where I met her. And Tiph, I met four years ago, two days after she arrived in Los Angeles to be the Marilyn Monroe on wheels. We met on my backyard porch, and there we made a soul-to-soul connection.

Tiphany: And I met all the girls that night.

Chet: Outside of now living your lives in front of cameras, what do you four do?

Angela: I'm a brain on wheels, Chet! [laughter] I model.

Mia: I'm a project manager for a graphic-design branding firm.

Chet: And what do you do, Auti?

Auti: I'm an all-around entertainer extraordinaire—actress, dancer, singer, rapper, producer of music. My husband and I are working on an album right now. He's a DJ and producer, and we both produce and write music together.

Chet: I noticed you have a pimped-out chair.

Auti: (laughs) I do have a pimped-out chair, provided by Colours Wheelchairs. Tiphany, Mia and I are all spokesmodels for Colours Wheelchairs. Thank God for that. Thank God for new technology.

David: Angela. You talk a lot about manifestations. In fact, I happen to know your nickname has become the Manifestor. What does that word mean to you? When did you start "manifesting?"

Angela: The word "manifestation," or being a "manifestor," as you call me, it's very powerful. I do believe in the law of attraction, but not just the law of attraction. With me, it started when I was a little girl. I realized that whatever I perceived in my mind, I could achieve. Then, just growing up, I realized that anything that I thought of, even if I thought of an outcome negatively, it would happen that way. If I thought of it positively, I would execute it, and 90 percent of the time it would be positive. So immediately when I got into the car accident, when I woke up in the hospital, I knew for myself, that I needed to go down that positive road. I had to take that route instead of going down the negative path, because if I went down that negative path, or even thought it, there was no one that was going to be able to bring me back.

David: Tiphany, you mention in the description of yourself "no labels." Why no labels?

Tiphany: Oh, wow. I feel that the world is very comfortable putting everything in a category or in a box and that labeling it just to make everyone else feel comfortable. The world's beyond that. We're in 2012 now, and we've evolved. That's the one thing in life that's guaranteed: change. It's constant. There's an amazing quote I just came across a few days ago by Deepak Chopra: "Equality is the first step toward acceptance." Totally connecting on a soul-to-soul level and taking away the superficial and just knowing that when this is all gone, we're spirit, we're connecting spirit-to-spirit. It's all an energy exchange. When you cross paths with somebody who's mad and angry, you're going to feel those vibrations, and you've got to make sure that you don't take that along.

David: You're also very health conscious. You eat wonderfully. You take care of yourself. You exercise. Why is maintaining a healthy lifestyle so important to you?

Tiphany: I'm a little bit obsessed with working out and eating healthy foods, because I know how it makes me feel. It makes my body feel well, and it responds well. I know if I'm going to eat a big slice of greasy pizza that it's going to really make me feel kind of groggy in an hour or the next day. So, I try to eat as cleanly as possible; and working out definitely gets my adrenals going. It just feels so euphoric, because it also makes me completely free, knowing that it's something I used to love doing when I was walking. It's a huge part of my life.

David: Watching you do it is having an effect on me. I eat seaweed every day now.

Tiphany: No way!

David: (laughs) I do! I buy it at Costco!

Tiphany: Seaweed—oh my gosh. It's just so many things! Before, I didn't used to like some of the things I now eat and indulge in all the time. Now my mind knows, "That has iodine in it. That's going to benefit my body in this way." Or whatever the nutrients, I know how it's going to affect my cells. It's just crazy. It's like retraining everything. You can retrain your taste buds. I never ate onions and tomatoes until I turned 19 or 20. Why? Because my father never ate them, so those were the two foods I never had to eat. But other than that, when I was younger, my mom made me try everything. I'm talking alligator, ostrich, buffalo and snake. I had to eat everything. Those [onions and tomatoes] were the two things I didn't have to eat until I got out on my own and I had my own place and I started cooking myself, and I realized those do enhance food. So now I'm very open to different foods.

Angela: How can you not love her?

David: I tell you, you could turn a gay man straight. [laughter] Mia, *Push Girls* fans have watched you get yourself back into swimming on the show. What is it about swimming that makes your soul sing?

Mia: That's a good question. Ever since I was young, I was always attracted to water It just made me feel peaceful. Water is very fluid; it always adapts. It adapts to whatever container that it's in. I find I resonate with that. Whatever happens to me, I find a way to adapt to it. When you're in the water, you feel lighter. You're the same weight, but it's all like a shifted perspective with matter, and I just feel that life is kind of like that. You could either feel like everything's a really heavy burden or you can feel like you have this buoyancy, and you can pop up from anything, because you do have a lightness. So I think I connect with water on a physical level and also a metaphysical level.

Angela: Mia's like Bruce Lee right now.

Mia: One with the water. [laughter]

Angela: "If there is a cup, be the cup. If there is a bowl, be the bowl. Be like water, my friend." [laughter]

David: Auti, I saw your first feature film *Musical Chairs*. What a wonderful film, and it was a joy to see you up there on the screen. I was kvelling.

Auti: I had an amazing acting coach named David Zimmerman who helped me get this role. [she winks]

David: You had the wings, I just said, "Hey, look, there's your wings. " Tell me about that experience, the movie. What was your favorite thing about it?

Auti: It's interesting, because I've been in the entertainment industry ever since I was young. My father was an aspiring actor, so I kind of followed in his footsteps. I started dancing first, and then I dipped my toes into acting, and I fell in love with it. When I went to different agencies, they never really captured the vision I had for myself. Finally, when I let go of one of my representations, *Musical Chairs* flew by and caught me by surprise, and the producers actually contacted me and said, "Wow, we think you are amazing" and "We saw your videos on YouTube. You should be in our film, directed by Susan Seidelman." And I responded, "Really? OK. I don't know what is." The role is completely—it's a little bit like me, but I'm more of a diva, and Nicky, the character, is so dark and doesn't want to talk to anybody. But finally—

Tiphany: You *do* have that side! I thought, "Wow, that's a side that people don't see of you."

Angela: We do! She's mischievous.

Auti: And being a dancer, I thought this character would be easy to get into. I thought, "No problem, piece of cake. I'm a dancer I can adapt to any kind of dance." I learned a whole new respect for the craft of ballroom dancing, because it's a certain structure you have to embrace. I'm used to hip-hop, where there's freedom of the soul to express yourself, and usually you're expressing yourself by yourself, and this time I had to actually partner up. This character actually helped me with my marriage, too, [laughter] because I had to learn how to follow and not always take the lead. So Eric, being my husband, was kind of happy about that.

David: Speaking of husbands ... what about sex?

Tiphany: Whoo! [laughter] What about it?

Angela: What about it? What not about it? What about sex, Tiph?

Tiphany: It's about creativity. How about that?

Mia: Use your imagination.

Angela: What about sex? People with paralysis have sex, David, and procreate. We have sex. We like it. Auti always says, "They sewed up our backs, but nothing else."

Auti: That's all you need to know. There's other . . . it's possible. [laughter]

Mia: But you know, I think people are really wondering if it is enjoyable. I would say yes.

Auti: Oh, yeah!

Angela: Yeah! There are a lot of women who are not connected to their bodies, and I think when you're in a position like this, you really focus on connecting fully and completely with oneself and with your mate, or whoever it is you're making love to. It's a learning experience for both individuals. Whether you're already married or you're starting a new relationship, it's like starting all over again.

Auti: Piggybacking off what Angela just said, before my accident I used to have sex just to have sex. It wasn't really that enjoyable. It was more about me figuring out how to please another person instead of me being pleased myself, because I was so insecure. Once I embraced my new body and became secure with it and found love ... to be honest, my husband Eric is the only one who has really made me [sings a high note]. [laughter] And it's because we have that connection. Prior to my accident, I had all the feeling and everything, but I didn't have that connection. Now that we are connected on a deeper level and I know how to tell him what makes me feel good and all that, it's all good. [laughs]

Angela: You learn a lot about yourself.

Auti: And we've been trying to make a baby. We practice a lot.

Angela: Good Lord.

Angela: After I was paralyzed from the neck down, I didn't move anything, nothing, so I literally just laid there like a bump on a log until after my stem cell surgery. I was able to start moving a little bit more freely, but it's all about communication and your partner understanding what it is and being educated. We still feel love and we still get it on.

David: If you had words of advice for someone who just had an accident or became paralyzed, what would you tell them about how to cope with the change?

Mia: I would just say, first and foremost, it's not the end of the world. I know when it happened to me, I felt that. I didn't see anything beyond it, because I didn't know there was anything beyond it. Your life is just starting. It really is. It's a beautiful life, and your world is going to get bigger, and it's going to be a beautiful world.

Tiphany: Look beyond the obvious. The only thing constant in life is change. Things change, and so will your circumstances at that time. One of my other favorite quotes is "Nobody likes a pity party." Stop crying and feeling sorry for yourself. Choose to see the optimistic side of life and know that there is always sunshine beyond the clouds.

Angela: I always say that life is a gift, and what we do with our life is our gift back. I learned within myself that you don't focus on the negative; you actually focus on what it is that you have and be grateful. Be grateful for the friends and family that you have around you. Be grateful that you are able to communicate. Be grateful that you are in a vessel and you're still living and you're still in this moment, and regardless of not being able to walk or not being able to walk as sexy or sashay down the runway like we used to, it doesn't matter. Focus on the positive, on things that you do have. That will help you get through whatever it is that you're trying to overcome.

> *Be grateful that you are in a vessel and you're still living and you're still in this moment, and regardless of not being able to walk or not being able to walk as sexy or sashay down the runway like we used to, it doesn't matter. Focus on the positive, on things that you do have. That will help you get through whatever it is that you're trying to overcome.*

Tiphany: A support system is huge. When you get into a circumstance that may seem detrimental, and you have no clue how you're going to get through it, you may feel like you want to alienate yourself, but what's best is to have a strong support system. It's OK to be weak from time to time, and it's OK to need that shoulder to cry on. Just feel those emotions and let them out, because if you're suppressing them, you're going to turn to other things that are going to numb you, and it makes the healing process that much longer. By allowing yourself to be vulnerable, it's healing for others, too.

Auti: Understand that you were left here for a higher purpose. You could have been taken out. Tiphany was the only survivor of a car accident. She survived for a reason. You survive this challenge, this obstacle, to use it as a tool to embrace others, use it as a tool to teach others. And like Ang says, give the gift back because you've been given a gift of continuous life. Find what it is that you have to offer and focus on that, because you have a purpose. Push forward just like the *Push Girls*. Sometimes people who have gone through a situation such as ours have lived through other life obstacles. I was molested. I was raped. My life was almost taken by my first husband, so those were all obstacles I overcame even before the wheelchair. You're pushed through life already. You keep pushing and you'll get past this other obstacle and you'll come out the other side with a victory and glory that are just unimaginable.

David: Angela, tell me more about your participation with the Christopher & Dana Reeve Foundation. You became an ambassador for their foundation. What does it mean to you to be involved?

Angela: Wow, David! OK, well, the Christopher & Dana Reeve Foundation is a huge, huge part of my life. When I got injured, Dustin was basically in the dark. When does your fiancé get paralyzed? When does your whole life change within a second? When the doctor came to him and said, "Your wife is going to be a quadriplegic for the rest of her life and she only has a three percent chance of moving or feeling anything from the neck down," Dustin looked at the doctor like, "Uh, you're speaking a different language." Dustin actually reached out to the Reeve Foundation and they educated him. People don't know this, but they actually are available for advice. There's an 800-number, or you can go online: www.reevefoundation.com. They were that light at the end of the tunnel for him. They were there. They were his resource, which was huge, huge.

Of course, I was in the rehab facility and the intensive care unit. I did not connect with them until three years later, when Dustin and I both went to our first Reeve Foundation event in Laguna Beach. There, I had the privilege and honor of meeting Dana Reeve, who was amazing. She was a real-life angel. When you meet her, just her aura, her energy, everything about her—she looks you in the eye. It's just you and her in your own little world. A year later—I believe that was 2004—the Reeve Foundation came to both Dustin and I and asked us to be their ambassador couple, because a year and a half later, Dana passed away. So, we basically stepped aboard the team and worked closely with them on their minority outreach campaign for the Asian community. A lot of people don't know this, but the Asian culture looks down on paralysis. They look at it as a bad omen or bad karma, and they shy away from it.

So, Dustin and I went into the Asian communities to educate and tell them, "Life still goes on. Don't shy away from this. Embrace it. Don't follow the old traditions. Break those stereotypes. Strip away the ignorance that you've been taught from your ancestors." In a nutshell, the foundation has been unbelievably amazing for both Dustin and I. A complete blessing. Also, another thing that people don't know, and especially in the Asian communities: If you speak any type of language, from Spanish to Tagalog to Korean to Chamorro, you can call the Reeve Foundation. They have staff members who speak over 50 languages. They will communicate and give you whatever it is that you need the answers for.

David: Auti, you have established your own foundation, too, the Save a Soul Foundation. What does your group contribute?

Auti: Save a Soul Foundation is a mentor-based program for at-risk youth. We reach out to the youth facilities to empower kids to follow their dreams and their ambitions. I'm following mine regardless of my onset of disability, so I'm using that as a tool to show kids that you, too, can follow your dream, no matter what you're going through at school, at home, mentally, physically. You can follow your dreams. On my way home, after I spoke to the kids at the LA Central Juvenile Hall, I heard, "save a soul," and I thought, "OK, do you want me to save souls?" Once you save one soul, it'll have a ripple effect, and that person will save another person, and that person will save another person. So, it's saving somebody through experience and teaching.

David: In the acting workshop that I teach, I start with the question that was passed on from the late Corey Allen, and the question goes to all of you: What do you want the most at this moment in your life?

Mia: True love. I just want to find my true love that I will be with forever.

Auti: I am honored to have sisters in my life like this and wonderful people who surround me and a wonderful platform to be able to touch the masses. So right now, at this very moment, I want to love. I want to heal the world with love.

Tiphany: At this very moment, definitely reaching the world, the global aspect, and to love freely. But, I would love to spend more time with my nieces and nephews while also continuing this amazing opportunity that I have right now with filming and interviewing, but still getting the chance to see them at least once a week.

Angela: Honestly, what I want most in this very moment, if this was my last moment, it's all about living for others, and to allow that ripple effect to float outward. And for those who are struggling, whether it's finances, finding a new job, finding true love, whatever it is, I would want them to attain what it is that they desire in this second. We all can do it together in this second, just like that. Snap your fingers for me, Auti! We all could just close our eyes, and when Mia makes her wish, we all could have our dream come true within an instant.

David: I have one last question. What do you want people to take away from watching *Push Girls*?"

Tiphany: I think one of the most important things that people will get from the show is learning that you can connect on a spiritual level, on a soul-to-soul level. You can connect beyond the physical level by shattering the stereotypes and breaking the boundaries. Everyone has something that they may be going through, something that may not be considered beautiful in someone else's eyes, but it doesn't mean they're not a deep person who has feelings.

Mia: I really want everyone to walk away with something that they've learned about which reflects within them internally, because I think there's a lot of healing we can do in the world. Ignorance is totally curable, and I think that this show could actually help. Hopefully viewers will see that in those moments when they think they can't get over something. *Push Girls* can become the example that they think of and use in that moment as a tool for themselves.

Auti: What I always say is, no matter what else comes your way, it can always be overcome. It's never too late to fulfill your dreams and your heart's desire, no matter what your circumstance or your situation. Once a dancer, always a dancer, and even though I don't have the use of my legs, I am still dancing. So, I want people to know that they, too, can follow their dreams.

Angela: Because I'm all about manifestation, it is all about focusing on exactly what it is that you want. My top three are educating and reminding and inspiring. We can open up our doors to our world and educate people about our lives. It's not even about the wheelchair. The common denominator is our wheelchair, but it's not about our wheelchair. It's about our spirit and how we live our lives. Then, reminding others that they can get through anything that they put their hearts, souls and desire into. It is about fading away the ignorance and realizing that you can step outside of the box, step out of your shell, fade away the façade and the masks and the illusions that cloak you in your own life. It's very simple. Just live it. Be. Breathe. That's it.

6

The Business of Reality Television

(© Billy Tompkins/Retna Ltd./Corbis)

Bret Michaels wins *Celebrity Apprentice 2010* in New York City on May 23, 2010.

The Real Business of Reality

Since the start of the twenty-first century, reality television has come to inhabit a large and lucrative segment of the entertainment business. The theme and focus of reality television programming has been wide-ranging. Reality TV shows have explored law enforcement, personal relationships, drug addiction, phobias, and unconventional lifestyles. Fans have followed adventure-themed competitions and musical performance contests season after season. The reality television genre has earned countless millions of dollars for its producers, stars, and advertisers. In addition to being big business, the genre has explored the business world. Contestants vie for a new job or to raise money for charity; restaurateurs and hoteliers work to save their establishments from obscurity; and work-a-day members of the labor force toil side-by-side, unknowingly, with their organizations' chief executives. Some reality television shows have become vehicles of charity in their own right, supplying new homes or windfalls of cash to individuals with financial or medical needs. As the reality TV genre has come of age, the business world has become a central theme of the genre. Business strategy, group decision making, product design, and concepts of corporate stewardship have become part of the culture of reality television. While business has inspired a variety of reality TV programs, considerations related to the business of television also continues to inform and influence the genre's content. The profit motive and commercial interests behind each reality TV project can have an exploitative impact on the individuals and cultures that they aim to celebrate.

One of the first business-oriented reality television shows was *The Apprentice*, which debuted in 2004. The show, which has since grown into a global television franchise, features a group of fifteen or more businesspeople who compete for a one-year job placement within the global enterprise of real estate mogul Donald Trump. The show also spawned a sister series, *Celebrity Apprentice*, which features well-known actors, musicians, and other celebrities competing to raise the most money for charity. In each version of the show, competitors vie to be the one spared from Trump's caustic catchphrase "You're fired!" The success of *The Apprentice* introduced other business-oriented reality TV shows. The program *Undercover Boss* debuted in 2009, featuring employees at major retail chains and restaurants who train and advise a new employee. In the process of training the new employee, viewers learn not only about the individual's job and company, but also about his or her life and personality. The twist of *Undercover Boss* is made known in the finale of each episode, when the employee is told that the new trainee is in fact a corporate executive, and in many instances, the chief executive of the company or franchise being featured. The stunned employees receive rewards for their innovative ideas and hard work.

Reality television has also featured business dynamics existing outside the employer-employee relationship. Producers have found much material in the service industry, particularly the restaurant business and the real estate industry. Leveraging the appeal and unique perspective of the reality genre, the Food Network reinvented the relationship between food and television, which for many years was limited to chefs taking the audience through the steps of recipes. While chefs like Rachael Ray found success in more traditional formats, the Food Network has also introduced audiences to a new kind of reality star: talented but unknown chefs who participate in cooking competitions. *Iron Chef America*, a takeoff of the Japanese television hit *Iron Chef*, debuted in 2005. In 2006, the Food Network debuted *Top Chef*. The popular culinary competition, which later moved to the Bravo network, soon became its own brand of cooking hardware and the basis of numerous spinoffs, including *Top Chef: Masters*, *Top Chef: Just Desserts*, and *Top Chef Canada*. British celebrity chef Gordon Ramsay has made a career in reality television programming in both the United Kingdom and the United States. His high-pressure cooking competition *Hell's Kitchen* features nervous chef contestants preparing meals for finicky dinner guests. Ramsey's other programs include *Ramsay's Kitchen Nightmares*, in which he helps to rehabilitate struggling restaurants, and *Hotel Hell*, where he works to reverse the fortunes of run down, struggling hotel businesses.

The real estate industry has also provided a wealth of material for reality TV. *Extreme Makeover: Home Edition* premiered in December 2003. For over eight seasons, the show featured a construction crew and host Ty Pennington overseeing major home renovation projects and the construction of new homes for families undergoing personal hardship, including medical or financial problems. Home improvement projects and the business of real estate serves as the basis for all the programming on Home and Garden Television, better known as HGTV. Shows like *Curb Appeal*, *Design on a Dime*, *All American Handyman*, *Holmes on Homes*, and *Love It or List It* look at real estate business strategies and home improvement techniques, providing viewers with unique stories and educating them on home maintenance, renovation, and home buying. Shows such as HGTV's *Selling New York* and Bravo's *Million Dollar Listing* provide viewers with a glimpse into the luxury real estate market, where wealthy clients trade high-end properties. *Million Dollar Listing* focuses primarily on California properties. The success of *Selling New York* has led to the spin-off shows *Selling LA* and *Selling London*. HGTV's *House Hunters* and *House Hunters International* tell the story of homebuyers with varying incomes negotiating space considerations, amenities, and real estate financing in property markets worldwide.

In addition to food and real estate, reality TV programs have featured other business endeavors, including pawnshops, exterminators, and antique dealers. The Discovery Channel has also aired numerous programs investigating the lives and works of people with previously untelevised livelihoods. These include the series *Deadliest Catch*, featuring Alaskan king crab fishermen, and *Dirty Jobs*, on which host Mike Rowe travels the country detailing occupations notable for their grease, grime, and general messiness. AMC's *The Pitch* pits real-world advertising agencies against each other as they work to earn the business of organizations seeking promotional partnerships.

Whether or not a reality television program is business-oriented in terms of content, its development, production, and success are all rooted in considerations of the larger entertainment business. These considerations have a lasting impact on the locations where reality TV projects are filmed and the people who live there. MTV's *Jersey Shore*, which debuted in 2009, helped to popularize the beachside hotels and clubs of New Jersey. However, critics of the show were quick to point out that the show did not feature residents of coastal New Jersey, but rather promoted cultural stereotypes of Italian Americans. In February 2012, New Jersey Governor Chris Christie stated that the show was "negative for New Jersey." Critics of the long-running MTV reality show *The Real World* questioned the legitimacy and authenticity of the show's storylines and claimed that its producers encouraged outrageous behavior to ensure the series remained lucrative for advertisers. Critics of vocal performance competitions such as *American Idol* and *The Voice* have claimed that while show contestants are indeed authentically talented, show winners are forced into rigid business deals ensuring that the majority of their record sales and performance income benefits the show's producers and their corporate partners. Programs like *Extreme Makeover: Home Edition* have been criticized for seeking out families coping with specific medical issues in order to exploit them for ratings and ad revenue. Critics have also pointed to the fact that many of the new homes built during the course of episode filming have been lost, because the families featured on the program cannot afford the associated upkeep expenses. Other contestants have reported that they felt forced to leave the homes built by the show because of neighborhood resentment.

Another common criticism of reality TV programming is that it is less a window into reality than a vehicle for product placement. The term "product placement" refers to the practice of corporations and companies paying to have their products and brand names featured prominently within a show's content. According to one study, the weight-loss competition program *The Biggest Loser* featured over one million product placements in episodes aired between 2007 and 2008. The same study reported that during the same period, *American Idol* featured over 500,000 product placements.

While reality television can serve as a promotional vehicle, it can also create new business opportunities. Many of the stars of reality television programs, previously unknown to audiences, have gone on to establish successful careers in television and entertainment. For example, television host Elizabeth Hasselbeck was introduced to audiences as a contestant on *Survivor*. Stars of *Jersey Shore*, such as Michael "The Situation" Sorrentino and Nicole Elizabeth "Snooki" Polizzi have become public speakers and entrepreneurs. Members of successful and wealthy families whose lives have been featured in reality TV shows have become a type of celebrity unto themselves. Examples include Paris Hilton, Kim Kardashian, and Kelly Osbourne.

The business of reality television is booming. Part of this boom is a result of decisions by producers to turn the camera on the business world itself, exploring the cutthroat nature of trade deals, product promotion, and commercial strategy.

Simultaneously, the success of reality television programming at large has generated lucrative commercial opportunities and influenced the landscape of popular culture. As reality TV continues to evolve, so will its associated business opportunities, both in front of and behind the camera.

Home Economics

By James Poniewozik
Time, June 25, 2007

The real estate boom may be over in your neighborhood, but the market for reality TV is going strong.

If you watch CNBC, you know that these are not happy times for American home-owners. U.S. home prices just fell for the first time in 16 years, new condos are languishing in former hot spots like Florida, and the subprime-lending fiasco threatens to drag down the wider economy.

But why listen to CNBC? Turn the dial a few notches to HGTV, and the housing boom has never been boomier. HGTV, the homespun redoubt of gardening and glue-gun projects that became a cable hit in the post-9/11 cocooning era, is now dominated by what it calls "Property Buzz" shows: series about buying and selling homes, which now make up six of the channel's 10 highest-rated shows. Shows like *Secrets That Sell!*, *Designed to Sell*, *Bought & Sold*, *Get It Sold*—notice a pattern?—offer a guide to tapping, Jed Clampett-style, the gusher of wealth sitting under your property. "What will people do to sell?" asks the intro of *Buy Me*. "How far will buyers go?"

Like CNBC, HGTV is a creature of a certain economic heyday (the early aughts housing boom, as opposed to the late-'90s NASDAQ bubble) that has had to adjust to tough times, in this case by offering escapism that turns head-on into the very thing people want to escape from. (Just as, after 9/11, terrorism became all the rage in pop culture.)

"Even a couple years ago, we got the sense that the market was becoming iffy for people," says HGTV senior vice president of programming Michael Dingley. "In times that are iffy, the stakes are very high, financially and emotionally, in buying and selling a home." The shows play on homeowners' nightmares—Will we get any offers? What if we have to carry two mortgages?—but there's usually a happy ending: the house is sold, the asking price met or exceeded. (Mind you, "happy" is relative. For a first-time buyer, low prices are good news. But more than 84% of HGTV viewers are homeowners, compared with roughly 68% of all Americans.)

The most mercenary, and irresistible, "Property Buzz" show is *My House Is Worth What?*, which is exactly what it sounds like. Homeowners anxious to cash in have their houses appraised, *Antiques Roadshow*—style. Features and renovations that add value—water views, granite counters—get a ka-ching! sound effect. (The premise is friendly to advertisers like Lowe's and Home Depot, since it helps viewers rationalize that spa bathroom as an "investment.") Minuses knock dollars

From *Time* 169.26 (25 Jun. 2007). Copyright © 2007 by Time, Inc. Reprinted with permission. All rights reserved.

Bravo, A&E, TLC and other channels have real-estate-oriented series, while HBO debuts the real estate satire 12 Miles of Bad Road next year. In FX's drama The Riches—about a con artist who moves to a gated community and passes himself off as a real estate lawyer— the buying and selling of land comes to stand for American dreams, appetites and origins.

off, especially anything that reflects the owner's individuality. "Your taste is very specific" is a death sentence on this show.

It all leads to the payoff, when an agent tells the breathless owners, "I would list your house for ..." It may not be realistic (how certain can an appraiser be that a half-bath is worth exactly $20,000?). But it's brilliant TV, allowing us to indulge a little jealousy (say, of the lucky bastard who bought a Manhattan apartment for $90,000 in 1990) and vicarious money lust. And it demonstrates how the housing boom changed the way people look at their homes: as an expression of their financial savvy rather than their creative selves.

And who can blame us for it? Social Security is endangered. Job security is a quaint memory. Upward social mobility is failing. (A new study by the Economic Mobility Project finds that American men in their 30s are worse off financially than their fathers.) Real estate may not offer double-digit returns anymore, but it does offer an atavistic promise of security, a nest egg embodied in Sheetrock that you can touch and dirt that can't be outsourced to Mumbai. Property fever is in our blood: this country made its fortune in sweet real estate deals—a Louisiana Purchase here, a few trinkets for Manhattan there—and these HGTV shows tap into something primal.

They're not alone: Bravo, A&E, TLC and other channels have real-estate-oriented series, while HBO debuts the real estate satire *12 Miles of Bad Road* next year. In FX's drama *The Riches*—about a con artist who moves to a gated community and passes himself off as a real estate lawyer—the buying and selling of land comes to stand for American dreams, appetites and origins. Creator Dmitry Lipkin says the pilot was shot in an exurb 40 minutes from New Orleans. "Everything around it was swampland," he recalls, "and in the middle of it was this very orderly chunk of land carved out for development." The setting, he says, captured the "quintessentially American" situation of building wealth out of nothing, imposing civilized façades on wilderness. One character gets her arm eaten by an alligator that emerges from the swamp.

That's homeownership in a nutshell: the dream of wealth, self-reinvention and security, combined with the faintest fear that something in your backyard may just come back to bite you. Welcome home, America.

Schlock and Awwww

By Jon Mooallem
Mother Jones, November/December 2007

Every week, Ty Pennington brings the American Dream to a deserving family. What a freakin' jerk.

"In charity," Francis Bacon wrote, "there is no excess." But then Bacon never saw *Extreme Makeover: Home Edition*, which since 2003 has been meting out garish and super-sized acts of charity—each more skillfully choreographed and excessive than the last—every Sunday night on ABC.

Each week, the reality show's "design team," led by cloying carpenter Ty Pennington, parks its tour bus at the dilapidated doorstep of a deserving, downtrodden family and unleashes a whopping assault of good will. After hugging the family, Pennington commiserates in his hushed tone of surferesque sincerity (he often talks to people as if they are crying, even if they haven't yet started) and then offers hope. "Here's the good news," he tells a single mother in Mississippi whose three children have learned to defecate in plastic bags because they have no plumbing. "We're here now, and things are going to get better."

Typically, at this point the family is whisked off to Disney World and the design team begins demolishing its house and building a better one—fully landscaped and prominently decorated with brand-name appliances and furnishings supplied by Sears, Home Depot, and the show's other sponsors—in one week. The family returns to a crowd of neighbors, volunteer builders, and well-wishers chanting "Move that bus!" before the team's motor coach peels away from the curb, revealing the new home.

Just like that, *Makeover* plucks poor or working-class people from their misfortunes and not only gives them a new Owens Coming roof over their heads, but—the implication is—newfound stability and comfort. Often the family also gets a new car, computers, or college scholarships for the kids. These changes can be profound. That Mississippi mom, reeling beside her new Ford Edge SUV while Pennington shouts, "It looks great, it's fun to drive, and best of all it's all yours!" mentions that she's never owned a new car before. Suddenly we grasp the life-changing enormity of just giving her a reliable vehicle. But wait—here are an iPod, modem art, bicycles, a karaoke machine, Panasonic flat-screen TVs, a collection of African percussion for her son, and a spacious new storefront for her fledgling business. Plus, gospel singer CeCe Winans has turned up to raise the family a nest egg!

From *Mother Jones* 32.6 (Nov./Dec. 2007). Copyright © 2007 by Foundation for National Progress. Reprinted with permission. All rights reserved.

We are increasingly tuning in to this brand of life-affirming transformation, whether it's Ty and the gang framing up a starter mansion, Madonna whisking children out of Malawi and into the tabloids, Oprah opening a school for impoverished South African girls, or Michael Moore—spouting the kind of schmaltzy platitudes Pennington has perfected—delivering sick and forgotten 9/11 rescue workers to the handsome Cuban doctors who will treat them for free.

These are feel-good narratives, meticulously polished to make us feel good about ourselves, too. With each cathartic conclusion, it's easy to believe that we are contributing to the healing when in fact we are just watching TV. Moreover, the ideal of domesticity into which *Makeover* deposits its families—the outsized house, the stainless-steel appliances and items from the Sears "Ty Pennington Style" collection-feeds our love of consumption and luxury; nobody tunes in to watch Habitat for Humanity build multiple modest houses. Frankly, the whole package is irresistible. More than once, I have caught myself mouthing "Move that bus!" along with the crowd.

> *And yet even as I am moved by such acts of kindness, I also feel an uncontrollable urge to cut them down. Makeover is schlock. But as reality TV increasingly concocts its schlock out of actual hardship and actual kindness, deriding it can open some unsettling moral terrain.*

And yet even as I am moved by such acts of kindness, I also feel an uncontrollable urge to cut them down. *Makeover* is schlock. But as reality TV increasingly concocts its schlock out of actual hardship and actual kindness, deriding it can open some unsettling moral terrain. I felt a certain smugness, for example, watching *American Idol*'s "Idol Gives Back" fundraising special last April. There was Ryan Seacrest, fresh from handing out meals to AIDS orphans in Kenya, clutching a child and urging him to just "let it out." And there I was: sitting on my couch, eating a tremendous burrito, scoffing at the man who had traveled across the globe to feed orphans.

Clearly, something was wrong. I have never fed AIDS orphans. I have never built anyone a house. By these measures, I don't stack up very well at all against Ty Pennington and his cadre of extreme prime-time altruists.

I feel only slightly less conflicted about mocking *Makeover* knowing that it can't always deliver the fairy-tale endings it suggests. Several newspaper reports have exposed how some *Makeover* families wind up unprepared for their new, exponentially higher utility bills and property taxes. A blind New Jersey man with three disabled children and a $14,000 tax bill on his new abode told one paper, "With all the taxes, it's like we're on a chopping block." Meanwhile, five siblings featured on an Easter Sunday 2005 episode recently sued their adoptive parents for driving them out of the nine-bedroom, six-bathroom house built for them. They also sued the show for rebroadcasting their episode knowing that its ending had soured. The kids' attorney happily revealed to the *Los Angdes Times* that the show's touching "door knock" scene, in which the design team first arrived at the house and dispensed hugs, took seven takes to shoot.

Even infrequent viewers will notice how the show has tightened its stranglehold on our consciences by gradually inflating its misery quotient. While the first season featured a couple that needed a larger home for its (surprise!) triplets, only two seasons later we were deep into a gallery of woe: twins with leukemia, the mother of a little girl who wandered off to catch fireflies and disappeared forever. In a memo acquired by the Smoking Gun website, a producer asks the show's casting agents to look for a kid with "congenital insensitivity to pain": "There are 17 known cases in US, let me know if one is in your town!"

It's easy to resent *Makeover* for the ways it simultaneously helps and exploits its beneficiaries. But when it comes down to it, I resent *Makeover* because it exploits me. I can feel it bullying me for my compassion, extracting it with a ham-fisted conspiracy of narration, editing, and musical accompaniment. What ultimately offends me about *Makeover* is that it takes humanity and turns it into bad art. It's an affront to my aesthetics more than my morals.

There's some solace, perhaps, in knowing that kindness is popular enough to be shamelessly commodified—that charity sells. And that thankfully, not everyone who comes into contact with the show is distracted by its wretched artifice. "I really think a community could do this without the cameras, without Hollywood," a Missouri woman told a local paper after *Makeover* wrapped an episode in her town. After all, all of the labor on the show is volunteer. And while few community groups could get the truckloads of lavish furnishings *Makeover* does without the kickback of prime-time exposure, not everyone needs cameras trained on them in order to act selflessly.

Wasn't it stirring to see so many people racing down to the Gulf Coast to contribute plywood, sweat, and compassion after Hurricane Katrina? Witnessing the efforts of volunteers in her hometown of Pass Christian, Mississippi, *Good Morning America*'s Robin Roberts felt compelled to remind viewers, "This is not *Extreme Makeover: Home Edition*. This is true reality TV."

But even "true reality TV" demands that no act of genuine altruism be left unhyped. And so Roberts signaled for a humongous banner to be pulled away, revealing the progress made on rebuilding one woman's home. But there was more. "CeCe Winans is going to sing for us," Roberts smiled. "She's gonna lift our spirits with song!"

The Situation for Reality TV Stars?
Money, Honey

By T.L. Stanley
Los Angeles Times, October 18, 2011

The Kardashian and 'Jersey Shore' clans aren't the only reality show players reeling in lucrative endorsement deals. Even lesser-tier celebrities are cashing in on the marketing magic.

If you're part of a reality TV show and might be famous for 15 minutes, tops, it's probably best to cash in while you can. But what if you're not a breakout star on the Kim Kardashian level?

No worries. Blue-chip national advertisers, nightclub promoters and book publishers still want you. And they're willing to fork over real money—sometimes six figures and up—for your recognizable face.

While the Kardashian klan is pulling down a reported $65 million annually and *Jersey Shore*'s Mike "The Situation" Sorrentino banked as much as $5 million last year alone, lesser players in the reality show game are riding their relative popularity to notable financial gain.

The list of second-, third- and fourth-tier reality show participants signing lucrative endorsements keeps growing, say Hollywood talent agents and other executives who barter the deals. And the trend is likely to continue.

"Every brand is dabbling in this area, and some want to glom onto any celebrity no matter how fleeting or newly minted," said David Reeder, vice president at GreenLight, a consultancy that marries brands with famous faces. "There's an insatiable appetite out there for new stars. That might even extend to the third banana on a truTV show, who all of a sudden has a big talent agency repping him."

As telegenic as they are outrageous, Sorrentino and Nicole "Snooki" Polizzi were the first *Jersey Shore* housemates to hook up with advertisers. (Among their stable: Wonderful Pistachios, Virgin Mobile, Reebok and Flow Formal tuxedos.) Then Paul "Pauly D" DelVecchio appeared in a Kraft Miracle Whip commercial, and Vinny Guadagnino used his signature "fresh to death" grooming habits to hawk Philips Norelco hair trimmers in a recent back-to-campus campaign. Sorrentino reportedly saw a six-figure payday from the tuxedo maker, as did DelVecchio from the Kraft ad. (Reps for the men declined to confirm specifics.)

Not to be entirely outdone, Sammi "Sweetheart" Giancola, Deena Cortese and Ronnie Ortiz-Magro are shilling energy shots and diet supplements.

From *Los Angeles Times* (18 Oct. 2011). Copyright © 2011 by T.L. Stanley. Reprinted with permission. All rights reserved.

Trista Sutter, the original "Bachelorette" in 2003, recently linked with General Mills' Betty Crocker to promote TV-themed recipes, "Dancing With the Stars" professional dancer Cheryl Burke is now touting Dole salads after hoofing it with Hoover upright vacuums, and "The Hills" alum Lauren Conrad is a spokesmodel for Avon and touts her own Kohl's clothing line.

Reality stars can earn anywhere from a few thousand dollars for mentioning a product on Twitter or online promotion to tens of thousands for personal appearances and media interviews on a brand's behalf. A minor star from a hit on the E! network could pull in as much as $30,000 for working the room at a Las Vegas club opening, provided there were promotional tweets beforehand and photos during the event. A lesser-known "Real Housewives" cast member could match that amount for selling exclusive photos to a supermarket tabloid.

> *Reality show stars also seem more authentic and less precious to the buying public, industry execs said. After all, some of them are famous only for their inability to self-censor. It doesn't matter that some of the stars have no discernible skills other than shameless self-promotion.*

This doesn't come close to the mid-six-figures and above that the crème of the reality crop can pull down. But there aren't many personalities at that level, where "Dirty Jobs'" Mike Rowe (Ford trucks, Lee jeans, Kimberly-Clark's Viva), "What Not to Wear's" Stacy London (Procter & Gamble's Pantene, Target, Woolite) and "DWTS'" Brooke Burke (Skechers, Unilever's Suave and Oral B) breathe rarefied brand air.

Bethenny Frankel, who has said publicly that she participated in "Real Housewives of New York" strictly to hype her businesses, is in that group, too, with ties to Pampers and Hanes. She created her own brand, Skinny girl cocktails, and sold it to Beam Global earlier this year; estimates of the deal price have varied wildly—from $8 million to $120 million—but Frankel will not disclose its value.

Reality personalities have become go-to brand ambassadors for several reasons, the primary one being that they work cheap compared with established stars.

"It's found money to them," said an agent at a major talent agency who didn't want to speak on the record because he represents reality stars. "They might not be able to retire on it, but they can cobble enough together to make a good living. And compared to what they had before, which was nothing, it's all cake."

It's also a good deal for marketers.

"If I pay a reality star 1/50 of what I'd pay Johnny Depp, my return is going to come back much quicker," said Mark Young, a professor at USC's Marshall School of Business.

Reality show stars also seem more authentic and less precious to the buying public, industry execs said. After all, some of them are famous only for their inability to self-censor. It doesn't matter that some of the stars have no discernible skills other than shameless self-promotion.

"Consumers can relate to that person," said Dari Marder, chief marketing officer of Iconix Brand Group, home to Bongo, Candie's, OP and other fashion labels that feature endorsers such as "Keeping Up With the Kardashians" Rob Kardashian, "The Osbournes" Kelly Osbourne and "The Hills" alum Audrina Patridge. "There's an Everyman quality about reality stars."

The deals are often short-term, to take advantage of a star while he's hot and to part ways before he goes off the rails. (Even risk-averse marketers are willing to take a chance these days with potentially volatile stars, though, since fans seem to feed on their bad behavior.)

Reality mavens are often heavy social media users, meaning their reach via Facebook, Twitter and other digital avenues far exceeds their TV time. Rob Kardashian has 2 million Twitter followers, and a recent tweet of his OP ad and retweet by his social networking sisters snagged millions of impressionable eyeballs.

There's near-constant coverage of these stars in Us Weekly and In Touch, TMZ, RadarOnline and elsewhere, stoking their popularity.

"The world has become more cluttered than ever, and brands are looking for any edge to separate themselves from their competitors," said David Schwab, managing director of Octagon First Call, which helps brands assess celebrity value for ad campaigns. "Reality stars drive awareness, and that's gold to a brand."

Television continues to pump out new reality personalities, enabling companies to find the perfect spokesperson to speak to a specific demographic.

For instance, Gerber Legendary Blades made a multi-year deal with "Man vs. Wild" host Bear Grylls for a survival gadget product line that carries his name. Grylls, who uses the knives exclusively in his Discovery channel series, takes home a piece of the sales, though the value is undisclosed.

"He's an adventurer, not just a TV star, and he was out there climbing Mt. Everest before the cameras were rolling," said Corey Maynard, Gerber's director of marketing. "He's different from a lot of reality stars who have very short windows in which they have any brand recognition at all, let alone credibility, if they ever had any. He's not just famous for being famous."

Philips Norelco chose to work with Guadagnino because the "Jersey Shore" cast member could reach out to the college crowd at the key back-to-school selling season. Known for his "short and tight" coif, he's a believable shill for do-it-yourself hair trimmers.

"He's very relevant to young male consumers—they want to hear recommendations from him," said Mike Schwartz, brand manager. "And he got massive amounts of media coverage for everything he did for us."

Do these deals move the needle? Marder and Maynard say they do, though for some marketers that can be a tougher question to answer. (Schwartz said he's still waiting on the data.)

"It's always up for debate whether the use of any celebrity sways consumer behavior," Reeder said. "But that's almost irrelevant in these cases. What's important is that you can grab a consumer's attention for 15 seconds."

USC's Young agreed, saying his informal on-campus research has shown him that young fans and even detractors are tuned in to what reality stars wear, buy and hawk.

"That's marketing heaven when even the people who don't like the shows care what kind of jeans the stars wear," Young said. "There's a good reason why reality people are called influencers."

With Reality TV, Is Southie about to Be New Jerseyed?

By Billy Baker
The Boston Globe, July 29, 2012

Hollywood captured and ruined South Boston at the same time. Now a slew of TV shows are going to turn "a Southie" into a symbol.

One night in 1994, when I was a freshman in college in New Orleans, I was in a bar charging hard at two young ladies. At some point in my game, one of the women stopped me.

"You're a Southie," she said.

I was a Southie kid, no question about it, all accent and attitude, me against the world. But I did not understand what she meant by "a Southie." I had never even mentioned Southie. They just knew I was from Boston.

I tried to educate the ladies, explain to them that Southie was the name for a neighborhood of Boston, a very particular one, but that I was from Southie, not a Southie.

"Yes," she said, "but you're a Southie."

I knew what she meant, and it was the first time I noticed how the outside world had begun to define a type, what they considered to be the authentic Bostonian. Accent and attitude. And they gave that type a name, put all the credit and blame on one neighborhood: South Boston.

I did not need to be told that the world was fascinated with people from Southie. It was always there, wherever I went, even in Boston. Southie triggers a reaction. Everyone has something to say about it, has his own idea of it.

During my senior year, I thought I'd try to do something with this Southie fascination, and for my senior project I wrote a screenplay about a guy who leaves the neighborhood. And I can tell you exactly when that project died: on Christmas Day, during my winter break in 1997, when I was home in Boston. That night, I went by myself to the Kendall Square Cinema in Cambridge to see a small indie film I'd read about, written by and starring two young guys from Cambridge. It was called *Good Will Hunting*. It was excellent. It took that type — all accent and attitude — and used it to create a classic cinema archetype, the charming rogue, and it gave that type a quest outside the neighborhood involving, of all things, math. But it worked. It was endearing, and it focused on the mostly likable qualities of the Southie guy without attempting to define the real neighborhood or bog the characters down in the streets.

From *The Boston Globe* (29 July 2012). Copyright © 2012 by Boston Globe Newspaper Company. Reprinted with permission. All rights reserved.

I left the theater and made other writing plans. It wasn't like Hollywood was ever going to make another movie about Southie.

The Real Southie. This is the catchphrase of the moment in Hollywood, for Tinseltown is not done with its Southie fascination. Not even close. Since *Good Will Hunting,* the Boston Irish have replaced the New York Italians as Hollywood's go-to for bad white guys. Despite their varied Boston neighborhood settings, *The Departed, Mystic River, Gone Baby Gone,* and *The Town* were all "Southie movies." And now reality television is coming. Anywhere from two to five shows could be about to drop, each one promising to deliver the *real* South Boston.

A few months back, I wrote a story for the Globe about this reality-show frenzy. At the time, there was a casting war going on, and when the people of Southie mostly balked at the idea of handing over their story to outsiders—this is a place that has long guarded its own mythology—the producers cast the net outside the neighborhood. That's because they didn't need to rely on the 33,688 people who live in South Boston to find "a Southie."

> **The Real Southie. This is the catchphrase of the moment in Hollywood, for Tinseltown is not done with its Southie fascination. Not even close. Since Good Will Hunting, the Boston Irish have replaced the New York Italians as Hollywood's go-to for bad white guys.**

You can definitely find that type in Southie, even after gentrification and the arrival of condos and the end of the Whitey Bulger era. But you can also find that type elsewhere. I was on a plane not too long ago and the in-flight magazine had a profile of Mark Wahlberg referring to him as "the hard-driving Southie" while making it clear he was from Dorchester. Brandon Kane, a cast member on the current season of MTV's *The Real World,* is being billed as a Southie, though he has taken great measures to note that while he spent a good deal of his childhood in Southie with his relatives, he is from Quincy. Kane was attacked all over the Internet for daring to associate himself with Southie; the rule is you have to be born there.

And now we're going to combine this type—no doubt in its most extreme form—with conflict, because reality television needs friction. Southie has been no stranger to conflict on a grand scale, most famously with busing and Bulger's Irish mob, but at the moment things are relatively quiet. All except for that low background hum, a sound heard in many Boston neighborhoods, but most vocally fought here: gentrification. Natives vs. the yuppies who have ruined the place. Us against them. Perfect TV.

Timmy Talbot is the most Southie kid I know. The 36-year-old bartender lives in Dorchester now because he's trying to stay out of trouble, something he's not usually good at. A couple weeks ago, he was with his girlfriend in The Playwright, on East Broadway, a fine eating and drinking establishment of the new Southie. When he was walking out, a kid, maybe just old enough to drink, hit him with the stiff shoulder.

They turned to each other, as Timmy tells the story, and the kid said, "Watch where you're going, you [expletive] yuppie."

"I turned toward him, Baker, and I says, 'What?' "

Timmy Talbot used to be this kid. He still is. "In Southie, you grow up in a tunnel," he says. "You think you're the baddest person on the planet. You're bad because you grew up in South Boston, even though you haven't done [expletive]. And in a way, that helps you, gives you that edge; you think you can do anything."

So when the kid replied, "You heard me, you [expletive] yuppie," Timmy smacked him. "Right in the mouth." Hard. "Stumbling off to the doctor's office." Then Timmy looked the kid in the face, told him his name, and instructed him to go home and ask his father about him. "It brought me to this place where I saw what the kids do to people. They're jumping people. You just don't do that. You're going to jump a yuppie because of the way they talk, because someone gets away and does something with his life?

"They should just change the name to preserve it, put it away somewhere. That *was* South Boston. They're fighting to protect something that ain't even there no more. That's a place people have memories of. And it's not what it was."

The real South Boston is the new South Boston, and it is a work in progress. Gentrification brought a very specific shift in the population: The size of the 25- to 29-year-old demographic jumped dramatically in the decade after the 2000 Census, from about 3,800 to almost 6,600. And South Boston changed because of them. Small homes became smaller condos. Three-bedrooms were priced not for a family, but three roommates. The waterfront, mostly overgrown parking lots and old warehouses, was redeveloped into an entirely new place. There was money to be had in the housing stock, and Southie people took it, cashed out, left. What remained was a different place. There's no going back. Unless — turn the cameras on, please — we fight them. That's what "a Southie" would do.

"The press releases [from one reality show] say, 'Can they fight off the yuppie invasion?' " notes Heather Foley, a lifelong resident who writes a humor column for local website Caught in Southie. "Why would you sign up for that?"

Nick Collins, a 29-year-old state representative, is the first of the younger generation to get elected in South Boston. He's a native; that requirement for pols hasn't changed. But his present and future will involve dealing with this new and evolving neighborhood. Collins actually believes most newcomers and old-timers get along in Southie, and he's worried the television shows will "try to highlight the negatives." He says: "People who make TV like people who fall on their face. And they're going to put these two sides on TV, and it will look like a longstanding battle royale that has to have a victor."

David Lindsay-Abaire, a Pulitzer Prize-winning playwright who grew up in the neighborhood in the 1970s and '80s and now lives in Brooklyn, thinks portraying the battle over gentrification is false, because the battle is over. "Now you're just pointing at people who are complaining," he says, and he worries the shows are "just going to make those people look stupid and close-minded, that there are still people in Southie who are fighting the wrong fight." This authentic Southie, this thing Hollywood seems to want it to be, feels like a stereotype from another era. "The world," says Lindsay-Abaire, "seems to think Southie stopped forming the day Whitey Bulger first walked into [the bar] Triple O's."

Still, for some residents, the fight will never be over. And sometimes the newcomers make it hard to move on. Recently, a 10-year resident wrote an open letter to the neighborhood on Caught in Southie, complaining of hearing the "yuppie" taunt "at least 20 times a week," despite owning a home and small business there and being active in community organizations. "When will I be accepted as part of the Southie community?" the person asked. Naturally, a war broke out in the comments section and on Facebook. Bringing it up doesn't help.

I understand the longing for what is gone. Southie is my hometown, and as such my reality is rooted in my childhood. I believe all people are this way. And your hometown is never like it was, can never be like it was, because you are not who you were. But childhood, oh, my childhood . . . there was nothing quite like it. It was the '80s and early '90s. There were kids everywhere, streaming out of the triple-deckers, and the streets were a stage for acting up. I ran with a crew that hung around the Tynan Elementary School — there could easily be 50 of us in a pack — and we wreaked havoc because that was really all there was to do. We were kids with no money and a thirst for adventure, so we created stories to live inside of, to see what we could get away with.

What's that you say? You did the same thing? Impossible. You're not from Southie. Beat it, before you get dope-slapped upside your head.

And that old gang of mine. Well, that's 50 different stories. They were all "a Southie," and they were all different. Some got into drugs, yes. It's a big problem. And, sure, some of that gang got into knucklehead stuff.

Here's the sad truth about most of my old gang: They're now kind of boring, like me. They have kids and jobs and mortgages. They are cops and firemen and municipal workers. Some go to work in a white collar. Quite a few of them have a raging addiction to golf and scratch tickets. None of them are as handsome as Matt and Ben. A lot of them left Southie, as did I. Sure, they still like to go out with the gang and act up—who doesn't?—but, as a firefighter buddy of mine likes to say, "If you stay up late with the boys, you've got to get up with the men."

Every happy family is alike, Tolstoy wrote, and every unhappy family is unhappy in its own way. Reality television does not like happy families; it simply doesn't work, because there is no conflict. I know a few nice families that sat down with the reality show producers; none of them was cast.

One of the reality shows is being developed by 495 Productions. It made *The Jersey Shore,* a show that features eight young troublemakers. Only two are from New Jersey. Doesn't matter. They helped define the Garden State to the outside world, and now the same thing is in store for Southie. A colorful minority will define the majority. We're about to be New Jerseyed.

Good Will Hunting has turned out to be a double-edged sword. It captured something great about Southie and at the same time ruined it forever. Because what I saw after that was unbelievable: Young women would get out of college and choose to move to Southie. Sure, it's close to downtown, but the real reason they were moving was because they were subconsciously thinking they were going to find "a Southie" like Matt and Ben. Everything else followed them, namely, young guys. That's how everything changed. That's how the old Southie reality ended. These reality shows will be part of creating the new one.

I'll probably watch them and probably hate them, for their reality will not be my own. But I don't doubt they will make for good TV. I'm surprised it took reality this long to come to the neighborhood. It almost feels like they're too late.

Southie by the Numbers

- Total population: **33,688**
- Median age: **32.4**
- Percentage white: **82.5**
- Percentage living in family households: **54.8**
- Median price of single-family home in 2011: **$400,000**
- Median price of condo in 2011: **$370,000**

Does Getting Laid Off Make for Compelling Reality TV?

By Dina Gachman
Forbes, September 9, 2012

If you've lived through a layoff, you know it's not a very cinematic experience. There's no rollicking soundtrack playing while you dramatically stride out of the office holding a banker's box full of family photos and a few office supplies you maybe grabbed in a moment of heated revenge.

When I was laid off from my job as a Creative Executive at a film production company a few years ago, I didn't escape with a stapler, but a few multicolored Sticky Note pads may or may not have found their way into my bag. They had been "downsizing" different departments on and off for over a year so the layoff wasn't a total shock, but as most people who have been through the experience know, it's still always a blow, even if you see it coming. So when I read about a new Fox reality show called *Does Someone Have to Go?* about dysfunctional companies asking co-workers to decide who should get laid off (rather than the bosses), I was a little intrigued, and extremely insulted. When you've lived the experience, it's tough to flip a switch and think of it as entertainment, unless that entertainment has integrity and involves George Clooney, like the film *Up In The Air*. This new Fox show doesn't exactly scream "integrity."

Fox picked up an earlier incarnation of the show three years ago, and back then it was called *Someone's Gotta Go*. Originally, employees at a real-life struggling company would cast their votes for who should get laid off. Mike Darnell, president of Fox's Alternative Programming, called it "*Survivor* meets *The Office*." Employees got to see each other's salaries and human resources files, and then divulge with relentless honesty what they thought about the co-workers that they said "good morning" to during countless elevator rides to work. They had the power to send them packing.

The show was shelved (it probably wasn't as hilarious as *The Office* or as entertaining as *Survivor*—what a shock!), but now it's back with some changes and a new title. This time around, the employees don't have to vote someone out of their cubicle if they don't want to, apparently giving human beings a chance to not be cold-hearted, water-cooler sadists if they so choose. This is reality TV though, so I have a hunch that sadism will trump sweetness most of the time. Who wants to watch Snooki making tea and knitting, right? It's entertainment—people want drunken, ridiculous humiliation. They want drama, and they don't really care if it hits a little too close to home for hundreds of thousands of people.

From *Forbes* (9 September 2012). Copyright © 2012 by Forbes, Inc. Reprinted with permission. All rights reserved.

> *Mike Darnell, president of Fox's Alternative Programming, called it "Survivor meets The Office." Employees got to see each other's salaries and human resources files, and then divulge with relentless honesty what they thought about the co-workers that they said "good morning" to during countless elevator rides to work. They had the power to send them packing.*

Fox and producer Endemol USA (*Big Brother*, *Fear Factor*) plan to air the show midseason, according to TV Guide and Deadline Hollywood. Part of me wants to "boycott" *Does Someone Have To Go?* by not watching, as if that's a radical way to protest the show. Me not watching *Here Comes Honey Boo Boo* obviously isn't putting a dent in TLC's profits, so is avoiding this new Fox show really going to do much? When a company starts having layoffs, the office environment can naturally just become sort of toxic. People are paranoid, looking over their shoulder, trying to cling to their jobs. It's not ideal, but it happens. Do we really need to exploit that dynamic?

Is it healthy to take a very personal, often traumatic situation like a layoff and turn it into "*Survivor* meets *The Office*"? Reality TV usually reflects the very worst in people through a mixture of sneaky editing, alcohol (though it's doubtful they'll be swigging mojitos in the conference room during this show), and casting. There's nothing "real" about reality television, and there's nothing entertaining about watching people getting laid off from their jobs in between commercial breaks. It makes sense that the show was shelved the first time around. The question is, why is it back? I think I'd rather watch Honey Boo Boo.

Reality TV Shows Teach a Lot about Money

By Ellen Roseman
Moneyville.ca, March 25, 2012

Here's a guilty pleasure: I love reality shows, such as *Dancing with the Stars* and *The Voice*.

When *Dragons Den* launched in 2006, I predicted it would be a hit for CBC. It's going into a seventh season with a new Dragon, personal finance author David Chilton (who replaces Robert Herjavec), and I can't wait.

I'm impressed by the potential of reality TV to help people learn to manage their personal finances. Entertainment is a key goal, but education happens along the way.

Til Debt Do Us Part, now in syndication after six seasons, was a huge hit for the Slice Network. Host Gail Vaz-Oxlade helped couples face up to reality after over-spending drove them apart.

I'm following a new show, *Million Dollar Neighbourhood*, which debuted last January on the Oprah Winfrey Network (OWN).

Co-produced by Corus Entertainment, this Canadian series is a winner for the struggling new network. It has just been renewed for a second season.

"We're delighted that Canadians have embraced the show and that it has in-spired people to take action in their own communities," said Vibika Bianchi, Corus vice-president.

The show follows 100 families in Aldergrove, B.C. (outside of Vancouver), as they try to raise their collective net worth by $1 million. One lucky family wins $100,000 if the goal is achieved.

The last of 10 episodes runs this week. All 10 will be aired back to back on Good Friday, April 6.

I spoke to co-host Bruce Sellery, a former Business News Network reporter and a personal finance author (*Moolala*), about what makes this different from other personal finance programs.

It's not just "schadenfreude stories," he says, referring to a German word that describes taking joy in the misfortunes of others.

"We want people to watch the show and learn something. We don't want them to say, 'Well, at least I don't have $60,000 in credit card debts.'"

Families face individual challenges each week. For example, they have to stop buying groceries, beer and liquor and eat only what's in their cupboards and fridges at home.

From *Moneyville.ca* (25 Mar. 2012). Copyright © 2012 by Toronto Star. Reprinted with permission - Torstar Syndication Services. All rights reserved.

> *Net worth—what you own minus what you owe—is an academic concept. But you finally understand how it works in practice as you watch families try to apply it to their own activities.*

They also have group challenges, such as staging a wine-and-dine event to raise money. They're judged on whether or not they increase their net worth by $100,000 in each episode.

Net worth—what you own minus what you owe—is an academic concept. But you finally understand how it works in practice as you watch families try to apply it to their own activities.

Did Aldergrove manage to turn itself into a Million Dollar Community in a three-month period? I'm sworn to secrecy. But I'll be keen to see which Canadian city is chosen for the next series in 2013.

Another reality show I like to watch is *Canadian Pickers* on History TV, adapted from a popular U.S. show. Scott Cozens and Sheldon Smithens drive across Canada to find antiques and collectibles they can resell.

I've learned a lot from seeing how they negotiate with collectors who want an inflated price for their stuff. It's an elaborate dance.

Here are a few tips from Smithens, an experienced auctioneer:

- Buy a few minor items to get things rolling. You want the seller to see you bend at first. Then, you can take a more rigid stance when negotiating on major items.

- Humour is an essential ingredient in negotiations. The best deals happen when everyone is having fun.

- Treat every negotiation as if it's not the last. You'll do business again with the same people (and their network) if you're fair and respectful.

- Don't take advantage. You can insist on paying more than expected if the seller doesn't know the value of the merchandise and is prepared to take any offer.

With a house full of collectibles—which my husband calls junk—I like to see how these pickers value their discoveries. Maybe one day, I'll be able to sell my stuff at a profit.

How Much Are Financial Reality TV Stars Paid, and Does It Interfere with Reality?

By Amanda L. Grossman
Houston Chronicle, Monday, August 29, 2011

I sat down to watch the first episode of the new season of *Downsized*. My eyes widened when the father, Todd, decided that it was time to start looking for a home to purchase. Not only did they just have a foreclosure 18 months earlier on top of a bankruptcy, but his argument to purchase a home was that the children now owned about 5 vehicles between them (they worked hard and paid for their own vehicles) and there was no room to park them all.

The wife was not keen on purchasing a home after just getting out of such a rough period in their lives (listen to your gut Laura!) and so they decided to discuss their finances and home purchasing outlook with their financial advisor. During the sit down, it came to light that they had received money from starring in the first season of *Downsized*. The amount of money was not disclosed; however, they were able to pay off their debt, their debt to their children, and still had $18,000 in the bank. In my mind I think they were paid around $50,000, but this is just speculating based off of the debts I remember from the first season. Needless to say, they are in a much better financial situation due to their involvement with the television show...but I am still completely against the idea that they should purchase a home.

Reality television shows to me are sort of like terrariums. Through the glass we are given a sneak peek of a different ecosystem, however frail or robust it may be. Because of the recession we are seeing reality shows pop-up that are based on people whose finances are in disrepair. However, by paying them money to be on a reality TV show the producers jeopardize the terrarium environment that we all find so fascinating or gut-wrenching to watch. It's like when you watch one of those Renovation Reality TV shows and you know that there just has to be a handyman behind the camera—wouldn't it be nice if they swooped in and pointed out what they were doing wrong before they hurt themselves or their wallets? But if they did...then it wouldn't be reality anymore.

This made me wonder about financial reality television shows: how much money do financial reality TV stars make for being in the shows, and how does this affect their reality and the 'reality' that we are witnessing? From what I have seen and researched online, reality TV stars are compensated in some way for their participation. I think whether or not this affects the reality that we see is based on many

From *Houston Chronicle* (29 Aug. 2011). Copyright © 2011 by Hearst Corp. Reprinted with permission. All rights reserved.

factors, such as the type of payment, time of the payment, and the amount of the payment.

Time of Payment

I think the time of the payment is key in whether or not it interferes with the reality that we are viewing. Is the person paid per episode, before taping, or after the episode/season? This could have a lot of bearing on their lives. I think if the people are not paid during the tapings, then that holds a little bit more reality than those who are paid per-episode.

> *During the show there is typically no money exchanged between the producers and the person. However, several times she has had to give a person monetary loans against their potential $5,000 earnings at the end (every time she does this she informs the viewers and subtracts it from any money earned at the end of the show).*

For example, Gail Vaz-Oxlade's show *'Til Debt do Us* Part pays the person at the end of the show *if* they made the improvements and changes she was hoping to see. The payout from this show can be up to $5,000, and she often throws in a monetary gift of some sort like a weekend getaway or paid-for classes to further someone's passion. During the show there is typically no money exchanged between the producers and the person. However, several times she has had to give a person monetary loans against their potential $5,000 earnings at the end (every time she does this she informs the viewers and subtracts it from any money earned at the end of the show).

The show *Downsized* is another example where the people were not paid during the season; however, this one has a twist. For the first season the family was unpaid. Then they were paid an undisclosed sum of money at the end of the first season, and WETV is now airing a second season. This means that their reality has now changed dramatically as they were able to pay off their debts and have $18,000 left in a savings account. How would their family have fared without this money? What would their reality be then?

Type of Payment

Some people are paid for their appearance and participation with cash, while others are given non-monetary compensation such as a new home and a vacation while the home is being built (*Extreme Makeover Home Edition*). While not having a mortgage to deal with each month arguably gives you a huge financial leg-up, the families also have to cover higher property tax, utility and maintenance bills (it is typical for a home to go from being 1,200 square feet to over 4,000 square feet, which ends up raising the property taxes for not only the owner, but in some cases the neighborhood). Also, there are tax ramifications for someone giving you such a large gift. However, this show stops taping after the owners are given their new house, so we don't really see the results of people being given such a large gift.

Amount of Payment

Depending on how much money the show is bringing the network, industry experts say that reality TV stars are paid anywhere between $750 per week (*Big Brother*) to $75,000 episode (Jon and Kate at their height of notoriety).

Teen Mom on MTV reportedly pays $60,000-$65,000 per season. This is a lot of money for a teenager (heck, it's a lot of money for someone my age!), and would certainly change their financial circumstance. In fact, this would seem to backfire because it could show other teenagers that it is not that tough to make it as a teen mom (which undoubtedly it is incredibly tough to do so, especially due to finances, but for other obvious reasons as well).

Anticipation Factor

I'd like to discuss one other thought I had: the anticipation factor. I am not sure how much reality can be in what we are viewing due to the fact that it is human to make financial decisions based on what you are anticipating. If you know that you are going to receive monetary compensation at the end of the season or show, then perhaps you will spend money as needed or wanted. This would certainly change the reality of the terrarium.

After all is said and done, I feel that paying financial reality television stars is going to change the reality that we are watching, whether it be because of the anticipation that they are receiving payment after the show is finished, or because they are being paid all along. Yet I do believe that they should be paid for their time and willingness to bare their lives on television—after all, networks are making money off of them. I guess I need to have a dose of skepticism for shows that I watch and remember that primarily they are for entertainment purposes.

Bibliography

Andrejevic, M. *Reality TV: The Work of Being Watched*. Oxford: Rowman and Littlefield, 2004. Print.

Bignell, Jonathan. *Big Brother: Reality TV in the Twenty-First Century*. Basingstoke: Palgrave Macmillan, 2005. Print.

Clissold, B. D. "Candid Camera and the Origins of Reality TV: Contextualizing a Historical Precedent." In S. Holmes and D. Jermyn (eds.). *Understanding Reality*

Curnutt, Hugh. "Durable Participants: A Generational Approach to TV's 'Ordinary' Labor Pool." *Media, Culture, & Society*. 33.7 (2001): 1061-1076. Print.

Dovey, Jon. Freakshow: *First Person Media and Factual Television*. Sterling: Pluto Press, 2000. Print.

Dvorak, Ken, and Julie Anne Taddeo. *The Tube Has Spoken: Reality TV & History*. Lexington: University Press of Kentucky, 2010. Print.

Escoffery, David, ed. *How Real Is Reality TV? Essays on Representation and Truth*. Jefferson, NC: McFarland, 2006. Print.

Essany, Michael. *Reality Check: The Business and Art of Producing Reality TV*. Oxford: Focal Press, 2008. Print.

Ferguson, Galit. "The Family on Reality Television: Who's Shaming Whom?" *Television & New Media*. 11.2 (2010): 87-104. Print.

Furedi, Frank. "Celebrity Culture." *Society*. 47.6 (2010): 493-497. Print.

Glynn, Kevin. *Tabloid Culture: Trash Taste, Popular Power, and the Transformation of American Television*. Durham, NC: Duke University Press, 2000. Print.

Hall, Alice. "Viewer's Perceptions of Reality Programs." *Communication Quarterly*. 54.2 (2007): 191-211. Print.

Hill, Annette. *Restyling Factual TV: Audience and News, Documentary and Reality*. New York: Routledge, 2007. Print.

Homes, Su, and Deborah Jermyn. *Understanding Reality Television*. London: Routledge, 2004. Print.

Kavka, M. *Reality Television, Affect and Intimacy*. Basingstoke and New York: University of California Press, 2003. Print.

Kuppens, Ann, and Jelle Mast. "Ticket to the Tribes: Culture Shock and the 'Exotic' in Intercultural Reality Television. *Media, Culture & Society*. 34.7 (2012): 799-814. Print.

McGee, Micki. *Self-Help, Inc.: Makeover Culture in American Life*. Oxford: Oxford University Press, 2005. Print.

Negra, D., and S. Homes. "Introduction: Going Cheap? Female Celebrity in the Tabloid, Reality, and Scandal Genres." *Genres* 48 (Fall 2008). Print.

Ouellette, Laurie, and James Hay. *Better Living through Reality TV: Television and Post-Welfare Citizenship*. Oxford: Blackwell, 2008. Print.

Skeggs, Berverley, and Helen Woods. *Reacting to Reality Television: Performance, Audience and Value*. New York: Routledge, 2012. Print.

Smith, Mathew J., and Andrew F. Wood. *Survivor Lessons: Essays on Communication and Reality Television*. North Carolina: McFarland and Company, Inc., Publishers, 2003. Print.

Websites

Reality TV World

www.realitytvworld.com

Offers a broad scope of information on reality celebrities, exclusive interviews, and message boards for fans. In addition, the website highlights updates on the latest ratings, casting news, and scheduling.

Reality TEA

www.realitytea.com

Listed by reality show, news of the latest developments in front and behind the camera.

My Reality Television

http://myrealitytelevision.com

One of the major online resources for all things reality, the website offers video celebrity profiles, updates of the major shows, and the latest "celebribuzz" fit to print.

RTVC: Reality TV Calendar

www.realitytvcalendar.com

An online magazine that claims to be written for and by fans of reality television, RTVC is primarily devoted to recaps with commentary of many of the major shows.

Index

❖

WITHDRAWN

JUN 1 7 2024

DAVID O. McKAY LIBRARY
BYU-IDAHO